P.O. Box 2381 Oceanside CA. 92051

Contact:

thesilentgladiators@gmail.com

THE SILENT GLADIATORS

Wrestling is not a sexy sport. It does not sell in Los Angeles. It does not get play in New York. It will not get you laid, made or paid.

Baseball will do this.

Soccer will do this.

Wrestling will not do this. Wrestling will challenge you. It will break you. It will humble you. Wrestling will ask you to train like a madman and then give up the necessary things for survival. Food and water for hours-days on end, when it is the only thing your body and mind wants, so that you can wake on the morning of competition and enter a room full of half-clothed bodies where you will countdown to competition by spitting into a plastic cup, running laps with plastic bags underneath your sweats while ignoring your thirst and hunger so that you can make the weight cut.

This isn't fun.

This isn't sexy.

This is the furthest thing from getting laid.

An hour later, wrestling will send you out on the mat alone to face a supremely-conditioned athlete. It will ask you to face an opponent but also face yourself. It will hold you accountable for partying the night before, for drinking and smoking, for dogging it in practice, for not pushing hard enough in the weight room, for not being good enough, focused enough, tough enough.

This isn't fun.

This isn't sexy.

This is the furthest thing from getting paid.

You will reach a point in the match where your lungs will burn like the virgin inhalation of a cigarette, your legs will want to give out, and every muscle in your body will tell you to walk away and quit. In fact, it will be easy to quit. All you have to do is lay down for your opponent, let him pin your shoulders to the mat and the match will be over as quickly as the referee stamps the surface with his approval. You will go sit in the stands and everyone will quickly forget. Your teammates will be still be your teammates. Your parents will still be your parents. Your girlfriend will still be your girlfriend.

Or maybe not.

Maybe your teammates will realize you're a quitter. Maybe your parents will tell you that they didn't raise you like this. Maybe your girlfriend can't quite look at you the same. This is where wrestling starts asking questions and you're the only one who can answer them. This is where you get stronger or weaker. Where the hard work pays off or goes to waste. This is the breaking point and this is where champion wrestlers are made.

Wrestling is unlikely to bring you money or celebrity status but it will make you feel like you can survive anything, will stop at nothing and it will provide you the discipline to achieve your goals in life. If your good enough, if you're tough enough, if you have the guts to stick it out.

Baseball won't do this. Soccer won't do this. Only wrestling can do this.

Do you give a damn about wrestling? Does anybody? If the U.S. Olympic team walked in the room right now would you recognize any of them?

Probably not.

Yet, you would want these guys on your side in a fight. You would want your child to grow up one day and have their work ethic. You would want them to own the skills that can be applied to any obstacle.

I wish people could understand wrestling. I'm frustrated with its lack of recognition. Because I knew. I understood. I'd been through it. Because I once competed on a high-level, but have since moved on. I left wrestling where it was at and entered the working world after college with an internship at the U.S. Olympic Training Center. I work a career job that looks good on a resume but has no challenge. The world is boring to me. So I race cars at late hours. I struggle to replace the rush of competition. I keep denying this part of myself but the sport keeps creeping back. I see *Fight Club* and relate. I watch *300* and it had the same effect. I know that aggression and cutthroat competition is not right in the daily world but it was my world for eight years.

I'm not a tough guy. I'm not a meat head. I get mistaken for a baseball player. But my co-workers say I have an edge. I don't go around telling them the reason but somehow, eventually it comes up. I tell them I used to compete as a wrestler. They mention the *WWF*. I shake my head. They laugh about the uniforms. I mutter to yourself. I wish they could understand. I want them to understand. But I've moved on.

A week later the USOC internship program sends me to New York for the World Wrestling Championships. I walk into the arena and the atmosphere, the passion for the sport sucks me right back. So I decide to write a book. I now have purpose. I'm on my way. I have no idea what I'm getting into.

It takes me across the country and back on several trips. I do things that would be unnecessary in more prosperous times. I sneak into the OTC mess hall. I sleep on floors. I put off a real job. I swear off attachments. I overdraw my bank account and overstay my welcome more than I wish to recall.

I report to the practice room every day and sit on the sidelines taking notes because I know there's a story and I know I'm the guy to tell it. I want to reveal wrestling's virtues. I want people to measure themselves in it. But most of all I want people to understand. This is the fuel that keeps me going.

I need money to make it to the Olympics, but I don't have a trust fund. So I work three restaurants jobs, getting canned from two. I gamble on pool. I ignore the law. I ditch out on rent and bail Colorado. One way or another, I get the money. Then I dart through the West, stash my belongings in California and fly across the Atlantic. A week later I'm in Greece. I cover the Olympics. I get the story. I leave Europe broke and crash with a friend in Chicago. I write in bars. I write in kitchens. I write while stuck in traffic. I feel like a bum. I have a falling out with my friend, so go back to California and keep writing. I write in San Francisco, I write in San Diego, I write in New Orleans, South Carolina, Washington D.C., I end up in Los Angeles and I'm still writing.

I'm given an inspirational wrestling book by Rulon Gardner. I respect Rulon, but I read one paragraph of his book and it's a joke. I'm arrogant. I know I can write about wrestling better than it's been written. I'm still penniless, I'm still unpublished, but this is the fuel that keeps me going.

I finish the book and now I want to pass it on to the world. I send it out to the heavy hitters in New York, the William Morris Agency. Six weeks later it's returned to sender. WMA compliments. WMA praises. But then WMA apologizes. They can't represent the book. "Not enough of a built in audience," they say.

I think about the massive crowds at the NCAA Championships. I recall 20,000 competitors at Fargo Junior Nationals. I know there's an audience. But I'm rejected. I burn the letter and plot revenge. The most important lesson of wrestling comes back to me: You gotta do it yourself.

A year later I self-publish one rough copy. And now I want to pass it on to heavy kids who need to lose weight, skinny types who need to learn to defend themselves, to wrestlers up and down California, throughout Ohio and Pennsylvania, to anyone who ever was affected by the sport, who understands it, who went through it, I want to tell the story of the greatest wrestlers in the world.

But it's not done. It's not over. This book has become the longest wrestling match of my life. I question it all. I want to quit. I want to walk away. But I can't. I'm still arrogant. I still believe. I'm still a wrestler that won't quit. So I get my head together. I keep going. Four years after I started writing, I'm finished.

This is a story about the toughest wrestlers on the planet. Wrestlers who were honorable. Wrestlers who were valiant. Wrestlers who were nice guys, tough guys and pricks. This is a story about trying to achieve your dreams. About those who reached and missed, and those who got made. This is a story about the world's oldest sport. This is a story that you haven't heard before. This is my story of wrestling.

Take it or leave it. Read it and weep. I don't really care. I'm done with it.

To Coach Mullen, for not kicking me off the team.
And Laura Paull, for kicking me out of writing class.

In the world's most famous city, in its most famous arena, man's oldest battle is taking place. Four hundred wrestlers from eighty-nine countries are colliding head-on to determine who will be champion of the world. Five elevated wrestling mats, with colored circles marked like a helicopter launching pad in red, yellow and blue, smother the floor of New York's Madison Square Garden. A crowd of Iranians have taken over one side of the arena.

"I-RAN! I-RAN! I-RAN!" is the chant.

Americans pack the other end of the Garden.

"U-S-A! U-S-A! U-S-A!"

On the mat below, Iranian Hadi Habibi and American Joe Williams are locked in a titanic battle. A roaring chant rises up again from the Iran section as the match goes into overtime.

"HA-BI-BI! HA-BI-BI! HA-BI-BI!"

As the referee blows the whistle, Habibi locks his arm around Williams chest, which resembles that of a comic book beast. Williams follows suit, and a fatal dance begins. They struggle and pry for position until Williams collapses under pressure and is dropped on his back for the loss. The Iranians are on their feet, violently whipping their national flag side to side. It's the first American loss in the tournament. As Habibi exits the mat, Iranian men grab his hand to kiss it; they are in tears over the victory. *"Ma'shallah!"* they cry. *"Ma'shallah Habibi!"*

It is clear that this battle, this sport, represents much more to the crowd than two athletes on a mat. It was the second anniversary of Sept. 11, 2001 and the warm weather of the city was eerily similar to the fateful day two years prior. Former wrestlers and current U.S. Speaker of the House Dennis Hastert and Secretary of Defense Donald Rumsfeld, were in attendance. With a Middle Eastern opponent, an American counterpart, and the paranoia that surrounded the city, all of these elements were charging into the electric atmosphere. It's as if the two country's prejudices, fears, their true feelings were furiously boiling to the surface and the wrestlers were settling the argument. People press into the barriers of Madison Square Garden like political demonstrators converging on squads of police in riot gear. They watch and cringe and exult, they scream and yell and hurl insults, but the gladiators remain silent because they are too busy fighting and scrambling and trying to advance forth, pushing and tugging and battling with intense force. The patriotic chants of the Americans, the passionate cries of the Iranians clashing together, sparking, igniting, lighting up the Garden; the fighters fight, the crowd salutes, the arena is in a frenzy.

"I-RAN! I-RAN! I-RAN!"

"U-S-A! U-S-A! U-S-A!"

For the men below, for the chosen few on the mat, this is the fight they have been searching for all along, they-the silent gladiators-were symbols of ancient calling, one that had withstood the test of time and the crowd, the witnesses hovered over the spectacle like some medieval battle in the Coliseum of ancient Rome.

On mat five, U.S. wrestling star Cael Sanderson is dominating Iran's Majod Khodaei, scoring off his unstoppable ankle pick. Long-limbed like a boxer, Sanderson hunts the legs, aggressively swooping down on the attack, catching his opponent by the hook of the ankle. Occasionally, Khodaei turns and bails immediately to his stomach and surrenders the takedown and other times, it's a tiger-by-the-tail scramble, with Sanderson locked on like a sprung trap, countering every counter and refusing to be denied his points. As Sanderson prevails the American crowd lets everyone know it, standing and breaking into another round of patriotic approval.

Later in the press gallery, the square-jawed champ from Iowa State University is polite and self-deprecating, sweat dripping off his brow. When a reporter asks Sanderson about his trademark move, he replies with little emotion: "It's about all I know how to do, so I have to go for 'em."

The Freestyle Wrestling World Championships, originally scheduled in New York for September 2001, were changed, as was everything else, after 9/11. On the eve of the 2002 Worlds, the day before departure to the Middle East, the U.S. team received word from the State Department of a threat against its safety and pulled out of the tournament.

Now, three years in the making, with powerful politicians and dignitaries sitting mat side cloaked by security, two Americans capture silver medals. Sanderson, wearing the look of a man carrying the burden of a publicity starved sport, loses to Russia's Sajid Sajidov. Teammate Kerry McCoy, despite also losing to a Russian, captured his first World medal but, as the rest of the wrestling community was soon to find out, McCoy wasn't the only American heavyweight whose stock was rising.

For the seven members of the U.S. World Team, the Athens Olympic Games were less than a year away and while they were ranked on top of the Olympic ladder, they were being hunted within their own borders. For there were others out there, some lurking in the stands, spying their movements, style and attacks; scouting, training and preparing to beat world team members and capture an Olympic berth by any means necessary; honing their skills in places such as Stillwater, Ames and Iowa City, but mainly at the United States Olympic Training Center in Colorado Springs.

During OTC practices there was an underlying tension and endless mind games among U.S. rivals. During the daily training sessions they refused to spar together for fear of telegraphing moves before competition. The upcoming freestyle season was a prelude to the

Olympic Trials and while past success would get this group of wrestlers on the mat in the Indianapolis RCA Dome, once there, they had to fight to earn the U.S. Olympic spot; a life's training boiled down to one weekend. Everything leading up to it-open tournaments, practice sessions and international tours-was geared toward three days of wrestling.

The wrestlers worked throughout the year with a one-track mind, prevailing over injuries and doubts, hardships and tragedies, forging the toughest collection of wrestlers America had to offer. Ultimately, only seven wrestlers make the U.S. Olympic team. Few would endure the cut, yet each would pay the price, walk the path and sacrifice. The others, no matter how close they got, would falter. Some athletes would burn out quickly, whether from injuries or personal matters. Others, within a grasp of their dream, would be dropped, perhaps in overtime in Indy, leaving an undeniable scar on their psyche.

Once on the Olympic team, lives change instantly. Athletes are celebrated in hometowns and their life stories spun to the public by the national media. However, the fans did not witness the everyday sacrifice of the body, the outpouring of sweat, the endless attention to detail.

But I did.

And at times it was boring and monotonous to watch. At times I questioned it. I questioned why they would dedicate so much time to a sport that, in all likelihood, would never make them rich or famous. And in other moments I was flat-out awed. The pure power of Daniel Cormier. The quick, cat-like movements of Stephen Abas. The showdowns of Abas versus Henson, Fullhart battling Sanderson and Mocco facing McCoy.

At these moments, I believed there was no greater sport, no better way of life than to dedicate oneself to rigidness of battle, to train to beat another man, not to score 40 points in a basketball game or run for three touchdowns in football, but to use an opponent as your tool to torque, twist and turn, to outwit one-another in a physical chess match.

I sensed something true and holy within the sport of wrestling, something million-dollar shoe contracts and celebrity can't touch. It tests the individual in ways other sports don't. On the world-class level, one move is just a set-up to another and no one gets away with sloppiness; to succeed one must be in peak form. Every day these wrestlers are consumed by perfecting their technique. The business of building Olympians is a fragile one, a fusion of mind and body, ligaments and tendons, spirit and soul and finding the right combination is a formula that takes years, even half a lifetime, to yield results.

As I set out to cover the story, I wondered who would withstand the pressure and outlast his rivals? Who would earn the right to realize his dream and walk into the Athens Olympic stadium in the summer of 2004 wearing the red, white and blue? Who would emerge?

"It is not the destination, but the journey."

-BOB BEAMON, U.S. GOLD MEDALIST 1968

USOTC

I

There are 200 days, 12 hours, 23 minutes and 36 seconds remaining until the opening ceremonies of the Athens Olympic Games as the giant score clock proclaims just inside the white, iron-rod gates of the United States Olympic Training Center. The top clock counted down to the Summer Olympics, the bottom clock to the Winter; everything within the complex is geared toward these two global events.

The USOTC is home to a carnival of athletes, many among the best in the world: towering volleyball players, hulking weightlifters, wide-backed swimmers, para-Olympians and fierce wrestlers; all sharing the commonality of sport. At the Olympic level, where the difference between winning and losing could be decided by a hundredth of a second, the timepiece is an inescapable reminder to all within its OTC boundaries that every moment, every second counted.

Colorado Springs is located on the eastern edge of the Colorado Rockies and on the western edge of the Great Plains. Its population hovers around 360,000; the state's second largest city behind Denver. Pikes Peak mountain looms over the community like an overprotective parent, always present even when out of sight. Most live or travel here for one reason: the mountains. Their presence is undeniable, they are the backdrop of everything in Colorado. Even at the state's lowest point, 3,300 feet above sea level, the sky is closer here than most places in the nation. The mile-high elevation starves the thin air of Colorado Springs, which is especially evident with any attempt at physical activity; much like the mountains, it can't be ignored. The elevation is one main reason that Colorado Springs is the epicenter of America's Olympic athletes.

Within the OTC's fenced-off grounds, is a sport science facility that tweaks and tests the athletes, addressing areas of strength and weakness by assessing the body's physiology. There is a hyperbaric chamber that could alter the relative altitude from sea level to 8,000 feet. The recently upgraded weight room has treadmills, stationary bikes, dumbbell racks and an Olympic lifting stations that cost nearly half a million dollars and were fronted by a corporate sponsor in exchange for affiliation with the Olympic brand. There is a health-conscious cafeteria, a library filled with historical Olympic books, videos and computers, residential dorms, apartments, volleyball and basketball courts, gymnastics and boxing facilities, office buildings and an athletic treatment center.

On the walls of various OTC facilities, there are posters that read, 'The Olympics are held not every four years, but every day.' They are placed next to miracle moment Olympic photos, the gold-medal winning snapshots that display the peak human body. But they are not miracles at all. Like an image of a climber conquering Mount Everest, these snapshots belied the behind-the-scenes training and the grueling energy applied while striving for the pinnacle accomplishment. When an athlete commits to the USOTC, athletic greatness is not a surprise or a miracle, but the end result of countless hours of physical and mental preparation.

The OTC was a place so professional in appearance, so legitimate in structure, that for any athlete with Olympic aspirations it represented a steppingstone to athletic Babylon. The facility looked like it had never taken a day off. The windows glistened, the grounds were immaculate and if a nation's athletic prowess were to be judged by its Olympic training facilities, the U.S. was clearly a world superpower. But for the OTC's inhabitants the new car smell eventually drifted away. The food menu ran in cycles. Practice followed a strict schedule. And the reality of being an Olympic hopeful was one of work and rest, training and recovery and everything else was secondary.

Few of these athletes attempted to blend into the Colorado Springs population. It was a transient place to begin with. Military personnel were constantly being funneled through the city for boot camps and then shipped to Iraq or other outposts, and it was also a city layered with many secret worlds unto themselves: the U.S. Air Force Academy, the Fort Carson U.S. Army base, the high-security sector of Norad Mountain and on the corner of Boulder and Union streets, the U.S. Olympic Training Center.

Colorado Springs was originally established as a resort community, drawing tourists to the Garden of the Gods, a nationally renowned public park with red rock formations, the COG Railroad that offered rides to the top of Pikes Peak mountain, among other attractions. There were several small colleges, numerous bike trails and open-area spaces spread out over 186 miles. With its central U.S. location, a large reserve of educated workers and a mild weather climate by Colorado standards, Colorado Springs developed a vibrant business, commerce and entertainment sector over the years. Hewlett-Packard and Intel, military defense heavyweights Lockheed Martin and Boeing, a large number of religious organizations including the Christian & Missionary Alliance, Young Life and International Bible Society have made the city their home.

A large portion of the Colorado Springs economy is fueled by the military, which has a long, established relationship with the city. In 1942, shortly after Pearl Harbor was attacked, Colorado Springs opened its first military base. The U.S. Army established Camp Carson near the southern borders of the city and prepared and housed troops in the event of the Second World War. In 1951, the U.S. Air Defense Command opened what is now named Peterson Air Force Base and later, President Dwight Eisenhower selected it as the grounds for the Air Force military academy. In 1963, North American Defense Command, short for NORAD, built their main facility in Cheyenne Mountain, permanently securing the city's military occupation. Many residents of Colorado Springs are paranoid that if World War III were to occur, Colorado Springs, with its heavy military presence and NORAD mountain, would be one of the first cities targeted for destruction.

Colorado Springs was dry until the end of Prohibition in 1933, but things have changed drastically since the liquor began flowing freely, and now downtown Colorado Springs can be found on many nights of the week with hordes of military personnel packed into two-story nightclubs that blast music loud enough to piss off residents several blocks away.

But Olympic hopefuls did not come here to socialize or to become part of the crowd. There was not a strong sense of community throughout Colorado Springs, there was the threshold of people trying to achieve something, trying to get ahead, trying to gain an edge in a competitive world and that was especially true at the OTC where displaced athletes trained with global ambitions and everything within the grounds is geared toward accomplishing this goal. The city is far from home for most of the resident athletes and they are generally neutral on how they felt about it socially. For America's Olympic hopefuls, Colorado Springs is neither good nor bad, but a place to be endured; the U.S. Olympic Training Center is a place to get better.

In the shadows of Pikes Peak, amid the thin Colorado air, is where American wrestlers dreamed of golden medals and athletic immortality. They went to bed early and woke at the crack of dawn. They watched their diet and nursed the smallest injury. They trained vigorously, pushing their bodies and potential to the limit.

Total commitment is demanded and essentially, all the athlete has to worry about is performing. The United States Olympic Committee takes care of almost everything else: housing and elite coaching, sports seminars and mental preparation classes, equipment is sponsored, meals are prepared, every injury professionally treated and cash stipends are provided according to status, ranking and sport.

The wrestlers were different from the other athletes on complex. Many OTC resident athletes were on leave from professional sports, as evidenced by the parking lot spaces occupied by expensive vehicles belonging to female volleyball players, who were regularly courted for lucrative off-season contracts in foreign countries.

For U.S. wrestlers, the Olympic Games are not a brief, patriotic diversion from a professional league but a four to eight-year pledge. Every day was a commitment to excellence, translating into grueling weightlifting sessions and lung-searing exercise routines, dorm rooms, cafeteria food and endless stacks of laundry. The Olympics is an American wrestler's one shot at national glory, their one chance to become a star. The brief opportunity comes every four years, for most it is a once-in-a-lifetime chance before they move on.

There was financial incentive for Athens Olympians, winning a gold medal was worth $25,000, the silver $15,000 and a bronze $10,000 in the USOC's Operation Gold program. The OTC provisions are a tradeoff, intended to get results. Like the athletes, the USOC had a bottom line as well. If it weren't for the Olympic logos stamped everywhere, the OTC could easily pass for a corporate business park. There was a security check point at the foot of the grounds. ID cards were required to enter the offices. Many of the building structures resemble each other and the employees tended to dress in uniformity.

The training center is home to the U.S. Olympic Committee headquarters and national governing bodies for 23 Olympic sports. NGBs receive funds from the USOC, but also raised their own revenues with sponsorship and membership fees. After walking through the complex it is evident that numerous facilities were funded in one form or another. The Richard M. Schrushy Health South building, part of an empire in which Schrushy would later face some of the most massive fraud charges in American corporate history, provided a glimpse of the other vibrations running through the OTC complex. Where power lies, the struggle for it follows.

The purpose of Olympic employees is to serve, protect, develop and promote Olympic athletes, but at times this duty was distorted by power struggles and good ol' boy tactics. In the international sporting world, there were prestigious positions of employment similar to the slots on the Olympic athlete ladder; each rung offering new perks, higher salaries and serious competition. It is here, in the offices and boardrooms of the OTC, *'Where the Olympics were not every four years but every day.'*

The U.S. Olympic Committee is in the business of producing medals, facing a new test that comes with the Winter and Summer Games every two years. The Summer Games are the cash cow, the bonanza for sponsorship rights and blockbuster television deals. "We can win both the total medal count and the gold-medal count in Athens," Jim Scheer, the U.S. Olympic Committee Chief Executive

Officer, said. "We think we've already put the carrot out there in terms of resources we provide."

Scheer, a former Olympic wrestler, was a principal of sorts for one of the most powerful sporting organizations in America. His replacement of former CEO Lloyd Ward and the subsequent organizational changes that followed were a bandage for an organization bloodied by a string of scandals.

The world invariably gets a three-week snapshot of the Olympic movement every four years, complete with controversy, rivalry, politics, hope, humanity, triumph, failure and glory. What went on at the Games was once a microcosm of the USOC. For all the inspiring gold medal stories, there was a dysfunctional sporting committee. For all the athletic triumphs, there was a misuse of funds. For many remarkable athletic feats, whispers of steroid use were raised.

In years past, the U.S. Olympic Committee resembled a large dysfunctional family. In 2004, with more than 120 members on the board of directors, the USOC was wrought with scandal. Accused of buying votes for the Winter Games in Salt Lake City and a misappropriation of funds, the USOC became associated with corporate wrongdoings that had plagued American businesses. Rumors flew within smaller circles about the dirty laundry of several national governing bodies. Soap opera stories told of employee affairs. An anonymous USOC telephone hotline was created where employees could tip off human resources of any unprofessional or illegal activity that occurred at the OTC. But, like feuding parents whose children continued to achieve high marks at school while their home life was a mess, the athletes continued to perform.

Each day tightly wound bodies fly smoothly through the air, cut across the water, and tangle on padded mats. As athletes interact on a world-class level sweat begins to bead on foreheads. With each consecutive drill, the lungs become more strained. As the coaches pushed and prodded, the lactic acid washed through the athletes' bodies like antifreeze.

In the practice facilities, where physical laws rule, there was no politicking and deception. The athletes were the sole reason for the existence of the USOTC and the true spirit of the Olympic movement. Everyday tour groups visited the complex and saw workers dutifully putting in their hours, but it was the athletes who drew the longest stares, were requested for photos, autographs and strode around the facility like it was their personal kingdom. They walked taller, leapt higher, but in actuality, they were chained to personal ambition and had little else to do but put in their work until their brief chance to seize athletic glory.

In-between workouts, they passed the time playing pool and watching TV in the lounge, using the Internet or reading books at the library. Some joined a church group, others took courses at a local college or online. For the resident athletes, this was the bulk of their social interaction and while college teams brought in for training camps drew a brief curiosity, the OTC was the resident athlete's turf. In the cafeteria many lingered long after meals were finished, playing chess, scanning the newspaper or watching the big screen TVs that is always tuned to ESPN.

But mostly they worked.

Each day, the process started at dawn. From the practice facility to the weight room, to several-mile runs around local parks, then back to their residences to recuperate before the afternoon cycle. Rarely a moment passed at the OTC where the athlete was not striving to improve. Even in sleep some could not escape; dreaming about their sport.

It was difficult not to. U-S-A signs were imprinted on gym floors and billboarded on the side of each building. The urging, the boosting, the influence was everywhere on complex. The OTC had a serious energy where one could hear, smell and feel something happening: The weights banging on the floor, the oxygen that left one hungry for intake, the athletes of extreme intensity and utmost belief, but sometimes it became too much. Sometimes, in the midst of a four-year Olympic cycle, one has to escape, drive past the security gates and head north for Denver. Or hit up the downtown nightspots. Retreat to the mountains, the ski slopes, go fly fishing, anything that might temporarily erase the endless reminder of what nearly every waking effort boiled down to. But for many athletes who made the OTC their home, the atmosphere was exactly what they needed and wanted all along. There were no academic classes to complicate their schedule, no distractions from the goal at hand. Surrounded by world-class competitors, they were right at home.

In this setting, at this level of sport, there were few excuses. From the world class facilities and top flight trainers, to the daily all-you-can-eat meals; at the OTC all amenities are taken care of. The preparation, the legitimacy, the endless attention to detail carried into the practice room where, for the Athenian wrestling hopefuls, Kevin Jackson was the tone-setter.

"It is a lovely thing to live with courage, and die leaving an everlasting fame."

-ALEXANDER THE GREAT

Kevin Jackson
II

In many ways Kevin Jackson was an ordinary man. He lived in a modest two-story home in a residential neighborhood. He dropped off his kids at school before driving to an office where he sat at a desk and filled out paperwork, made phone calls and attended company meetings. But Jackson could not walk through the wrestling room doors at the OTC and be ordinary. Jackson had to control the room, he had to fill it with a presence, he had to be a champion among champions.

Inside the Olympic wrestling facility there is tremendous ego and ambition, varied opinions and rivaling tactics, and amid this environment someone had to consistently take charge. Jackson had to be the type of man who not only listened to advice but followed through with it. Who would avoid traps and vices. Who would work when no one was watching. Who would compete whether he was sick, down or having an off day. Who would deliver at all costs.

Jackson would walk in the wrestling room barefoot or in sandals, wearing shorts and a workout t-shirt, clutching the minimum requirements of his coaching profession: wrestling shoes, socks and a whistle. He would scan the perimeter quickly and joke with one wrestler or another, but when addressing the group he took on a definitive tone.

The OTC athletes thought of Jackson as a brother, an uncle, an alpha male example of what they wanted to be because in the corner of the room they saw the picture of him kneeling down on the mat after his 1992 Olympic gold-medal victory. Jackson was a decade removed from his last competition, but he remained in good enough shape to spar with the athletes. During his career, Jackson was not devious with his intentions and he communicated the same way. He wasn't known to sugarcoat his advice; he was as direct in his approach to coaching as he was as a competitor.

Yet, there were few world beaters among the OTC resident team, few capable of clutching gold, and that was another challenge of the U.S. resident wrestling program. Jackson had athletes who were not going to the Olympics but as training partners were essential to the Olympic operation and Jackson had to coach, motivate and engage these men just as well.

Jackson's world as a wrestler was one seeded a generation ago in East Lansing, Michigan. He got involved with the sport as a young boy, following in the footsteps of his older brother, eventually winning two state titles for Lansing High School, then moving on to the Louisiana State University, where he was a three-time NCAA All-American. When LSU dropped the sport due to budget cuts, Jackson still had a final year of eligibility remaining. He wanted to transfer to a college where African-Americans could feel comfortable and a team that wasn't afraid of the powerhouse Iowa Hawkeye's. "I was sick of guys lying down to the black and gold singlets," Jackson said.

Iowa State fit his needs. It had elite coaching. It had talented training partners. It had the kind of program that could challenge the Iowa juggernaut that had rolled over the sport with nine consecutive NCAA team titles. The ISU Cyclones won the NCAA title the next year, preventing Iowa from winning ten in a row, but not before Jackson lost in the national finals, to a Hawkeye no less. This event produced an insecurity that haunted him until he won a world championship in 1991.

Before his gold medal match in the 1992 Barcelona Olympics,

Jackson recalled, "I tried to control my emotions, but I just had to put my hands on somebody." He defeated his Russian opponent by scoring the only point in the bout. Jackson stood unfazed on the top of the Olympic podium as shoes were thrown to the surface by a jeering Spanish crowd. It became all the sweeter when the taunts were snuffed out by the Americans singing their national anthem.

That was Jackson's moment.

He went on to win another world title, then, after a failing to make the 1996 Olympic team, Jackson went into coaching. In 2002, he was named the head coach of the 2004 Olympic freestyle wrestling team. Somehow he needed to bring his athletes to the Olympic podium; somehow Jackson had to get them there. But just as Jackson made the journey on the mat alone, the wrestlers were the only ones who could venture out on the Olympic process; Jackson could push so much. The athletes he dealt with were no longer supported by college scholarships. The monetary sacrifice to continue competing was amplified by adult responsibilities. They had to want this.

The wrestlers could train at colleges while working as assistant coaches, or move to Colorado Springs to join the resident program. Jackson's base was the OTC and like a wise man doling out knowledge to whomever came to him, his job was to assist each Olympic hopeful with guidance and encouragement; up until the completion of the Olympic Trials Jackson was paid to be neutral. "I want whoever is going to be the world champion," he said.

In addition to not having all the potential Olympians in his stable, Jackson faced another uphill battle coaching the American team. U.S. high schools and NCAA wrestling, the feeder program for potential U.S. Olympians, spent much of the year wrestling collegiate style and a quarter of the year wrestling freestyle. Every other country in the world competed in freestyle year-round. As NCAA wrestlers graduated into Olympic hopefuls, they had to adjust their technique and change their mentalities to the highly technical freestyle wrestling.

Lacking a professional sport, NCAA wrestling was the marquee level in the states. For elite college wrestlers, there is no annual professional draft or free agency period. The glorified transition for NCAA football, basketball, baseball, and hockey stars did not exist in college wrestling, leaving many competitors with few options.

Ultimately, they had to choose between pursuing a sport with little financial incentive or moving on with their lives.

That left only the elite, the cream of the crop, to continue. They found access to the best training and coaches. They were able to garner sponsorship to finance their quest. The pursuit of many of these athletes was singular. The gold medal was the only goal that seemed to matter and the U.S. system only benefited those who had the potential to reach it.

In a perfect world, Jackson would have all the prospects under his guidance at the OTC. They would devote themselves solely to the sport. Money would not be an issue. But Jackson knew better. He knew Olympic hopefuls had wives, children and professional obligations to worry about. He understood why they trained with college programs. He knew some wrestlers struggled to make ends meet. Jackson knew he had choir boys and he also knew he had boys who would be boys.

Jackson searched for character flaws in his wrestlers. He talked about life imitating sport on all levels and how all champions he'd known were at true with themselves. Jackson embraced different techniques of training, but believed that it all boiled down to who was willing to make the ultimate sacrifice. "Everything is a carryover," Jackson would say.

The U.S. system is democratic. Any wrestler in the nation can enter a regional tournament and qualify for the Olympic trials and, if they conquer the trials, to become the Olympian. This left America's best wrestlers open to the laws of nature, not the politics of man.

In other countries, the national team could be selected by a committee. In the U.S., there was nothing of that sort; just athletes, their college coaches and the OTC where Kevin Jackson oversaw a system that, at times, didn't make sense.

The team would be formed on the final day of the Olympic Trials in a best-of-three championship. The first contender, the national champ, would watch the other wrestlers to battle in a two-day tournament with the winner of the challenge tournament earning the right to face the national champ the following day. But before this day, Jackson would have to coach, observe and wait for his Olympic team to form.

Although there is an open circuit for freestyle wrestlers in the states, it is hardly a professional league. NCAA Division I is the highest amateur level in the nation. As powerhouse NCAA programs wage battle each year, their philosophies and styles spill over to the open wrestling stage. Select NCAA coaches have a large stake in America's success because if their athlete could win an Olympic spot or Olympic medal, it legitimizes the school, its coaches and style of wrestling. The Olympian often returns as an assistant to train with current members of the NCAA team and top high school recruits are lured by the presence of world-class training partners. Success breeds success, a program is built and patterns begin to emerge.

Jackson's challenge was to lure athletes to Colorado Springs and make each feel welcome in an environment where rivals trained only a few feet away. He was the assigned leader of the Olympic project, and how he handled the various coaches and wrestlers was vital to the U.S.'s international success.

*"Earliest man, full of the sense of his own worth, screaming
into the blackness, needing no God but himself..."*

-HUNTER S. THOMPSON, GONZO-THE ART

The Forgotten Discipline
III

To the untrained eye, wrestling might be nothing more than awkward
uniforms and smelly gyms. At times, the competition is boring and
confusing, even tasteless. Perhaps it was too complicated initially, that
many never gave it an opportunity, as if it were a dusty book with a
tattered cover buried in the corner behind rows of glistening hardbacks.
Maybe wrestling was too raw, un-glamorous, too rough around the
edges and the athlete moved onto something more acceptable, more
popular, more fun. But beyond first impressions, those who take a
chance on the sport also have taken the first step toward understanding
its virtues.

The deeper one went beneath the surface, the more complicated the
sport became. Those who have lived the story, all wrestlers have one,
were forever changed by it and when they met other wrestlers, they
shared an unquestionable bond; only they truly understood the story,
only they knew what had been endured.

Wrestling is unlike any other American sport. In football, the
hyped match-ups of two stars are often lost in the crisscrossing of
bodies. In basketball, players can disappear in the flow of the game.

But with wrestling, by removing the team, by reducing the field of play to a cage of boundaries, there is no downplaying, no denying the individual duel. One cannot hide behind a wall of blockers or be aided by the screen of a defender. There is no armor to soften contact, no playing balls to distract the eye. The expectations, the pressure, the responsibility is all on the individual's shoulders and as a a result, no sport is as pure in its individual competitiveness, as direct in its conflict, as raw in its exhibition of the survival of the fittest. Wrestlers come face-to-face with their doubts. If there is uncertainty, it shows. If there are flaws, they are personally exposed. If there is weakness, its story would be told.

When 75,000 people fill a football stadium or basketball arena to cheer a team, they are in essence pulling for what it represents: their city, organization, or school. But when 7,500 knowledgeable wrestling fans pack an arena to watch two competitors engage in battle spotlighted under a set of glaring lights, all eyes are upon two athletes, the intensity, the sensation, the sheer violence of it all is hard to match.

The sport does not discriminate against shape or size, color or creed, background or origin. In a martial art where contact can not be averted, where one can neither run nor hide, where wins and losses reflect, superficially, who you are, wrestling demands a certain type of person, although it draws all types: gangsters, preppies, cowboys and surfers, inner-city youths, farm boys, wise-guys, tough-guys, rebels, Christians, and atheists, tall, skinny, fat, short, long, lean, stocky, squat, all shapes, all sizes, all individuals.

While football players are defined by their physicality, wrestlers are by their mentality. They were, by nature, loners, their foundations predicated on self-reliance. Before matches, they pace back and forth like dueling gunmen, fate awaiting them, time drawing them closer, their names called out for all to hear and while they are given strategies by coaches and teammates come up to offer encouragement, wrestlers settled their debts alone. Their reputations rise and fall with each performance, a hero or legend can be disgraced with one defeat.

One could walk into any building, high school-college-or professional and witness the same cold-eyed menacing stares, nervous energy and primal intentions preceding showdowns on the mat and through these one-on-one alterations, distinct psychological and physical characteristics form. A sense of independence and confidence grows with each battle in the circle, with the knowledge that victory is one's own doing. The wrestler is mentally stronger from having endured practices and matches where every muscle was fatigued, every ounce of energy drained. Discipline comes with the ritual shedding of weight before competition, when a wrestler's insides growl for food and water but the circumstances call for more work. The sport develops V-shaped backs from the constant pushing and pulling that makes their arms stick out like a cowboy in search of a gunfight. Many wrestlers attain grips strong as a climber from the relentless tugging and bracing of limbs and necks. Ears form the shape of cauliflower from the banging of heads and use of it as driving force on execution of moves; some wrestlers taking pride in the disfigurement, the way a young boy honors a well-earned scar.

Many develop strong egos. Wrestlers learn to trust in themselves because out on the mat there is no one else to believe in. To be the best in the world requires a strong sense of self, a component as vital to a champion as a work ethic. Before stepping out onto the mat, wrestlers convince themselves of victory. Some build up hate for an opponent, others are indifferent, but nearly all choose not to engage in verbal conflict with the competition, preferring to let the battle play out in the only place that matters.

***

The human body, the way it twists and turns, the flexibility of its limbs, the uniqueness of each build plays a significant role in the style of each wrestler. Strong hands aide the ability to control the opponent. Long arms can be used to fend off attacks or cut down the distance needed to reach an opponent's leg. Powerful hips allow one to maneuver and explode on moves. The back is used to lift, pull and tug. The neck is a tool for positioning, a spear to drive with.

Wrestlers are adept at using their physical dimensions to form a technical advantage. They understand technique can negate strength, power can offset skill, and conditioning can overcome both, but it's what's inside the head that narrows a country full of hopefuls down to a single Olympian. Strategy, talent, skill are all factors, but mental toughness is the biggest factor in the wrestlers' success.

Here is a sport where individual athletes excel with the agility of a gymnast, the lung capacity of a swimmer, the fast-twitch muscles of a football player and the discipline of a black belt. On the international level it is rare that one move will be enough to score; it often takes three to four set-ups and exchanges, hedging on an opponent's reactions.

Any abnormal physical characteristics can be used to the athlete's advantage and styles develop that play to each athlete's strength. Those athletically limited remain in solid positions, glued into their stance, taking few chances as they try to wear down opponents with physical beatings and superior conditioning. There are wrestlers whose technical skills are so refined it is only a matter of time before they prevail. Some rely on athletic ability, always trying to force a position that will be decided by it. When wrestlers face an opponent with an opposite style, they probe and bait one another into positions that will weaken their opponents. Wrestling technique doesn't come as naturally as a throwing a baseball or catching a football. Initial practices appear as awkward as children learning to ice skate. Technical moves have to be taught and executed in a slow-paced fashion, requiring strenuous, focused repetition until the day when the muscle memory was trained to react smoothly, naturally to the savage rhythms of the sport.

At the high school level physical maturity and experience is enough to set top athletes apart from their peers. Those who were well coached have a technical edge, but the kids with physical maturity can sometimes overpower that and the ones with both physical and technical edges usually advace to the next level. Like the martial art academies of Japan, the best prep wrestlers in the U.S. head off to universities to learn discipline and techniques on how to defeat opponents. College level coaching is more advanced, the workout partners higher skilled and athletes have the benefit of rigorous weight training programs. While high school athletes develop at different ages, most NCAA athletes are physically mature with their peers. With a more level playing field, mental toughness separates competitors more than ever. Athletes enter top collegiate programs and face a new level of competition.

Steel sharpens steel. Champions develop champions. Trained fighters grow by being beaten. In a sport that does not rely a ball or stopwatch, a training partner is essential to development. For an NCAA wrestler to succeed, they must be pushed to ever-increasing levels in practice. Every year, they grow stronger and more experienced. A freshman becomes a sophomore, then quickly a junior and senior. Those that continue training usually fall in as assistant coaches and with each passing of knowledge, the seed is nourished, the athlete develops and when his eligibility was done another champion emerged. With elite competition, academic studies and two-a-day practices, wrestling burnout is common at the collegiate level. Owing to the effects of Title IX and subsequent budget cuts, NCAA competition is fierce as ever. In 2004, there were 107 Division 1 slots and there were far fewer scholarship programs and opportunities than a decade ago.

NCAA head coaches are in charge of overseeing an entire wrestling program, often leaving young assistants in to run practice and serve as workout partners; the assistant's main job function is to beat lessons into fresh recruits and battle with starters. Most wrestlers don't find much success in the initial sparring battles with coaches. For some, taught to believe in themselves and re-enforced by age-group dominance and a knack for the sport, the college transition is seamless.

With the collision of bodies, the clash of styles, something has to give. Sometimes wrestlers will crack and break their opponents and nobody, during the period of 1976 through 1998, did this with more frequency than the Iowa Hawkeyes.

Iowa
IV

In the community of Waterloo, a young Dan Gable followed in his father's footsteps and chose wrestling as his sport. Wrestling came easiest to Gable among other activities where athletes had to wait their turn; he was captivated by the sport's continuous action.

"Wrestling engulfed me," Gable explained. "The whole time I wrestled I was working for better control, for domination even when I was in control. A lot of guys let up when they get in control." Gable's goal was to always have his opponent reacting to him and. At Iowa State, his college coach, Dr. Harold Nichols, encouraged his individuality by telling him never to rely on anybody but himself.

In 1970, as a college senior, Gable entered his final college match with an undefeated record, and only to lose to Larry Owings 13-11. It was a defeat Gable never seemed to get over and he channeled the pain of the loss into training seven hours a day for the 1972 Munich Olympic Games. At the Olympic Trials and Olympic Games combined, he won 21 straight matches, capturing the Olympic gold.

With each win, with each lesson on the mat, Gable was also taking notes from his Olympic coach, Bill Farrell, who had a reputation as an astute businessman. After four years as an assistant at the University of Iowa, Gable took over the head coaching position in 1977. Like a Fortune 500 CEO, Gable took all the lessons of leadership, politics, education, and management that he learned from his own coaches and incorporated those principles into the Hawkeye program. J. Robinson became his top assistant. Mark Johnson took over the strength and conditioning program. Gable set the goal of winning every weight class at the NCAA championship. "The more leaders you got on the team," Gable said. "The less you have to take that role."

As the components fell into place, the Hawkeye's trained so hard that when they were let loose on the competition, they ravaged the sport like attacking barbarians, never stopping, running up scores and taking over gyms. In the process, Gable built an empire that would dominate the sport for two decades. When he retired after 21 years as Iowa's head coach, the Hawkeyes won 15 NCAA team titles, 21 Big Ten Championships, producing 78 individual NCAA Champions and 152 All-Americans.

There were few insurgent uprisings against the Hawkeye's. Oklahoma State, led by Joe Seay, won a national title before NCAA recruiting violations temporarily handicapped the program. Seay arrived at OSU from Cal-State Bakersfield, where he had built a Division II powerhouse that rivaled many Division I programs. One long-time observer of the sport believed things could have been different.

"If Joe Seay had not been made an example of, had Joe Seay never gotten into trouble, Gable would have never done as well as he did," Gene Guerrero said. "Joe was naïve and gave up too much, too many scholarships and the school didn't back him. The university protected Gable."

But comments such as these would inevitably be directed at a man whose influence dominated an entire American sport; programs cannot be built with this mentality. Great feats are never accomplished along the lines what-if, they rely on doers, closers and leaders, and in that light, Dan Gable had no equal over his career.

His presence went beyond recruiting and speed, his coaching transcended power and force. Part psychologist and full-time motivator, Gable's Iowa teams physically and mentally dominated, creating one of the most successful dynasties in American sports history. As the athletes came and went with each recruiting class, the system, the pillars of strength remained intact. When the Hawkeye's had a down year, Gable always had dominant leaders on his team to pick up the slack, such as Tom and Terry Brands whose intensity and relentless style fit right in with their coaches and carried over to the international level. Tom Brands won an Olympic gold in 1996, Terry a bronze in 2000; both won world titles in 1993. But under Gable's reign, no single athlete was bigger than the program.

The Brands brothers, the Zaleskys, the Steiners, the Banachs, the Williams, the Zadicks, McIlravy, Alger, Davis all came from the Hawkeye lineage. Conditioning and strength provided the foundation for their style and they had the attitude to back it up. Hawkeye wrestlers bullied there opponents off the mat, running back to the center and waiting to attack again as a result, many opponents were intimidated beforehand. When asked by coaches at a wrestling clinic what the Iowa secret was, T.J. Williams, a two-time NCAA champ, said there was no secret. "After being pushed passed the point of exhaustion during practice, a match didn't seem like much," Williams said. "You just knew that you weren't going to hit that point in competition."

A standard developed in the Iowa program that nothing less than a national title would be acceptable. If the goal was not accomplished, some athletes fell into various stages of depression. "If you fell short of your goal," Lennie Zalesky, a former Iowa All-American, said. "Something was wrong with you."

The Hawkeyes broke the sport down to a battle of attrition and this dominance ceded in the Olympic arena where the U.S. wore out their foreign counterparts. Gable emerged as the American face of the sport, one courted for Presidential dinners and capable of transcending wrestling's close-knit community; a leader of men that rivaled General Patton to his troops.

After the '97 season unfolded with another NCAA championship, Gable retired and long-time assistant Jim Zalesky was selected as his successor. Iowa won three more NCAA titles while Gable kept close watch of the program. When his former recruits graduated and moved on, so did their overwhelming success. The empire had weakened. The dynasty lost pillars of strength. Faults began to show.

Some pointed to the rise in mechanical farming and Iowa schoolboys, the breeding ground of Hawkeye recruits, not being as tough. Some say it was the ascension of other programs that was bound to happen. Others pointed directly at Gable's replacement Jim Zalesky. But there was no denying that the University of Iowa got too big to retain its success; Iowa City was too small a place to cradle the energy of the program. Over the years, similar to the NFL 49ers dynasty, valuable assistant coaches began taking higher-paying head coaching jobs elsewhere. Tom Ryan went to Hofstra; Mark Johnson went to Illinois; J. Robinson took over at Minnesota; Barry Davis went to Wisconsin; Lennie Zalesky took over at U.C. Davis; Terry Brands took the head coaching position at Tennessee-Chattanooga and his brother Tom went to Virginia Tech; at least twenty former Iowa coaches or wrestlers went to other programs. The black and gold cloud that the Hawkeyes had cast over the sport parted with Gable's absence, and tensions rose in Iowa City as other NCAA teams broke through.

As Iowa struggled to return to what it had once been, there was another great American wrestler turned coach leading a Midwest school that would break the Hawkeye stronghold on the NCAA team trophy. After shifting to the University of Minnesota for two years, the balance of NCAA wrestling power returned to its origin, the native lands of Oklahoma.

"There is no one like him and there will be
no one else like him."

-LEE ROY SMITH SR.

Stillwater
V

Like the skyscrapers that tower over America's cities, the athletic complex at Oklahoma State University, with its concrete corner pillars rising from the red-dirt flatlands, trumps all within Stillwater's city limits.

Just past the entrance into Gallagher-Iba Arena, beyond the glass-encased Barry Sanders' Heisman Trophy, rests the OSU athletics Hall of Fame where many of the 32 NCAA wrestling champion trophies are housed; vacant stones await the engraving of new championship teams. Passing through the elaborate, maze-like athletic shrine, with its streaming video screens celebrating OSU alumni, beyond the long stretch of windows of the training facility, through another hallway where a giant bronze statue of cowboy mascot Pistol Pete lurks over visitors, and finally up a set of stairs to the second floor, there is an obscure door in a hallway that, if it weren't for the orange Cowboy Wrestling door sign, could be mistaken for a storage closet. Yet through this door, past the team lounge and down the low, narrow hallway, is where the power of American wrestling resided in 2004.

Athletes are spread across three full mats, going through drills after brief instruction from the coaching staff. Afternoon sunlight shot through the windows, slicing across portions of the surface. Orange protective padding clings to the walls. C-O-W-B-O-Y-S is spelled out in large block letters stretching the length of the ceiling. The room is big, wide, massive, but the ceiling is low and the windows that provide a view of Boone Pickens football stadium are closed, trapping the body heat.

Crouching next to an orange pillar, a man drapes a hand across his jaw and scans the room in the manner of a rancher eyeing stock. Not a word is said. Not a moment wasted. For twenty minutes athletes worked at three-quarter speed and there was only the pitter-patter of steps and the hollow sounds of bodies hitting the mat; a symphony at work. The wrestlers continue drilling their moves, each as calculated and precise as the one before, then the training partner takes his turn, everything-everyone in aggressive unison and the man next to the pillar continues hawking the mats, continues his search for clues among the bodies spread across the room.

Upon visiting the training grounds of the reigning NCAA wrestling champions, one might imagine snarling brutes thrashing each other across a dungeon-style room, barrel-chested dumb jocks who cut class and got their grades taken care of, picked on smart kids and pirated kegs from frat parties, but this assumption fell far short. There was a deep physiological tension evident in several of the wrestlers; some were talking to themselves as they pushed through the workout. The struggle in the room was not to win a takedown or score on the training partner, it was remaining focused on repetition of technique.

Their coach, John Smith, kneeled down, listening intently to the sounds of the room as if he were Frank Sinatra in front of a 50-person orchestra, searching for the slightest off-beat. He scanned the surroundings, sizing up the group before halting the action and bringing them together. Like Sinatra, Smith was often the shortest but most powerful presence in a room and he seemed to have a psychological grip on those around him. Heavyweights, physical specimens twice his size and strength, defer and wait silently as Smith pointed out mistakes.

He moved with a bit of a hitch and he didn't have the type of build that would warrant attention, but when he lowered into his wrestling stance he was suddenly fast and slick and had a way on the mat that made his All-American demonstration partner look as dangerous as any regular college kid who got his muscles from the schools rec center.

Smith's voice was even and un-emotional; there were no traces of anger or aggression, just the steady flow of instruction as he addressed the group. He knows attention spans are short and action is paramount in the training facility. Smith had his wrestlers for two hours before they went to class or returned home to their wives and other occupations, so he did not waste many breaths in getting his point across and the room was swiftly at work again.

He is one of the most accomplished American wrestlers in the history of the sport, but it is difficult to gauge from his appearance. His face fit one observer's description of feminine and does not bear the excessive scars that the trade often yields. His ears are cauliflowered like many wrestlers but are not mangled, appearing smoothed over as if by an iron. In plain clothes, he appears ordinary, neither overly powerful nor slightly intimidating. He owns a full head of curly dark hair, showed few signs of wear and tear and held a youthful look. At 5'6" and 140-pounds, Smith is an inch shorter and weighed less than the average American male, but he was ever anything but average.

He won six straight world titles and two straight Olympic Games and was highly revered in international wrestling circles. "He won six in a row, nobodies done that," Jim Ravanack, founder of the OSU's Gator wrestling club, said. "In Iran, Bulgaria and wrestling rich cultures like Turkey, everybody tried to beat him and they couldn't. There isn't a country in Europe where somebody doesn't know him."

Smith, a devoted Catholic who is married with four children, was known to have few personal interests outside of his family, wrestling and the outdoors. He hosted visitors to his wrestling room like any Southerner would to his house and as he offered a tour of the facility, Smith pointed out multiple award plaques, the team lounge room full of leather coaches and memorabilia, but there was a part of him that never left the coaching process and didn't appear as leisurely as his outfit of shorts, t-shirt and untied jogging shoes might suggest. As he passed wrestlers headed to the showers, he offered bits of advice, stopping one with a tap on the shoulder for assurance that he was headed to study hall.

Smith gave the impression of one extremely at ease with himself. He was engaging in conversation, always looking one in the eye and when praise was directed his way, he deflected it smoothly, crediting his athletes, the OSU program and assistant coaches he was surrounded with. But there was a ruthlessly competitive side that he reserved for his athletes and he could be fierce and ornery when unsatisfied with his wrestlers. He realized that some athletes were afraid to ask how to achieve greatness and perhaps more were afraid of the answer and while Smith knew that athletes could be taught to train and taught to wrestle, the desire to win was not an educational matter; it had to come from within.

He hails from Dell City, Oklahoma, where a life-size sculpture of him stands outside his former high school. When John Smith's older brother Lee Roy was in the fourth grade, he was hanging on the monkey bars during recess when the school's wrestling coach was recruiting kids in the yard. A group of young wrestlers crowded around and asked him if he wanted to go a takedown with another kid. Lee Roy Smith won the takedown and joined the school's team soon thereafter; one of the most successful wrestling families in American history had emerged.

Lee Roy, the second oldest of ten children, had four sisters before his parents had another son they named John. Lee Roy looked forward to coming home from school and working moves on his younger brother. Lee Roy was a three-time All-American and an NCAA champion for OSU and went on to capture silver at the World Championships in 1983. The Smith's passion for the sport passed on to younger brother Pat, who in 1994 became the first four-time NCAA Division I champion. Mark Smith would earn All-American honors as well, but it was John who would make the biggest impact of the Smith's on the sport. "From a young age," Lee Roy said. "John had the ability to watch someone wrestle and then without practicing go reproduce the move, he knew how to do a half-nelson before he could walk. John might tell you different, but he was a stud from the time he started."

Lee Roy recalls how wrestling had been somewhat of a burden for his younger brother and he was always pushing him to work harder. While John had shown traces of potential, it wasn't until his sophomore year at Oklahoma St. when he was forced into an unwanted red shirt year by his coach, that he took his talent to another level. After being forced to sit out a year and just practice, Smith was determined to never be denied an opportunity to compete. His life began to revolve around wrestling and a rare level of work ethic followed. Smith spent so much time in the practice room, a former teammate joked that his best friend was the school janitor. "I no longer worried about getting tired in the practice," Smith said. "I worked like I never worked, I was motivated like I was never motivated and I couldn't get enough."

Instead of trying to be the best in the nation, John Smith wanted to be the best in the world and for six years on the international level he was nearly unstoppable. He won the World Championship four times and captured gold in the 1988 and 1992 Olympic Games. He won 436 out of 458 high school, college and international matches and along the way, carved out a niche in the sport.

If Gable represented American wrestling's blue-collar toughness, Smith was its gunslinger. He relied on a mix of speed and precision, mat savvy and balance, and a low-single leg shot that blew away the competition. During his many hours on the padded mats Smith began to get creative, developing what became the most unstoppable shot in the world. Positioned in a low wrestling stance, Smith would open-hand jab at his opponent's head, fake at his legs, anything to create the slightest opening or hesitation. Blessed with lightning quickness, Smith would burst in, latching his hand around the ankle like a grappling hook and catch his opponent flat-footed, making their legs appear to be weighted to the mat. Often times the opponent draped over Smith's back, trying to salvage a stalemate, but Smith would remove his limbs like a magician untangling himself from a straight jacket. When his prey attempted to flee, Smith leveraged his opponents leg the way a fisherman would a pole, jerking and reeling it in to score his catch.

America's elite wrestlers were drawn to Smith and the OSU tradition. From 1924 through 2004, Oklahoma State won a record 32 NCAA team titles, 152 All-Americans and 34 alumni wrestlers become Olympians. OSU Olympic hopefuls had financial support through the Gator Club freestyle program which was funded by Jim Ravanack, a wealthy Southern businessman who made his fortune in the oil business. For Eric Guerrero, Jamill Kelly and Daniel Cormier, three top-ranked American wrestlers, Stillwater was where Olympic dreams began each day. In the glass-walled weight room below Gallagher-Iba Arena. On the track of the football stadium where they ran sprints and climbed the bleacher seats. In the wrestling room where the top NCAA program held sparring sessions. Surrounded by elite wrestlers with the comforts of home, they choose to live and train here. Guerrero had a wife and daughter. Cormier recently lost a young infant in a tragic car accident. Kelly was viewed as having the least chance of all the world team members of being an Olympian; all felt more comfortable training here than in Colorado Springs.

Similar to the OTC, greatness was not a miracle in this environment, it was expected and U.S. Olympians were sure to come from this wrestling room because OSU is the NCAA program of the present like Iowa was of the past. "There's always more to achieve, always something bigger to win in John Smith's eye," Mo Lawal, a former OSU All-American said. "If you capture the NCAA title, he wants you to win another. Make the world team, he sets the goal of capturing a medal. Qualify for the Olympics, go for the gold. He doesn't accept anything but winning, he never settles for anything but being number one."

After practice, many athletes stay for additional mat time. Spread across the room are the nation's best high school recruits, NCAA Champions and All-Americans in every weight. Several assistant coaches, each multiple NCAA champions, were also immersed with this group. Many of the OSU wrestlers had long, lean frames and were known as offensive technicians; even the heavyweights in the room seemed to have a lightweight's footwork. Early in his coaching career, Smith molded many of his wrestlers in his low-level offensive style but he has distanced himself from this approach, realizing that not everyone could emulate his ways. He is quick to shoot down the notion that OSU is one-dimensional. "The OSU style was about scoring points," Smith says. "As many as possible."

The action continues in the practice room long after it is required. The athletes and young coaches swirling together, the daily competition between the fresh-faced high school All-Americans who were now nobodies, the NCAA All-Americans who were somebodies, and the Olympic hopefuls who had been both and were now trying to take on the world; the three ladders of the athletic food chain-prep, college and professional-grinding together in the OSU room and Smith being the main ingredient.

"Get em' drunk and get em' laid."

-UNOFFICIAL RECRUITING SLOGAN FOR NCAA WRESTLING POWERHOUSE.

The Campus Platoon
VI

The coaches preach of higher education and elite facilities, of storied tradition and program values, but some NCAA wrestling recruiting trips turned into booze and broads, high times and wild nights, in hopes that by the next morning the blue-chip recruit was sold on the wrestling program, was ready to sign and commit right then and there.

But when the wrestlers finally got settled onto campus it was a fight for the starting spot, it was a daily justification for scholarship money, it was bruises and cuts, stretched ligaments and black eyes, six am practices and afternoon wars; a daily physical regime of a boot-camp Marine. In college, many wrestlers struggled with this balance of academic and athletic excellence, drifted away from the sport for the first time, and couldn't cut it. With NCAA rosters stacked with high school All-Americans and ambitious walk-ons, academic schedules jammed with required units, several hours of training in the weight room and the mat, there was little time for the usual college vices. For schools boasting year-round vacation weather such as Tempe or San Luis Obispo, the sport could be a viewed as a grinding duty, keeping young athletes from the warm sunshine and campus parties, beautiful women and casual decadence, requiring wrestlers to exercise even more discipline and self-restraint.

So many prized recruits ended up in the Midwest, where long, harsh winters hibernated these indulgences, put them on ice during the winter season, and made college wrestling a more justifiable passion. Where the tradition of Big Ten and Big XII programs and the influence of coaches like Gable, Smith, Bobby Douglas and J. Robinson could override youthful desires to go hell-bent on the party route, and athletes from schools in Oklahoma, Iowa, Minnesota could buckle down, focus solely on the sport and carve out gladiator legends of their own.

They could put on headphones in the morning and pound out long sessions in the weight room. They could throw on hooded sweat shirts and bini-caps and run down dark roads at night, miles at a time, locked into cultivating their championship desires and not feel as if they were missing out, as if there were some party to be at, not have them conflicted like a celibate in the Garden of Eden.

Oklahoma State.

Iowa.

Iowa State.

Minnesota.

Among these four NCAA wrestling programs, they have traded 54 of the last 69 NCAA team titles. OSU has taken home 34 championships, Iowa has 20, Iowa St. has eight crowns and Minnesota emerged at the turn of the century with back-to-back NCAA championships in 2001-2002.

Years ago, Olympic dreams were spawned and nurtured across the country. From the shores of the Pacific to the muddy banks of the Mississippi, from the blue-collar regions of Ohio and Pennsylvania to the small valley towns of the Central California and for many young Olympic aspirers, there came a time when they had outgrown their surroundings and had to take their talents to the next level, leading many to the four points across the country where wrestling is known, understood and appreciated. Along the dusty backstretches of Oklahoma, amid the Great Plains of Iowa, in the northern isolation of Minnesota, wrestling was home. Many of America's past Olympians had trained here and it was where many more would emerge.

Many Athens hopefuls would split their time between these four points and the Olympic Training Center, doing whatever it took to reach Athens. With no representation to rely upon after college, it was up to each athlete to find his way. Wrestlers were paid respect wherever they were recognized, but they were not paid much else. Surviving on assistant coaching salaries, camp appearance fees, USA Wrestling stipends, personal t-shirt sales and individual sponsors. Full-time careers are out of the question. Rest and recovery fill the time between practices. Training is their job. But even at the biggest events, wrestlers' accomplishments remain unhallowed. With rules that are both technical and confusing, with uniforms appearing awkward to the uninitiated, the sport is out of the mainstream. National title results are not posted in the sports pages. Outside of the wrestling community, no one knows where to watch, nor would anyone know how to watch.

***

"There is no great genius without some touch of madness."

-SENECA, ROMAN PHILOSOPHER

Wrestling was not art, wrestling was not image, feats cannot be accomplished by a romantic lost youth, by staying up all night and partying all day, by following in the footsteps of Spicoli from *Fast Times At Ridgemont High* or the decadent path set by rocker Pete Doherty; Sid Vicious was not an appropriate role model either. There was no escaping the code of discipline and the sport weeded out the weak, but the role models in wrestling might be possessed by the same obsessive demons as those in art, music and film.

Gable ran four miles *the day after* he won Olympic gold. Tom Brands ultimate fantasy was to O.D. on a workout; to train so hard that he had to crawl out of the practice room from exhaustion. Cael Sanderson broke one of the running machines at Iowa St., wore it out in the words of his former college coach. "All these guys have nothing in common, except for a crazy drive to win," Sonny Greenlagh, of the New York Athletic Club said. "John Smith wants to pick you apart, the Brands brothers are like bulls in a China shop, but really they have nothing in common, I guess wrestling is the only thing they need."

There are three major wrestling clubs in America which supported aspiring Olympians: Team Sunkist run by Art Martori; the NYAC managed by Greenlagh; Team Gator under the guidance of Jim Ravanack. Neither of the leaders of the teams express animosity with the other clubs, athletes frequently train in each others camps. Many American athletes felt more comfortable training exclusively at their clubs or the OTC and often times both.

American wrestlers' greatest asset, champion training partners, is also its biggest vice. The very people they needed (elite wrestlers) were also their rivals and had to be avoided. Wrestlers prefer to keep techniques a mystery and top U.S. wrestlers ditched their fiercest competition until the most important moment.

So they cross paths in airports and hotel lobbies. They eye each other at weigh-ins and warm-ups, as the confrontation on the mat is unavoidable. Collisions are forecast in the bracket sheets posted on gym walls like exam times on a professor's office door. When the two finally meet on the mat, their moves are more potent when unexpected. This made things difficult to set up and control, more challenging to predict and at the Olympic level of sport, split-second hesitation can be the difference between victory and defeat.

Even when the tournament ends, wrestlers never really leave each other. They return to separate training grounds, but are still ingrained in each other's minds. Indirectly, they push one another through workouts, their opponents faces showing up on days their bodies don't want contact, their rivals pushing them through strained moments of practice.

On the open level families, careers and other priorities complicated Olympic dreams. Few could make a living off the sport. For some ex-wrestlers there were opportunities down the line, openings for athletes such as Chuck Liddell, Randy Couture, Dan Henderson and Brock Lesnar who had conquered the Ultimate Fighting Championship. Or Olympic gold medalist Kurt Angle who landed a million-dollar World Wrestling Federation contract. Or former freestyle world champion Stephen Neal, who moved on to the NFL after walking away from the mat. But these successes were scarce.

Being an Olympic wrestling hopeful in the U.S. was all about survival. It meant getting by on minimal funding. It meant outlasting fierce rivals. It meant going for the gold when all conventional signs pointed in other directions.

The Silent Void
VII

Other than the battered ears and stout physiques, no one outside the wrestling community would recognize elite wrestlers by name; they are professional athletes in caliber only.

There are places out there, tiny towns, dots on the map in deep stretches across America, places where if accomplished wrestlers were due in the room, hundreds of parents would show up with their kids and be willing to fork over money to watch them train, compete, be willing to pay several hundred dollars in camp fees for these wrestlers to teach their offspring skills. Afterwards, mothers and fathers would point toward these wrestlers and the kids would takes photos, get their t-shirts signed and it would be a moment to look back on for the youth, a reference for motivation in their careers, but Colorado Springs is not one of those places. Colorado Springs is far from those places. Outside the gates of the OTC no one knew who these wrestlers were, no one interrupted their dinners for an autograph, they were not a cause for civic celebration; people were grinding their own lives in this city.

Somehow a sport with legions of troops and strong youth participation across the U.S., had failed to hire a public relations gun to toot its horn. Somehow wrestling drew less TV viewers than the country-club cocktail sport of yachting and had gotten flat-out pinned in its battle with exposure. It was a fact that perplexed many within its ranks, especially with the rabid popularity the World Wrestling Federation.

Some felt the real sport needed a Vince McMahon, the brash, outrageous, all-or-nothing leader of the WWF who knew how to seize an audience and did it one way or any damn other with all the decency of Blackbeard the pirate, who took what he wanted and answered to no one. McMahon, for his entire bombast image, should be applauded for creating a fake drama dynasty from a sport whose origins were real and Kurt Angle, Brock Lesnar, Sheldon Benjamin and other former NCAA wrestlers couldn't be shamed as sell-outs for taking WWF money because their talents were not compensated by USA Wrestling. So they cultivated alter-ego's and performed flying roundhouse kicks, camel clutch contusions and belt-buckle debacles that were a theatrical hoax but enthralled a public audience that did not understand freestyle or NCAA wrestling or had been failed to be informed by the powers of the sport, had failed to do what McMahan did and that was simply… *entertain.*

USA Wrestling needed to attract a new audience with a dynamic marketing plan with the same vigilance that their athletes went after opponents.

But USA Wrestling didn't do this.

USA Wrestling didn't create villains.

USA Wrestling didn't promote bad guys.

USA Wrestling promoted the family sport.

USA Wrestling folded on an Ace-King hand, walked away from the table with a modest earning, called it a night in Vegas at nine p.m.; played it safe when the play called for fast and loose. USA Wrestling, for all its fearless champions, *was scared.*

But USA Wrestling did have hope. They had an athlete with the potential to captivate an audience, deliver under pressure and become a household name in the sport that needed a star as surely as *Playboy* needed a centerfold. But USA Wrestling also had a problem.

If the best wrestler in the United States walked into your classroom right now you wouldn't even notice because he was known to slip in quietly, find a corner and sit with a ball cap tucked low on his head like an undergraduate trying to doze through study hall. But with his height, build and squared-jawed gaze Cael Sanderson couldn't be mistaken for anything but an athlete. Sanderson didn't match comparisons to the public perception of a wrestler as a barbarian hulk. He was tall, sturdy, but lean like a graceful shortstop and looked the part of a perfect All-American hero, having one of those clean-cut faces that made millions in Hollywood for portraying Superman, Batman and other recycled action hero flicks. USA Wrestling was in the promotion business and did not miss the connection with Sanderson, putting him on posters, advertisements and making him the frontrunner to sell the sport.

But USA Wrestling's greatest marketing chip was also its most reluctant hero. Like a great artist devoted solely to his work, Sanderson's fame interfered with his passion. The more the attention came, the further he withdrew. The pressures and expectations were the desires and motivations of others, and Sanderson would just as soon as stash them under his bed like his oldest brother Cody once found him doing with the Danny Hodge Trophy, college wrestling's equivalent of the Heisman Trophy.

Sanderson stiff-armed the notoriety he received, knowing that to indulge would only dull his sharpness, waver his focus and detract from what he really wanted. Sanderson was more laconic than iconic, his eyes more alert than telling, and when he entered rooms he was more likely to be seen than heard and unless you knew his face, unless you followed the sport, Cael Sanderson was more likely to sit next to you and not say a word, than tell you that he was America's best wrestler in a decade.

"No one knows what kind of pressure he's facing because none of us has done what he's done before."

-OLYMPIC COACH KEVIN JACKSON

The Champ, The Underdog
& The Future
VIII

They came onto the scene like three forces of nature: The champ rising like the early morning sun behind the Utah Mountains to shed a new light on the sport. The underdog steadily building like a Midwest storm that ravaged the Iowa fields pushing forth, shadowing opponents like a black cloud. The future arriving boldly, like the thunderclaps that stuck down on the open plains of his native Texas, making noise, disturbing the peace.

Wrestling had once been very simple for Cael Sanderson: Playing. Competing. Fun. The third of four brothers, Cael Sanderson was always around the sport, enrolled in recreation programs at a young age. He was a coach's son; his father won a conference title for Brigham Young University in the 1970's and instilled a battle cry into his four sons: "We came here not to win," Steve Sanderson said. "But to fight."

Quietly competitive, Sanderson's father was never jumping up and down on the sidelines when coaching, a trait that carried over to his sons, neither of whom displayed much emotion; they came off the mat with the same manner in victory as in defeat. "I never twisted their arm," Sanderson said. "I let them play and learn to love the game. We never talked about winning or losing we just played. They were never afraid of challenges. They were never cocky, couldn't tell whether they won or lost. Sometimes I don't understand the mentality of Gable and Brands who treat wrestling as life or death. It's just a game, play it as well as you can."

Cody began to take the sport seriously in fifth grade and his younger siblings followed. Competitive by nature, an intense rivalry developed among them. Wrestling, football, chess, Nintendo, the brothers were always trying to outdo one another; the Sanderson's were not dedicated sports fans they loved to compete. Separated by a year in age, the three Sanderson were roughly the same size. The oldest, Cody was small for his class, Cole was average and Cael, the youngest, was ahead of his peers in growth. The three brothers were the perfect workout partners, each offering a different challenge. Cody was the technician, Cole was the bruiser and the precocious Cael would try and find a way around his two older siblings as a form of survival and as a result he developed a different style of competing.

His older brothers made it a point not to give Cael easy points in the wrestling room. At times, he had to be separated from Cole, leaving the mat in tears, wanting to go one last takedown. During this process, Sanderson learned to work smart, developing an ability to know what he needed to do to get ready. "Cael was pretty much unstoppable since he was a little kid," Cody Sanderson said. "He had uncommon leverage and quickness for his size, with an extra sense of his body and how to push it." Unlike his brothers, Cael inherited his father's height and his natural athletic ability transferred to other sports, earning a reputation as a hard hitting strong safety on the football field, taking down ball carries with single leg tackles, rarely letting offensive players past him.

As a high school All-American, Cody Sanderson had his pick of colleges as a senior in 1995. He visited Oklahoma State, North Carolina and several Ivy League schools and he chose a school not just for himself, but for his siblings as well. "Cole and Cael would have gotten in anywhere in the country with their grades," Cody said. "But there weren't athletic scholarships at Cornell and the distance from home did not fit Cael."

Cody signed with Iowa State. Cole came the next year. Cael would follow his brothers to Ames. Once reunited, they moved into the same house and rarely a moment passed where they weren't hanging out or training together. During Cael's freshman year, his two brothers lived in a house together. When Douglas recruited Sanderson, Cael told him he wanted to be an Olympic champion. Still, Douglas did not know what to expect. "I saw Cael as a freshman," Douglas said. "He was getting scored upon more than he was scoring on people in the wrestling room. His practice partner, Barry Weldon, pounded him. It wasn't till after his freshman year that I knew he was special. Guys train at a certain level of intensity to be a champion. Cael trained above that level of intensity. He had an eight-year plan from day one. After going undefeated as a freshman and winning the NCAA title at 184-pounds he came out as a sophomore and turned it up to where no one could score on him. After practice I would come out of my office and the treadmill was smoking, he broke one, literally wore it out, never seen anyone run as hard on a treadmill."

Sanderson's non-stop attacking style kept opponents off-balance and like Gable and Smith, he developed a signature style. When performing his ankle pick, he would grip the collar of their neck, shift his opponent's weight from their toes to heel, handicapping their balance, before dropping and picking the ankles off, leaving them little choice but to bail to their stomachs and concede the takedown.

Sanderson entered the 1999 NCAA Tournament as an unbeaten freshman. Always wary of people thinking he was cocky or arrogant, Sanderson made a point of humility when talking to the media. In the wrestling program that previewed the tournament, he felt his words were taken out of context in a story that had him bashing his competition, quoting him as saying, "The only reason he wasn't ranked No. 1 was because he hadn't wrestled the best guy." When Cody found out about the article, he tried to hide it from Cael but it was too late. As Cael read the words, "His eyes became teary and he got up and left the room," Cody said. "He had been burned early and decided not to give the media any more information than he had to."

It was a long time before Sanderson began doing interviews again; he found that it was easier to say nothing at all. He won the NCAA title convincingly his freshman year, appearing to be smiling in the championship match. As a sophomore, Sanderson went undefeated again and the Cyclone program was surging. Then things changed. Cody and Cole graduated. Questions about going unbeaten and breaking Gable's record intensified. Now there was pressure and attention he didn't want. As it came, he pulled back. Half of the wrestling fans wanted to see Sanderson break Gable's, the other half wanted to see him fail.

In 1970, Steve Sanderson was a high school senior when Gable lost his last college match to Larry Owings in the finals of the 142-pound NCAA Championship. As the pressure began to increase on his son Cael, Steve Sanderson brought out a newsreel of Gable preparing to wrestle Owings and showed it to Cael. They watched the image of Gable sitting against the wall before the bout and the intense national media coverage that surrounded the event. "This is what it could be," Steve Sanderson told his third son. "But it doesn't have to be like this."

Cody also worried about the effect and noticed changes in his brother's personality; Cael began seeking ways to escape the attention. "Every chance he got, he'd get in his car and drive right out of town," Cody said. "In five minutes he'd be out on the river." Unsure of how to deal with the pressure, Cael closed in and his artwork became a release but he was a perfectionist at this, too, remaining frustrated with his work; Cody can't ever recall Cael finishing a drawing. His professor told him he could do something with his art if he put more time into it, but that he had to choose between the two passions: "Can't be a wrestler and an artist too," Sanderson teacher said. Sanderson would wear his hat low to his Iowa State classes and students generally left him alone. "People were intimidated by him," Cody said. "His smile and joy for the sport disappeared."

Unwilling to embrace the spotlight, he pushed harder, focusing solely on the sport. When Sanderson won matches, he didn't leave feeling exalted. If he was ridden for too long in the bottom position, he would be furious in the locker room. If he defeated his opponent by technical fall, ending the match early, he worked harder in practice the next day to make up for the lost mat time. Cael moved in with Cody, who, along with his coaching duties, became his bodyguard from the media, going to the point of shutting the doors on cameraman who wanted footage of Sanderson. "He didn't dislike the media," Cody said. "He just couldn't believe how stupid their questions were. *Are you better than Gable?* Cael didn't know how to respond to that."

As Sanderson's undefeated record continued, there were faceless opponents gunning to break his streak. Opposing wrestlers knew their place in history would be cemented by just one win; they could become the modern-day Larry Owings if they could take Sanderson out. Sanderson became a target and had the same deer in the headlights look of American baseball player Roger Maris, who in the summer of 1961, would break Babe Ruth's single-season home run record under intense media pressure. Like the Yankee slugger, the situation might have had something to do with the receding of Sanderson's hairline.

One slip-up, one twisted ankle, one wrong turn and Sanderson's record chase would have been over, but through midterms, summer workouts, seasoned opponents, beating three future Olympians in the process, Sanderson sustained perfection. Along the way he received standing ovations in rival gyms. By his senior year, he had his own BobbleHead doll. With every match the streak and the pressure grew, but Sanderson delivered each time, winning 158 straight.

When he stepped out for his last college match at the 2002 NCAA Championships in Albany, N.Y., going for win number 159 against Lehigh's Jon Trenge, the atmosphere was a Ringling Brothers event.

Cameras popped and flashed, the crowd wouldn't sit down, it was as if a giant slayer was going to be introduced; the lingering presence of Gable's last college defeat in the same circumstances amplified the setting. Tiring of the speculation, Sanderson headed out after the introductions and just before he reached the platform, a video of him wrestling as a youth began playing on the arena screen. Cody, incensed, blocked the ESPN cameraman who tailed his every move. Not even in the escape of competition could he find solace. No matter how much the press hounded him, no matter how much pressure he felt, when it mattered, Sanderson delivered. He defeated Trenge 12-4 to become the first undefeated, four-time champion in NCAA history. A five-minute, nonstop standing ovation followed. In a sport in need of a hero, still searching for the next Gable, the next Smith, Sanderson became the chosen one.

ESPN gave him an ESPY.

Wheaties put him on a cover.

He had his picture taken with the President.

Sports Illustrated listed his feat as the second-best of the century. And the attention that followed his achievement can only be matched by Greco-Roman wrestler Rulon Gardner. Gardner's feat, beating the unbeatable Russian, was the moment that defined the Sydney Olympics. Gardner and Sanderson each faced attention uncommon to the sport, but handled it in different ways. Rulon, amiable and outgoing, embraced celebrity, did cartwheels over it; Sanderson shunned it. While people looked up to Rulon, they stared at Cael, as if searching for what made him great: What was his secret? His athletic ability? The way he trained? Not even his own coach, Bobby Douglas, the one who knew his ability best, had the answer. All he could come up with was simply: "He has the heart of a champion."

Sanderson was an exception in a sport where sound bites, big-city headlines, savvy public relations agents didn't apply. Multi-year contracts, jersey sales, controversial commercials? *Not a chance.* Not unless you broke an unbreakable record, not unless you one-upped Gable and while his potential implied this burden, Sanderson moved on to the next challenge, but international wrestling was different. The rules, the style, were not the same. Adjustments were needed. Instead of dueling Iowa and Oklahoma State, there were powerful Russians and the world champ, Yoel Romero, from Cuba. Sanderson's first international loss was in overtime against Romero at the Titan Games and after his defeat, the Sports Illustrated headline read: 'Can't Win 'Em All.'

The pressure to succeed rose, still Sanderson delivered, capturing the U.S. national title in 2001. Then the World Championships were cancelled in wake of 9/11. In 2002, the U.S. State Department issued a last-minute warning that the U.S. was a target for terrorists. "That was such a frustrating and helpless feeling," Sanderson said. "To get to the point of leaving and be told it wasn't happening. The World Championships and Olympics are what you spend all your time working for, everything else is just practice." It is only when Sanderson is engaged in a meaningful battle where he seems to lose himself in the blood-rushing, mind-numbing realm of the sport.

Wrestling consumed Sanderson away from the mat. He would be on vacation with his wife thinking about opponents. He felt obligated to the sport but questioned his desire to compete. Several times in the past year, Olympic coach Kevin Jackson came to his office at USA

Wrestling convinced Sanderson was finished with wrestling.

In Sanderson's stature lay opportunity for rival wrestlers and coaches. The more attention and expectations that come, the more Sanderson withdraws. For every moment the champ's passion fades, someone else is training. For every moment Sanderson wavers, somewhere in the broad sweep of American landscape, the underdog trains.

***

A broad-shouldered, square-jawed rock of a man exhausts himself before practice even starts, circling the OTC wrestling room one time after another, running stiffly as if all his muscle fibers were in knots, slowing around the turns and bursting up the straight-aways until the panting of his breath could be heard throughout the facility. He trains as if a storm was swirling inside of him, letting out occasional screams and yells in frustration. When he has broken a sweat that seeps through his shirt, he pulls his shorts high like a boxer and grabs a partner.

His machine-like wrestling style is cold and hard and every every point of attack for Lee Fullhart points to the Hawkeyes and specifically the Brands brothers, whose coaching is so intense, so involved, it seems like they are out on the mat with him. His defeats become theirs, and in victory they triumph with a pounding fist or look of clenching satisfaction.

Fullhart graduated from Iowa with a degree in computer science, but is holding off on a professional career. Number two on the Olympic ladder, he faced the most daunting task of all challengers in seizing the Olympic spot, but instead of running from the challenge, changing weights or giving up, Fullhart's pushes to another gear; in his path is the most successful collegiate wrestler the sport has ever known.

***

"I don't give a fuck..."

In a humble sport whose roots lie in conservative middle America, Mohammed Lawal is not exactly walking the company line. He's young, black, ambitious and has no problem telling it. He swaggers onto the mat with a frame over six feet and arms thick as a pythons swaying by his side, approaching his bouts with the mentality of boxing idols Muhammad Ali and James Toney, wanting to inflict pain, relishing physical clashes. "When I step on the mat it's Showtime," Lawal said. "I'm gonna kick some ass. I'm a soldier. I'm not gonna be a coward. I'm vocal. I'm the most hated guy in wrestling."

What lay ahead of Lawal was an athlete who was everything he wasn't: established, crowned, on top of the Olympic ladder, but Lawal was not silent about his goals. "Cael's the greatest," Luwal said, mocking others. "I respect him, but we don't talk. What's the point of respecting him? You have to disrespect him to beat him so let it be known. The best overlooks everybody, looks down on people. There's no secret plan to beating somebody, just go out and do it. Brandon Slay and Kevin Jackson overcame adversity. If I thought like other people, I would never beat Cael but everyone gets beat. I have to give it to him. He's good, he's good, but I'm gonna rise to the occasion. I'll be up and people come up. All it takes is a throw and a couple turns. Yeah, I'm going to be physical. If I'm gonna come, I'm gonna come hard. I'm not dirty, but if I have to I will. I want what Cael's got. He's wrestling's Oprah Winfrey or Bill Gates. Yeah, I'm jealous, yeah, I'm hatin' a bit, but I want that cash, I need that cash. How am I going to wrestle when I'm worried about bills?"

The number three ranked wrestler in the U.S. receives a $330 stipend plus six months medical insurance from USA Wrestling; number one receives $900 a month. "I'm not trying to get sympathy," Lawal said. "Can't expect someone to be the same, just two different mentalities. Compare our two careers, our families. Cael's mom knows about wrestling, he has family support, my mom's from Africa."

USA Wrestling, a non-profit organization, gives a $1000 dollar stipend every six months to the top-ranked competitor but they cannot offer nearly as much money as the UFC, which they are losing many of their best athletes to.

"I could get $12,000 for my first fight in the UFC," Lawal said. "Wrestling just has an old-school mentality. In America if you're good, I guess they want you to say you're not good. But wrestling will never grow this way. UFC grew when Tito Ortiz started running his mouth. Matt Linland told me that he started getting paid in the UFC when he started talking. Look at boxing, Floyd Mayweather Jr. played the bad guy for a reason. If he hadn't said, *'Money Mayweather,'* nobody would have watched his fights. The people who have the money in wrestling keep it, the athletes busting their ass don't. Ken Chertow paid me $200 to coach a session of his camps, but he's making the big money. I drove all the way down from Oklahoma to Texas to do a camp with Al Rodges, who is a part of USA Texas Wrestling. He paid me $50 bucks! What the f*ck am I going to do with $50 bucks!?!

Lawal was introduced to the sport as a sophomore at Plano East High School. His football coaches wanted him to stay in shape, so he attended wrestling practice in the morning and ran track after school; eventually Lawal had to pick between the two sports. "Everyone went to track, wrestling was too early, it started at six a.m.," Lawal said. "I showed up barefoot, I had no shoes or nothing, but I was hooked when I discovered that wrestling was like a fight."

Lawal was an All-District linebacker as a senior. Texas Tech, SMU and Fresno State showed interest in recruiting him but Lawal was not swayed. "Football got boring," Lawal said. "We made the playoffs but lost to Tyler, Texas every year. If I lose, I want it to be because of me." In his final wrestling season, Lawal went 50-0 and qualified for senior nationals, a showcase tournament of the best prep wrestlers in the country. The tournament exposed Lawal to a level of wrestling he had never seen before but he finished 3-2 and was not offered a full scholarship. "I knew I had a lot to learn even if I had more talent," Lawal said. "I wondered how good I could be if I had a little more wrestling."

Through the recruiting grapevine, Lawal's name was growing and one day while shopping at the grocery store, his cell phone rang. "How would you like to be a Bronco?" Central Oklahoma coach David James asked. "Do you want me to send a videotape?" Lawal replied. "Nah, no tape," the coach replied. "We heard about you."

Central Oklahoma promised to pay for books and out-of-state tuition, the rest he would have to earn. Following the last of his high school final exams, Lawal stopped at Oklahoma University to practice with All-American Byron Tucker. "I was basically a practice dummy, but I soaked up everything Tucker did. As the day's passed, I failed to get one takedown, one day, I got one, I felt like a college wrestler already."

His freshman year at Division II Nationals, Lawal lost in the 30-second tiebreaker for a chance to be an All-American. "The next season I hit puberty," Lawal said. "I had never even shaved before." By the end of summer, Lawal was nearing 200-pounds and growing fast. As a sophomore, he finished second in the country and became a takedown king, notching 255 in one season. After defeating starters from Division I powerhouses Iowa and Iowa State, Lawal knew it was time to face stiffer competition and calls from Oklahoma University began flooding in, but Lawal was not receptive to being a Sooner. "Coach Jack Spates treated me like a scrub," Lawal said. "He wanted me to walk on and didn't offer any scholarship money, it bothered me." Oklahoma St. entered the picture and Lawal quickly asked for his release from Central Oklahoma. "The next day they mailed the papers. I signed, mailed them back. Bam, I was a Cowboy."

John Smith and the OSU program had a green talent to shape. There were times when Lawal's emotion and boldness worked against him, as Jim Ravanack, a financial booster of the Cowboy wrestling said, "Sky is the limit for Mo, or he can fall off the ship." But Lawal didn't lack ambition and was drawn to anything that would make him better. While it was only a 45-minute drive from Central Oklahoma's campus to Stillwater, Lawal might as well have been entering another wrestling world. While he had dominated the past two years in the Central Oklahoma room, OSU was a different story. He sparred with All-American Daniel Cormier and NCAA Champions Mark Munoz and Mark Branch; Cormier overpowered him, Munoz worked him with technique and Branch destroyed him from the top position. "They beat me up," Lawal said. "But I kept working and finally I broke through."

After holding the NCAA top ranking at various points throughout his senior season at OSU, Lawal lost to Damion Hahn of Minnesota by a point in the NCAA semi-finals, finishing third. "Coming out of high school Hahn was the biggest name ever and I was nothing," Lawal said. "But I didn't deserve to be a national champion."

Lawal could be brilliant and foolish in the same sentence, in one moment saying he respected Sanderson and the next minute admitting envy, but he had what many of Sanderson's opponents didn't and that was a lack of deferential respect for the American champion, making him as dangerous a challenger as any within U.S. borders.

At 185-pounds, there was one spot for three men and each would have to go through the other two to become America's Olympian. If Sanderson were in another country, his top slot might be protected and assured by a committee or coach that would look at past accomplishments and deem him the country's best shot in Athens. But in USA Wrestling's democratic system, Fullhart and Lawal would get their shot.

"It is said that victorious warriors win first and then go to war,
while defeated warriors go to war first and then seek to win."

-ZHANG YU, THE ART OF WAR

Resident Hope
IX

Through a set of glass-paneled doors, past the expansive weight room and inside the wrestling room at the OTC's Irwin Belk Complex, the temperature immediately rises, slightly suffocating any visitor not used to the heat. Near the entrance, there are several framed photos of 1992 Olympic champion Kevin Jackson, on his knees, clenching his fist after his triumph at the Barcelona Games. There is an image of Dan Gable on top of the gold medal stand in Munich. There is Zeke Jones, Dave Schultz and a host of others, but this room is hardly a shrine to former U.S. champions, it is a training ground for future ones and its ambiance is all business; filled with only what was required.

Three full-size wrestling mats stretch the length of the facility. Padded walls coat the perimeter. While circles indicate out of bounds in competition matches, the walls and posts are all fair game at the OTC. Barbells, jump ropes and other training contraptions are found at the foot of the mats. There are two trash cans, one for miscellaneous use and the other marked with a red bio-hazard waste symbol. A set of old yellow gym lockers stand next to the coach's office. One set of silver metal bleachers face the mats and two water coolers and four stationary bikes are tucked into a corner. The facility spoke of regiment and regime, order and purpose, but the only posted rule is: 'Absolutely no street shoes on the mats.'

The wrestling room morphs easily from one day to the next. There are no windows to alter the lighting. There is no weather to change the playing conditions. The mats are cleaned and sanitized daily. The music playing from the speakers is randomly arranged-rock, techno, rap and country-but after several practices it was cyclical. Like the coaches words, some tunes strike a chord with the athletes and others go in one ear and out the other. At some point the music will grow stale. Over the grind of a training year, the powers of rhetoric fluctuate. In the end, the wrestlers must rely on themselves for motivation.

Next to the stereo is the single most telling piece of insight to what U.S. Olympic wrestling hopefuls go through. Tacked on a bulletin board between the coach's office and the lockers is the practice schedule leading up to May 10-11, the date of the U.S. Olympic Trials. For the resident Olympic hopefuls, there lives will be dedicated and restricted to the contents of several 8 ½ x 11 inch sheets of white paper. Sleep, eating habits, social lives and families revolve around this. If they veer from the path the coaches set and cut corners, they will, in effect, cheat themselves.

Wrestling is their life. Wrestling is their duty. Wrestling is their job. And unless you walk through the door with these ambitions, you are not one of them. You will look different. You will act different. You will go about your day different. They might talk to you and hold a conversation for a moment or two if so inclined, but this will not be the tie that binds; wrestlers are a species altogether their own.

It's early January on the OTC mats and the number one-ranked 121-pound wrestler in America, Stephen Abas, is dragging. While Abas is in good shape, he's not in wrestling shape. He has just arrived to the OTC and his body has not acclimated to the high elevation; for now, his lungs are burning. He gets up slower after each move drilled with former college teammate Yero Washington and his face has the bitter beer look of exhaustion, but while he wilts with fatigue, he manages to remain controlled and executes each drilled shot with ingrained precision.

When the action ceases for a rest break, Abas momentarily disappears back into the crowd of thick-necked brutes. He is visibly tired and water seems to be the only thing on his mind as he drags his feet over to coolers. He wears dark blue workout shorts and has just removed his red Fresno St. wrestling t-shirt, revealing a hairless upper body adorned by tattoos on his back and left arm. His limbs sway easily off his thin frame and his chest and shoulders are cut and framed to a fine edge, but his lack of bulk would lead one to think that he has never spent a serious day inside a weight room.

Soon thereafter, he is performing Capoeira moves; a free-flowing, Brazilian martial art that's a cross between kickboxing, break dancing and gymnastics. Two other resident athletes join the improvisational talent show, spinning low with high leg kicks and one-armed cartwheels with a twist, but it is the lightest wrestler in the room whose movements draw the heaviest attention. Abas makes two quick, loaded steps as if ready to dunk a basketball and kicks his right leg high in the air. Momentum carries his body up and over for a sideways flip before landing softly on his feet.

More Bruce Lee than Hulk Hogan, everything about Abas points to a martial artist: his thin, floppy black hair; his quick, fluid movements; his face a combination of sharp features and a pointy two day stubble beard. With a body fat in single digits and standing no more than five-feet-five inches tall, he's not physically intimidating. Run into him at a local pub and one wouldn't think about it twice, but watch Abas on the mat and they'd never forget.

While there are high-caliber athletes in the room, many former NCAA All-Americans, they do not move like Abas, who is dancing around his opponent, fooling him with his rhythms, failing to follow anyone's code but his own. Armed with cat-like quickness and the agility of a gymnast, he appears comfortable in any position, seemingly always landing on his feet. He changes levels so fast it is difficult for the untrained eye to catch the details. Hovering somewhere around his opponent's waist, his re-shot is vicious, coiling back and striking like a snake, or slithering around for the takedown. Abas, like the state he hails from, is different.

He moved to Colorado Springs earlier in the year from Fresno, California but other than himself, the OTC resident team, once a staple for elite talent, is now a mixture of challengers and long shots, champions and also-rans, a place of the Olympic hopeful here and there.

The room was filled with several NCAA champions and many bit players, those at the bottom end of the nation's top ten ranks, many of whom could only be considered workout partners, bodies, guys who used to compete in college and knew the drills. Moving amid this atmosphere were short men, tall men, powerful wrestlers young and old, those with prior knee surgeries and ankle braces and limbs that took 25 minutes to get warm, harsh defeats they were trying to avenge, goals they spent a life chasing and rivals standing several feet away; pain, execution and repetition part of their daily existence.

Open level wrestling was a close-knit group of athletes who were all chasing the same thing. Nearly all had come up through USA Wrestling's freestyle ranks, going on international tours and competing at the same national youth events and through the course of the next several months, many American wrestlers would be walking through these doors with an open shot at making the Olympic team, but on May 10-11, there ambitions will be realized or not. The wrestlers were not any different from other athletes on the OTC complex, their Olympic spots were not solidified, and the pressure of this pursuit was stressed every day in practice.

The Olympic training center was far from stagnant, it was a living, breathing American muscle, getting stretched and pulled and pushed to the threshold, soothed and massaged and treated with care, and the sound of the contractions, of bodies being developed was hard to miss. Olympic weights crashing to the weight room floor, athletes screaming at the climax of a squat lift, the military squad sound of feet shuffling on the mat, the smell of sweat and astringent, body heat and manufactured ice, evident throughout the facility.

At the moment, the wrestling room, as far as sounds go, was a library filled with the silent friction of labor. Yet, it held few athletes with gold medal potential and appeared capable of duplicating the feats of the coach overseeing their movements on the mats.

America is a consistent world wrestling power. While the Iranians produced stiff competition and the Cubans often provided fantastic athletes to contend with, it was the Russians who were the rival target, which makes it all the more perplexing to hear a far Eastern voice governing Yankee athletes on the mat.

Sergei Beloglazov moves briskly across the surface, to four different groups in a span of a minute. He does not show allegiance to one wrestler in particular, but whoever happens to be within his reach. Beloglazov is listed at 5'4", but he appears taller because he walks on the balls of his feet. As he works with athletes in 30-second spans, it becomes obvious that many of the U.S. wrestlers have quickly accepted him. They trade jokes when he is pulled into groups for instruction and when Beloglazov brings in his twin daughters to practice the wrestlers become protective older brothers, making sure the young girls avoid the potential danger of the practice surface. After many practices Beloglazov will sit with a group of wrestlers and tell stories or offer advice for any problems they may be facing.

Beloglazov has had to make the typical communication adjustments of any foreigner (his English is rough; he makes an extra effort to enunciate his words) but on the wrestling mats the Russian's skills require no translation. Fearless and peerless in him prime, Beloglazov competed with technical proficiency unmatched in his era, smashing through Olympic brackets with the same ruthless authority as the American legends Gable and Smith; pinning five of six challengers in the 1980 Olympic Games alone. During the several times a week that he spars with competitors half his age, it's not hard to imagine him dominating the world in earlier years. When an American wrestler arrived to train at the OTC Belogalzov took no stock in their NCAA accomplishments, he liked to personally engage them himself. "I test you out to see if you any good." In any position, he has five or six moves to choose from and he executed with a crisp, explosive style packed into a short, compact frame.

Beloglazov was brought in by USA Wrestling, the national governing body of the sport, in late 2003. The U.S. needed his technical knowledge to combat the skill of Russia and its former Soviet Republics. While few in the U.S. could compete with this technical brilliance, the Americans focused on wearing the Russians out and for a period of nearly a decade, the U.S. nearly matched the Soviets tally of world and Olympic champions. Their dual matches consistently filled American gyms for exhibitions but with the fall of the Soviet Union in the early 1990s, the U.S. versus Soviet Union rivalry lost marketing power; U.S. coaches speak of this rivalry with the nostalgia of grown men remembering lost high school football days.

Watching Beloglazov work through the different groups in the room he communicates with an easy charisma. "I love Sergei," Ron Groves, a OTC resident athlete said. "He's really about enjoying what you're doing, enjoying life, he doesn't put a lot of stress on himself. He always tells me to relax with the sport. Dissociates the sport from the person very well. He always asks me about my family and stuff going on in my life and he tells me not to stress out so much. He sees you as a more complex individual. He lets you know that he relates to you on a different level. He's not just a coach, he's a friend. He's concerned about the complexities of people's lives. Even if a person doesn't like his training methods, it's difficult for people to say I hate Sergei, he's an asshole. Sergei's not a kid, he's an adult, he's experienced enough to know life is more than wrestling."

While many American athletes speak in reverential tones of Beloglazov's accomplishments, there were those who looked past his charm. Few questioned his coaching ability, they debated something more personal, something that went deeper than world titles and international experience, something that speaks to pride and prejudice, deception and spy tactics and would spark both truth and rumors that would swirl and gain their own life during Beloglazov's tenure in Colorado Springs.

With a whistle from the resident coach, practice is over. Weary wrestlers trudge over to the water fountain, replenishing fluids they spent the last ninety minutes losing. Moments later, the room is deserted. A shower, food and rest beckon. Training resumes in four hours. Shortly thereafter, USOC employees enter the room to mop down the mats. Each day, each practice, the athletes come in and pour energy out to perfect a sport that has consumed them, coming in and pouring out like the ever-flowing ocean tides that crash upon the Pacific coast. The sweat, the energy that has been exerted onto the mats, only to be washed away by employees' mops like waves wiping away footprints from the sand. With the Olympics, the names, the bodies, the competition sites have changed, but the games, the sport of wrestling will go on.

Beloglazov
X

Growing up in Kiev, Russia, Beloglazov spent his youth consumed with athletics while his parents worked long hours in a furniture factory. Many of nights Beloglazov's father would return home exhausted, but pleased that his twin sons, Anatoly and Sergei, were keeping busy.

"This is after World War II when people work all day," Beloglazov said. "My mother, father work all day, everybody work. We were lucky, lots of kids have no parents or alcoholic parents. I hav nothing to do after school. Totally independent, we choose. Some guys choose good, some guys choose bad. We go buy soccer ball, train soccer all day. At 14, my friends and I walk by big window basement where a wrestling practice was being held. So we work out. Nobody have wrestling shoes. The next morning my brother, two friends wake up completely sore."

The Beloglazov brothers and their friends began to practice three times a week and his father was happy because it was a way for kids could stay out of trouble. Word of Sergei's wrestling prowess began to spread at the same time he came to a crossroads with athletics. A doctor diagnosed him with an overworked heart and told the young wrestler he had to quit playing sports due to the danger. Beloglazov hid the news from his mother and for six months he could only watch practice. After another round of tests the doctor cleared Beloglazov to compete with the stipulation that he pick one sport. Beloglazov choose wrestling over soccer and after winning several amateur tournaments, was invited to a camp with 400 other Soviet Union wrestlers.

"All the Russian champions there," Beloglazov said. "I was so impressed, so professional. Nobody act like superstar, they talk to you. The competition was the best in the world and I was getting closer. In 1976 before Montreal, I beat guy who had placed in world three times. I think to myself, I can wrestle with these guys and in the next four years maybe I be on the national team, Olympic champ, world champ."

The wrestling mats were a way Sergei and his brother managed to escape the harsh factory work life of their parents. The wrestling mats were a way to stand out in a country of cold, isolated winters. For the Beloglazov brothers the wrestling room was a way out and he would go on to become, in the words of Bobby Douglas, "An icon in the sport, he was the one everybody watched and modeled themselves after."

Competing for the Soviet Union in the 1980's, he dominated the 125-pound division. In addition to winning Olympic Gold in 1980 and 1988, he also claimed six world championships, five European titles and a 1979 World silver medal. Since retiring from competition, Beloglazov has lived the young coach's life, moving and shifting from one opportunity to the next. He was Russia's head technical coach for five years. He was Japan's 1996 Olympic coach, staying for one Olympic cycle. He came to the U.S. and worked two years as an assistant at Lehigh University. He remains a sought-after clinician in many countries and his instructional videos float around the world's wrestling rooms.

But Beloglazov's home, his heart, his deepest ties are in Russia. He owns property near the Balkan Sea. His brother Anatoly, also a former world and Olympic champ, is one of Russia's head coaches. His mother and his sister are still there and some believe his allegiance is as well.

Beloglazov has not lost his fondness of the Soviet Union, he recites stories his homeland in quick, passionate bursts and he frequently wears his royal blue Russian national team shorts while working the OTC room. He holds his country's wrestling technique above all others and despite his genial nature, some questioned his motives in the U.S., they questioned whether blood was thicker than water and this is where the Russian's problems began.

***

The Cold War was a period of tension and competition between the United States and the Soviet Union that stretched from the mid-1940's to the early 1990's. A rivalry developed crossing into military coalitions and technological developments. While there was never a direct conflict, there was half a century of political battles and enhanced military preparations, mainly the two superpowers were in disagreement over how to reconstruct the world following WWII. Tensions between the two countries existed since the beginning of the 19th century and the competition extended into the Olympic arena as well.

U.S. wrestlers grew up learning the Russians were the enemy and many of these former competitors were now elite U.S. coaches. The Cold War was still etched in their psyches just as the 1980 U.S. Olympic hockey teams Miracle on Ice upset of the powerful Soviet's was ingrained into American sporting culture. And there are telling clues on the padded walls of the OTC practice room that the rivalry had not dissolved. Near the entrance, in standard size black poster frame, was a color picture frozen in time. Rulon Gardner, is suspended in air, rejoicing in the arms of two American coaches after beating the unbeatable Russian Alexander Karelin; a conquest imbedded in minds of anyone who tuned into the coverage of the 2000 Sydney Olympics, even those fans who normally wouldn't have watched wrestling, but were exposed to it after the American heavyweight's improbable upset.

It was not the U.S. versus Italy, it was not the U.S. versus Canada, it was the U.S. versus Russia and that's why Gardner's picture was on the wall and the entrance was lined with triumphant moments like this. But inside the Olympic wrestling room, working their coaching mats, was a rival in the flesh, a short powerful Russian genius of the mat, living on U.S. soil, with the keys to its athletic laboratory, eyeing, training, developing U.S. wrestling hopefuls; Beloglazov's new position, equivalent to the Russians hiring Dan Gable, raised eyebrows in the wrestling world.

Beloglazov was on par with any U.S. wrestling great. He had accomplished more internationally than Gable, had matched the tally of world and Olympic titles of Smith, and was not without his opinions and ways that would be forced to coincide with another great U.S. wrestler turned coach.

Kevin Jackson and Beloglazov, matched together by USA wrestling and the powers-that-be, couldn't be more different. Jackson was a physical presence, Beloglazov was technical. Jackson was American, Beloglazov was Russian. While both were in the business of building champions, they had clashing methods on how to do so and early on, there was a sense that neither Jackson nor Beloglazov was comfortable with the arrangement. This was beyond each coach's personality. Jackson was the type of patriot who had a U.S. flag flying on the front porch of his house. Beloglazov was a Soviet symbol of Olympic dominance. Opposites didn't attract, but a USA wrestling coaching contract did and suddenly Jackson had another large ego in the room, another world-beater to share the space.

"To give anything less than your best is to sacrifice the gift."

-STEVE PREFONTAINE, CHAMPION

Sunkist Open
XI

Tempe, Arizona: It's half past eight on a Friday morning in valley of sun and while Arizona State students are headed to class amid warming weather or just recovering from hangovers from the previous night's parties, a crucial battle is about to take place on their campus. Next to Sun Devil Football Stadium, inside Wells Fargo Arena, the 19th annual Sunkist International Open is kicking off the freestyle season, the beginning of an Olympic year where former champions come out of retirement, young talent attempts to make its mark, and veterans try to hold their top spots.

Not that anyone cared.

Tempe is a live college town with bars, clubs, coeds, big-time college football and many attractions to pass the time. So why would anyone want to fill an arena to watch nameless competitors duke it out for what...*$500 prize money?* There are locations in this country where the presence of great wrestlers would certainly cause a stir. But not in Tempe and not at nine a.m., where elite wrestling isn't even a good enough excuse to ditch class.

Like other things in the desert, wrestling seems lost, abandoned, eclipsed by the shadows of the colossal football stadium, in the echoes of the expansive basketball arena that it couldn't possibly hope to fill, in the lonely seats that gather dust until another more popular sport takes its place. Wrestling is the forgotten beast of the American sporting landscape. Somewhere in the rise of cable television and 24-hour news, wrestling missed the boat, failing to make itself known as a major American sport. And while NCAA coaches chant and preach and fight for its livelihood just like they inspire their athletes to on the competition mats, there's no denying Title IX's scent of death in the wrestling arena. From the empty grandstands to the local newspaper that barely paid note to such an event, to the number of extinct collegiate programs dropping off the NCAA map, wrestling was a species endangered.

In some places wrestling barely had a heartbeat, requiring a financial lifeline from other athletic programs to keep going, and in others it thrived. Building up until the annual NCAA tournament in March where the nation's top college wrestlers flock to a choice arena and collide at American wrestling's premiere event. Where fans claim sections of stands like real estate, where ten matches ran simultaneously, where contingents rise and fall as massive crowds cheer the gladiators still remaining, the survivors in a grind of a season, a sport that benefits those who were fittest. But American wrestling's greatest asset, the NCAA championship, is also its greatest deterrent to international success. NCAA wrestling competes in collegiate style while the rest of the world competes in freestyle year round.

After the last NCAA match the relationship between coach and wrestler instantly-undeniably changed. Whether ending gloriously or not, when the records they set could never be advanced further, when the college glow dimmed to a selection of memories, wrestlers were faced with a tough choice whether to continue competing. With a new crop of athletes to develop, they were no longer their NCAA coach's first priority. For some wrestlers, still believing the dream that was fostered years earlier in front of T.V. screens flickering with dramatic images of the Olympic Games, the choice was easy, but for the afflicted, family, careers and financial priorities tip the scale. There was also an adjustment period to the rules and scoring of freestyle wrestling. The athlete no longer represented the university that he lived and breathed and sweated for in college, now the wrestler was on his own, hoping to wear the colors of the red-white and blue. For most, the jump to international level was too large of a wager and the four years-for-one Olympic moment too small a prize. The gamble just wasn't worth it.

The competition in the U.S. for an Olympic wrestling spot is brutal; the 145-pound weight class had eight former NCAA champions ranked in the top ten alone. The system protects the richest talents, providing financial stipends and covering travel expenses for the top three slots on the U.S. National Team. The remaining athletes on the Olympic ladder must get private funding or be assisted with university club programs. Money is scarce. Opportunities are limited. Odds were not in the hopefuls favor. Wrestlers knew this reality, knew it all too well.

They didn't receive the adulation that professional athletes are accustomed to. They did not check into four-star hotels and have groupies hunting them in the lobby. They did not get interrupted by autograph seekers at dinner.

They were Spartan.

They were Gladiators.

They were alone.

On the open level, former NCAA stars seldom compete in venues that match their talents. There is little, if any, financial incentive. Without the crutch of a college scholarship, in terms of dollars and sense, wrestling made little. Still, many wrestlers in the ASU arena were chasing gold, a few foolishly.

Beneath the massive scoreboard five wrestling mats, connected two and three in a row, fill the bowl-shaped surface. Officials from FILA, the international governing body of the sport, file in wearing black jackets with gold buttons, gray slacks and bright canary yellow ties; one puffs on a half-vanished cigar as 80's music blares over the loudspeaker.

The action doesn't start until ten a.m., but a few competitors have begun stretching on the mats. At the moment they appear loose, relaxed, engaging. An hour later, faces have tightened, minds have focused, bodies are geared to explode. The public address announcer signals the start of the tournament with a greeting worthy of the Indianapolis 500, *"WREEESSSTLERSSS!! CLEAR THE MATS!!"* But when the tournament begins coaches shouts echo like crow calls in a canyon.

Melvin Douglas, a two-time U.S. Olympian, is on mat one, competing in the first match of his comeback attempt to make his third Olympic team. Douglas hardly looked the part of a former champion wrestler of the world, in fact, Douglas really didn't appear like anything out of the ordinary at all, except what he was: a 40-year old father of three who was a little overweight, a little rusty and a little out of place in a young man's game.

On the mat Douglas was a dancing bear, belying his heavy physique with a natural affinity for the sport, a control of his opponent and a love to entertain. He seemed to enjoy the attention that came with his return to the wrestling ranks. In between matches, he chatted up fans, vendors and anyone in his vicinity. He sat in the stands with his thick, muscular legs situated on the empty seat in front of him and his arms slung across the aisle spread eagle, displaying all the nonchalance required of a baseball bleacher bum.

Douglas wasn't like the other athletes in the gym. He spent little time warming up, lacking the restless ambition of the young sharks that surrounded him. He didn't nervously re-tape his shoes or pace anxiously awaiting his turn. He didn't worry about losing his sweat, concentration or the edge needed to survive. Douglas embodied comedian Bill Murray's look, appearing as if he just woke up, never thought about shaving and was going to show up at work without dressing properly or giving a thought to being two hours late. As Douglas stood around aimlessly waiting for his next bout, one fan joked that taking off his warm-ups was Douglas' warm-up. He cruised onto the surface, with his never rushed about walk, arriving the way one could picture Murray rolling onto a movie set; people were going to wait, watch and enjoy it just because it was him.

Earlier in the month, Art Martori, founder of Sunkist Kids Wrestling Club, urged Douglas to compete again and provided him with financial support. After three weeks of training, Douglas is toying with his first opponent, making a seasoned wrestler look amateur. He exerts little energy, never more than he has to, gliding on skill, experience and the lack of sufficient challenge, moving with the assurance of an old matador around a young bull, knowing the true outcome is soon to come, but content to let it pitifully attack to no avail.

The action on another mat becomes heated when an Army athlete hurls an insult at an Olympic coach who was once a top competitor in the world. The trainer, a prideful man in his fifties, hobbles onto the mat, dragging a bum leg, and shoves his antagonist. *"You don't tell me to shut up!"* Anatoly Petrosyan snaps. A shoving match ensues, members of the U.S. Army team get involved, but no punches are thrown. Martori streaks across the mats from the other side of the arena, his face reddening with each stride, until he reaches the U.S. coach and yanks him off to the side. *"You don't go on the mats!"* Martori yells. *"Don't jeopardize your whole f***king career for one match!"* The coach brings his hands up to his side like he was unjustly framed for a crime, but his mask is one of guilt and he knows he stepped out of line.

Martori, a silver-haired former ASU wrestler with thick shoulders and assured disposition, motions to the coach with his index finger, coaxing him to a hush like a snake getting hypnotized back into its basket by his master. Martori is an important man in this arena, an important man in this sport and he makes sure that Petrosyan gets the hint; do not bite the hand that feeds you. Petrosyan connects the political dots quickly and recedes his protest. Similar to other Olympic sports, USA Wrestling, with a lack of streaming revenue, relies on financial donors like Martori to help their athletes train for the Olympics, athletes like Marcus Mollica who now faced Lee Fullhart.

Mollica and Fullhart are no strangers to one another. They lived in Colorado Springs. They dined in the same cafeteria. They trained in the same facilities. Both men were after the same thing. There was a time when Mollica was the master of his peers. In the early 1990's, he was a two-time NCAA champ for Arizona State. His picture hangs among other championship Sun Devil teams in the circular walkway at the arena's entrance. The color in the photo has since faded and large crowds no longer cheer Mollica. He is several years removed from graduation, having left a coaching position at Harvard to join the OTC resident program this past year.

Mollica is just one of many who have given their life to wrestling. He has traveled the country for it, passed up career opportunities, but he cannot cut loose from what the sport has given him. Mollica has proven himself on the high school and college level, and he wants to be the 184-pound U.S. Olympian, and while he is strong, athletic and ranked in the middle of the Olympic ladder, he seems to have lost the bloodthirsty edge required for such a feat. Mollica wants to be the Olympian, but Lee Fullhart could care less. He has nothing to do with Mollica's dreams, Fullhart has his own.

He makes quick work of the former ASU star, pinning Mollica in the first period. Unsatisfied by the match, Fullhart is drilling by himself moments after, hardly stopping to catch his breath. He stalks around in circles, crowding a phantom opponent while others prepare nearby. Then he jogs furiously in pace, knees eclipsing his waist, with no place to go, no opponent in sight, yet pushing himself with manic passion. Fullhart did not train to beat Mollica. Fullhart did not train to win the Sunkist. Fullhart is training for someone, somewhere else, for the moment he could get his hands on the nation's crown prince of a wrestler and knock the immaculate shield from his grasp and seize the 184-pound Olympic slot for his own.

So Fullhart continued on.

Pushing to the point where his legs burned like a Tour De France cyclist climbing the French Alps, and his lungs seared like a freestyle swimmer on the last lap, and the physical torture Fullhart's body was feeling was a good enough excuse to pack it in, give up, sit down right then and there because weakness was present too, riding each shoulder like the Devil and the Saint, ready to free Fullhart from physical torture, ready to rescue him when all the energy deposits had vacated his body, yes, weakness was there as surely as a dive bar for a drunk or an all-hours slot machine for a degenerate gambler, ready to drown his sorrows, ease his fix, ready to be his sweet companion, ready to put its soft arm around Fullhart's strained muscled shoulder and guide him to the stands where he could slow down, rest and gloat in his tournament victory and count the day's check earned.

But Fullhart ignored easy street and took the hard line. He kept going, kept running in place like a madman because Fullhart had known physical torture, had gone into the practice room asking for it, looking for it, had found it and wrestled with it. He had struggled to not give in, had already pushed himself past the point where it could mentally break him, and after Fullhart had it out with physical torture, after he had experienced it so many times on the mat, then-soon physical torture became Fullhart's partner, his confidant, his only true companion, because physical torture was going to be the difference between fighting on the mats or sitting in the stands, between Olympic participant or observer, between Athens and agony.

During a break in his post-match workout Fullhart's short brown hair is matted with sweat and his cement-jaw expression is strained with pain. Like some dark brooding movie villain, Fullhart shared few words. As he pulls on his black warm-up pants, his dark eyes look off in the distance, not at the wrestling mats, not at the barren seats, not at any of the days opponents, but searching for something bigger, grander, something that would be the equivalent of a bounty hunter's chase of his life, that had swallowed his past and would consume the next crucial months of his life, and that something was a rival competitor that spurred him to continue training long after his last match completed.

As the bouts continue on, as action swirls around, Fullhart is not with his fellow competitors or in the arena either, but, in another setting, in his world of visions and goals, lost in the recesses of his mind where he is America's Olympian and gold medalist leaving everything around him irrelevant. The hallmark image of Cael Sanderson, a wrestler who had defeated Fullhart numerous times over the several years, was what continues to push him through his workout, that detached him from this setting, made him unaware of his surroundings and unaffected by the social norm of taking a break after a match, because Fullhart is not average and no one who is going to be a U.S. Olympic wrestler ever was.

It was not hard to tell where Fullhart came from. He had pale skin that comes from long winters of isolation. He had a wrestling brute's natural build. He was a workaholic as dedicated to the sport as a farmer to his crops. Surely there were other places where men of the mats trained hard. This was a given. But there was something about Fullhart that went a little further, that was just a bit more intense, that had a passion that bordered on downright obsession, and one knew by watching him train while most would be resting, that Fullhart was from the Iowa school of wrestling, that the words of the great Gable were ringing in his ear, that the powerful Brands brothers had stamped their hard-willed mentality into his head and then it was not hard to tell that Fullhart was a Hawkeye anymore, it was hard to imagine him as anything but.

***

Steve Mocco has all the looks and charm of a Sopranos hitman. He is not cordial. He is not sweet. He is not some pretty boy *Abercrombie* b*tch.

Mocco brooded, Mocco scowled, and came across as exactly what a mean, nasty heavyweight was drawn up to be. He kept his burnt blonde hair short and only seemed to shave his goatee when it was required for competition, leaving him with the gruff disposition of a longshoreman. He had a face that wasn't fit for smiling, arms the girth of motorcycle mechanic, chest as wide as a bear's and with the wrong set of homemade tattoos Mocco could intimidate with all the effectiveness of a lifelong resident of Pelican Bay. But Mocco was hardly the All-American hell-raiser.

He graduated from Blair Academy, a rigorous east coast prep school, with honors and spent his youth commited to disciplined-rearing sports of judo and wrestling. His father can't say enough of how good of a person he is, classmates describe him as hardworking, and he was easy for coaches to fall for. Mocco was a winner. He was 216-1 in high school and finished his sophomore year in college as the NCAA champion. His trainers never complain of his work ethic, even in pick-up basketball games at the OTC he played with an intensity of the NCAA Final Four.

He was raised in North Bergen, New Jersey, a township of Hudson County where he was raised as one of several children of Joe Mocco and Helen Peck. Born on December 21, 1981, Mocco shared the same birthday as actress Jane Fonda and the painfully annoying comedian Andy Dick, but he was not a social butterfly. He seemed to regard interviews as an enormous waste of time and he guarded himself in public but nevertheless, his presence is felt, he is known where he is seen, one could imagine him scaring off a whole playground of children.

Weighing roughly 270-pounds with a wide, burly frame, the Iowa heavyweight shifted restlessly before each match on each of his size-16 feet, ready, prepared and with all the pleasantries of a gravedigger; spooking many foes by reputation alone. Mocco knows this, plays up to it and uses it to his advantage, winning many bouts before the whistle ever blows. One of his best moves is a foot sweep, which left opponents falling back as if they slipped on a banana peel. For a heavyweight to have this skill was similar to a lightweight winning a power lifting championship; the concept was at odds with one another. Despite his technical proficiency, there was no denying that Mocco was a physical wrestler.

Since taking a red-shirt year to train for the Olympics, there has been rampant talk of Mocco taking over the U.S. heavyweight ranks, and when he strode onto the mat in Tempe his performance did not disappoint. He smashed his first opponents, looking every part the figure, the force hell-bent on being the next U.S. Olympian, whoever in his way be damned. But Melvin Douglas is not impressed. Douglas had battled Russians in Siberia, Iranians in Tehran and over the course of winning a world championship and making two Olympic teams, he had seen many heavyweight hypes come and go. When asked about Mocco by a reporter from *The Arizona Republic*, Douglas was hardly flattering. "NCAA champs are a dime a dozen."

Now it was the veteran experience of Douglas versus the power and youth of Mocco. In the 2000 Sydney Games, Douglas' last competition, he wrestled at 213-pounds. At Sunkist, he was closer to 240, with a Warren Sapp physique and a Fu Man Chu mustache. In the semi-finals, Douglas handled Kellen Fluckinger, the huffing, puffing, tattooed All-American out of ASU. With blurring speed and nimble feet, Douglas worked in split-second explosive shifts, bursting in on duck-unders, single-leg attacks and throw-bys, buying time with under hooks, snap-downs and lazy strides back to the center. Meanwhile, Mocco paced behind Douglas' mat, occasionally stealing glances at the former world champ as he warmed up for his own match. On his way to sign his bout sheet, Douglas strode a few feet away from Mocco, neither made eye contact; they would meet soon enough.

Like a pay-per-view boxing, the best fight is saved for last; it's nearly 6:30 p.m. when the main event begins. Mocco, like a bull let out of his pen, charges Douglas, shooting, ducking and trying to snap him out of position, but Douglas calmly brushes away the onslaught like a regal fencer, one leg forward, standing nearly erect, slowly back-peddling with each forceful rush.

The crowd quickly chooses sides. Each Douglas point is met with deafening cheers of approval, every Mocco score with grudging acceptance. In the second period, Douglas tries to duck-under the burly frame of Mocco three consecutive times, but is denied. Mocco captures a double-leg takedown with 40 seconds left to knot the score at three. Timeout Douglas. The trainer rushes out, but the old man is in no hurry. Searching for an injury, they eventually diagnose strained lungs. The referee, like a dignified servant, waits patiently by the seated Douglas, affording the master vet all the time he needs; oxygen is hard to come by at 40.

Minutes later, the action resumes. In one quick flurry, Douglas lowers his level, ducks under Mocco and whirls around his wide frame. In trouble, Mocco tries to spin away, but is corralled at the edge of the international mat, in between the first and third circles of the perimeter. Douglas is behind Mocco, who is in a tripod position, hips arched high in the air like a sprinter at the starting blocks. The referee frantically waves his arms before motioning to the side like an air traffic controller.

"No takedown! Out of bounds! Back to the center gentleman!"

The crowd, on its feet, boos in unison. Timeout Douglas.

"Fix the tank Mel!" one fan said.

"Re-tape your shoes," yelled another.

Mocco, shifting side to side in the center circle, hands on hips, is annoyed. Five seconds into overtime, Douglas attempts another duck-under, lowering, rising, but never stepping forward. Mocco, crouched like a linebacker, withholds the attack, before steamrolling the off-balance Douglas to win 4-3.

They shake hands, paying respects. Douglas gazes into the applauding crowd, sleepy-eyed and expressionless, as if searching for someone. Mocco, in typical Hawkeye fashion, bolts the arena, out of sight and into the warm desert night.

*"Many men die at twenty-five and aren't buried
until they are seventy-five."*

-BENJAMIN FRANKLIN

O.T.C.
XII

Former NCAA champions roll into the OTC room as if coming off an assembly line: Kerry McCoy, T.J. Williams, Marcus Mollica and Steve Mocco enter for the afternoon practice and a new hopeful has arrived. Yoshi Nakamura, a two-time All-American from the University of Pennsylvania.

Nakamura was from Elyria, Ohio, 25 miles west of Cleveland. His father, Ryozo, was an 8th degree black belt in judo and a well-known instructor in Kodokan School in Japan. He came to the U.S. by invitation from the U.S. Judo committee and began teaching his son Yoshi his skills at just two and a half years of age. "Basically at that point I made a dream of making the Olympic team," Yoshi Nakamura said. "My father trained me with traditional Japanese way; hard core, disciplined." The younger Nakamura did not disappoint. He won five age-group national titles by the age of twelve and was being groomed for the U.S. Olympic Judo Team.

When he was 12, his mother was driving him from basketball to judo practice when he found out that his father had lung cancer. After surgery the cancer disappeared for three months, but in October of

1991 it resurfaced. "It was growing so fast that they gave my father three months, maybe four, to live, I was on the verge of manhood and the greatest male figure in my life was going to die." In early December, Ryozo, was lying on his hospital bed, withered down from 180-pounds of muscle to a sickly 115. "He was skin and bones and one of the last things we talked about was continuing to train and reach my goals. I promised him right then that one day I would make it to the Olympics."

Ryozo was brought home from the hospital and on the fourth of January, 1992, around midnight, he passed away while being surrounded by his family. "With that a part of me died." Nakamura said. "I didn't know what would happen with our dreams." Before Ryozo passed, a good friend of his, Ichiro Hatta, an Olympic freestyle coach from Japan, was asked to look after his family.

Coach Hatta accepted and Nakamura continued to train in judo, winning two more national titles. Before high school, he took coach Hatta's suggestion and chose wrestling over basketball as his winter sport at St. Edwards, a national prep powerhouse in football and wrestling. His mother drove 30 minutes each way to get Nakamura to the all-boys school. Once the school year began, the family business Kiri Judo Dojo began to lose students. Attendance dwindled from 40 participants to 10, and eventually had to be shut down.

Yoshi continued to pursue judo and without training he won high school judo nationals as a freshman. As a sophomore he won again and placed fifth at the U.S. Senior Nationals. He was invited to the OTC to train with the U.S. World Team at the age of 14 while the other judo hopefuls were in their early-to-mid twenties. But the physical demand of wrestling captured Nakamura's passion and he began incorporating flashy judo throws and foot sweeps into his repertoire.

Nakamura, the oldest child in the household, was now saddled with part of the responsibility of his younger siblings. Father Larry of the local St. Agnus Church helped the family with food, but they stuggled to make ends meet living on one income. His sophomore wrestling season at St. Ed's was filled with a concussion, separated shoulder, IV treatment and torn cartilage in his knee. "I had to clean the house, wake them up for school, lots of stress and pressure," Nakamura said. "I realized how I felt and how I wanted to feel and I made a vow that

I would never let it happen again."

Putting judo aside and focusing solely on wrestling, Nakamura became obsessed with improvement. His mother would wake in the middle of the night and seek out the noise that would lead her to her oldest son's room to find Yoshi doing military presses and arm curls with weights he kept next to his bed. His mother would complain and order him to go to bed, but Nakamura didn't retire until he passed out from exhaustion. He went from 119-pound sophomore to a 140-pound Ohio state champion as a junior and senior. The nation's top schools began recruiting him, eventually settling on the University of Pennsylvania. Nakamura hadn't competed in judo in two years and he shifted his focus to making the U.S. wrestling team. His sophomore year in college he won University Freestyle Nationals and his coach Roger Reina, began to groom him for the Olympics. In 2001, he made the U.S. national team at 152-pounds, ranking third behind Ramico Blackmon and Chris Bono.

At the same time, U.S. college programs were being butchered and the International Olympic Committee knifed the sport, cutting the weight divisions from ten to seven, leaving Nakamura between two classifications and dropping him from No.3 in the nation to all the way off the Olympic ladder. Factoring in the weight class jump and the job prospects in Colorado Springs that were not exactly booming his fiancé's line of work, Nakamura gave up wrestling.

After graduating from Penn's prestigious Wharton School of Business, the couple moved back to Cleveland and got married. Amy Nakamura began working at a bank and Yoshi started his career at the Legg Mason financial firm in downtown Philadelphia. "Suit and tie job, the most money I was ever making," Nakamura said. "And we started our lives together." Following the 2003 World Championships, Nakamura's college coach called him.

"I think you can do it," Roger Reina said.

"Whatta ya mean?" Nakamura asked.

"I think you can beat Joe Williams, you have the ability with your style."

Nakamura didn't think much of the conversation, but over the next two weeks Reina made calls to donors from the Penn and St. Edwards communities who were interested in sponsoring Nakamura; fourteen days later, Reina called Nakamura back.

"Yoshi, would you ever consider training again?"

"Soon as I win the lottery!"

"Money? Is that all? What about in a perfect world with no monetary issues?"

"When he posed that question, I realized I would be training for the Olympics."

The Hunter & The Hunted
XIII

Like a rose that grew from Chicago's sidewalk cracks, once Joe Williams found wrestling, he flourished: winning four Illinois high school state titles and being voted 1993 Asics high school wrestler of the year.

In the sixth grade, competing for the Harvey Twisters freestyle program in Harvey, Illinois, Williams had already made up his mind about his future in the sport. "I decided what college I wanted to go to and what I wanted to accomplish in the world of wrestling. That was what my grade school coach, Quintroy Harrell, who instilled that in my brain. If he thought I could do it, I thought I could do it."

Raised by a single mother, William's father was never really around and wrestling became an escape from the pitfalls of negativity in the neighborhood. The Williams brothers, Steve, Joe and T.J., would rise early to catch the train or bus to Mt. Carmel, an all-boys private Catholic school on the south side of Chicago; getting in a quick workout before the morning bell. Joe would also run on the track a half-hour before practice or drill with his younger brother T.J. in the workout room. "Joe would kick my ass every day," T.J. Williams said.

"But that's what I needed. I would get so pissed off the coaches would have to break it up." After practice, Joe could be found running on the track again before the brothers would catch the train home to work out with the Harvey Twisters. "Practice was a dogfight," assistant coach Mark Antonietti recalls. "Both of them, it didn't matter who you were, they would tear you up and it was nothing personal. If Joe didn't think his partner was working hard enough, he would throw them around."

Joe Williams was just one in a long line of standout athletes from Mt. Carmel. In the hallways of the celebrated school, framed sports pages of alumni's athletic exploits line the area above the lockers, motivational quotes hang above bathroom urinals and glistening trophy cases sit next to statues of Jesus Christ. Williams' photo is across the hall from NFL all-pros Donovan McNabb and Simeon Rice, NBA's Antoine Walker, NHL's Chris Chelios, MLB's infamous Denny McClain and other professional athletes who once attended the school. Williams' photo is the largest of the bunch, with four gold state championship medals around his neck and a shy, almost embarrassed look on his face.

Williams, an African-American, was a popular student at Mt. Carmel, an intermixed high school in Chicago's heavily racially-segregated south side. From 1991-1994, Mt. Carmel won three straight Illinois high school state championships with the three Williams brothers and Tony Davis, who coaches regard as the greatest natural talent in the room; Davis would later win an NCAA title for Northern Iowa. "Physically Joe had un-naturally long arms and his quickness was head and shoulders above most kids his age," Frank Lenti, the athletic director of Mt. Carmel said. "He was a good student, we never approached any problems with Joe. He was very well-liked and showed absolutely no arrogance. If anything, Williams was so quiet, you wouldn't even notice him if he was standing next to you. He wanted to be one of the guys."

But on the mat, Williams was calculating.

"He had this poker face every time he stepped on the mat," a former coach recalls. "Almost a machine-like personality. From the moment I met the kid it was all business. Sprint on, win match, sprint off. If his opponent was stalling, Williams would look at the ref with his hand on his knee and just wait."

During his freshman year against St. Lawrence, in an old 1924 Hoosier-style gym that Muhammad Ali once spoke in, Williams lost the only match of his high school career on a disqualification for slamming his opponent to the mat; a rival coach telling the injured wrestler to stay down. "The gym was stunned," Antonietti said. "But Williams walked off quietly, showing no emotion. He was so much above anything I was in wrestling. There wasn't a lot of coaching with the kid. I was his English teacher and he would type up all his homework. He came prepared just like he was for wrestling, totally focused."

After winning his fourth state title, Williams had his pick of colleges and he chose Iowa, where he would go on to win three NCAA titles, the last of which came after defeating a burly, powerful senior from Penn named Brandon Slay. Williams moved onto the international level, but he has not had the same success, winning only one medal on the world stage.

While Williams competes in the 163-pound weight class, his arms fully extended, are long enough to reach his kneecaps while standing. His back is cut and shaped like a diamond and on the top of his right shoulder is an Iowa Hawkeye branded into his skin. His hair is cropped close on the top and tightly faded on the sides and with his square jaw and closely trimmed beard, he bears a striking resemblance to former light-heavyweight boxing champ Roy Jones Jr. Like Jones once was, Williams is enormously talented and almost unbeatable within the U.S.

He won three straight national titles after college and is still the top-ranked 163-pound wrestler in the U.S. It's not a surprise that Williams is in strong position to make the Olympic team, rather, more of a question why he failed to four years earlier. Leading up to the 2000 Olympics, Williams' face was in a McDonald's commercial featuring America's Olympians, but Williams never made it to Australia; Brandon Slay was there instead.

Slay upset Williams at the Olympic Trials and went on to defeat Buvaysa Saytiev of Russia, the returning gold medalist, to make it to the Olympic finals where he lost to Alexander Leipold of Germany. Months after the closing ceremonies, it was revealed that Leipold tested positive for steroids and was stripped of his medal; Slay was awarded the gold on a national TV show. "I'm watching a tape of the Olympics," Williams said. "I'm not even there."

Since 2000, Williams has gained a son, Kaleb, and lost a brother, Steve, to complications from asthma. He's still number one on the ladder, but there are several contenders training to defeat him, guys with the same ambitions Slay once had and who train in the same facility that Slay once did.

***

Yoshi Nakamura had the type of success in college that gave him enough to believe on the Olympic level. He was a multiple NCAA All-American at Penn and was consistently in the running for NCAA title. He had the type of explosive power and technical skill that went a long way on the wrestling mat and he was the model of what the NCAA drew up a student-athlete to be; juggling the rigorous demands of business school with two-a-day practices on his collegiate team. After graduation, Nakamura accepted a job in the financial world and got married, but the sport was still itching at him. On the mat Nakamura could stand out, could be a contender, so he committed to the OTC, but his current Olympic hopes appeared precarious at best.

Now, Nakamura finds himself locked into a new routine, things that involved numbers that the body-not the accounting spreadsheet-could feel, such as round red, yellow and blue rubber Olympic weights that he stacked onto metal bars in the weight room and performed clean and jerks, squats and other power lifting excercises; the wrestling mat where Nakamura dealt with dimensions of the body and how to break them down; in the cafeteria where the food is infinite and where Nakamura now sits after another workout.

Like the other OTC athletes, Nakamura doesn't have anywhere particular to be once training sessions are completed, so they take their time, slicking their hair back in the mirror and moving gradually from the locker room to the hallway to the outside of the gym where the air was thin and crisp and slowly they move up the steps of the complex, usually with a couple fellow wrestlers, cracking jokes or discussing practice while wearing the satisfactory expression of construction workers whose day is done and they carry gym bags like those carry hard hats and the wrestlers move to the cafeteria, which is visible once they reach the top of the steps, and they walk through glass-paneled double-doors and perhaps they pass other athletes and they nod, smile or hold quick conversations, but they keep going because they are hungry and they need to put fuel back into their bodies that they spent the last two hours breaking down.

They enter the cafeteria and grab trays, forks, knives and whatever they want from the assembly line: salad, vegetables, potatoes, pasta and marinara sauce, soup and bread, steak, chicken, fish, fruit, cake, jello and pudding as they make small talk with the chef. Some days the menu is different but with the cycle it's all the same, the food groups come back around: protein, vegetables, dairy and carbohydrates and there are Cheerios, Fruit Loops, energy bars and ice cream. The athletes grab whatever they want, however much they want and walk out to the seating area to find a spot to sit. And they usually stay there, sometimes for hours on end, reading *The Denver Post* or watching Sportscenter, talking with friends, playing chess, going back for seconds and thirds and some athletes trying to pick-up on other athletes, fellow attractive athletes, fellow supreme physical specimens like 6-foot-2 inch women's volleyball players or tightly wound female gymnasts or college types who are just at the OTC for a short training camp, and they develop relationships or flings or one-night things (or at least try to) or maybe they just meet a new friend that will help pass the downtime that is inescapable at the OTC, because while someone is always training at the training center it isn't all about training. It's also a community, sometimes all the social interaction they have between competitions, so they make the best of the OTC even when they aren't squeezing something out of this world-renowned facility because once they leave the cafeteria, there is not much else to do until they wake in the morning and have go at their goals again.

OTC resident wrestlers are provided with many things to succeed but they are not given belief, assurance or guarantees that they will be the Olympian. No lawyer could put it in writing, no coach picks the team, the Olympic spot is not up for bidding. Teammates couldn't reassure them because wrestlers on this level don't have teammates, they have practice partners, sparring mates, those chasing the same thing as them and right now all Nakamura had was the practice facility, his own belief and one shot at the Olympic Trials to prove it because as it is, Joe Williams is the guy, Joe Williams is the man who has owned the U.S. weight for several years and appeared to be as threatened by his

American competitors as Wal-Mart was by a mom and pop.

But for any U.S. wrestling challenger, the competition is visible and one can just tell what is going through Nakamura's mind during one afternoon practice. He is seated on the mat, staring down the length of the room at the nation's top ranked 163-pounder. Nakamura is thinking there is Joe Williams, the guy ranked above me, figured to fare far better than me, but right in front of me just the same.

Nakamura's body ached after what it had been put through during the last several weeks of training and while he diffused it with protein shakes and energy drinks, ice bags and training room remedies, he was stuck with a guilty feeling that any wrestler felt if they didn't go all out in practice, on the mats, on the god-damn thing that was the only reason he was here. At the moment Nakamura had to be questioning it all because while visitors to the OTC saw the glory filled photos and immaculate physiques walking around, they didn't see the x-rays of when things were peeled back, they didn't feel the muscle knots on the days when the body didn't want contact, they didn't have to deal with the mental frustration of OTC practices where former NCAA stars were routinely smashed like walk-ons. These things seemed to be filtering through Nakamura's mind and after his performance in practice he had to be thinking:

Today I was beaten. Today I made no progress. Today I got my ass-kicked. And while I'm ranked eighth in the U.S. right now, I didn't accomplish a thing today so how could I make the jump to No. 1? How can I make this happen? Am I training right? Am I training when Williams is not training? Can I beat him? *Wait! Of course I can beat him!* There, see, Joe Williams just got up and left the practice room before me. I know because I watched him leave, I'm aware of where he is. I know right now the best wrestler in the country was not training, was slacking, relaxing, taking a shower, and I'm here, I just dropped to the sit-up position and ripped out a set on the blue mats, putting more work in than Williams is, which makes me more dedicated, more prepared, in better condition because I just sprinted the length of the room five times while Williams was turning the knobs on the shower dials and now I'm doing pushups until my chest screams while Williams is unlocking his locker and now I'm doing stance drills while America's No. 1 is sitting down tying his shoes, yeah, I'm doing it while Williams is not, that piece of paper that holds the rankings doesn't mean a fucking thing, might as well torch it with a match, because right now the only thing that matters is work and right now, I'm working and Williams isn't. As Nakamura watches Williams walk out of the practice room his face says it all: *I'm the Olympic hopeful? Joe Williams better hope he doesn't run into me.*

If one were a betting man they would have to say Nakamura's Olympic pursuit was a waste. He should go home to his wife and return to his job. Leave wrestling behind. He didn't have a chance. But betting men were usually fat slobs who rose in the late afternoon and sat in casino gaming rooms watching TV screens day and night, sucking in Marlboros and scratching their afternoon shadows while sifting through sports pages attempting to gauge the merits of winners and losers, college basketball players and stud racehorses, while part-time cocktail waitresses, who were one bad shift from being full-time strippers, dropped off watered down martinis and bowls of stale peanuts. But these men weren't the gladiators in the arena, they weren't built to fight, they didn't wake early in the morning to train or sneak into the weight room late at night and Nakamura didn't think like these men.

Nakamura thought like a wrestler. He knew it was up to him and he believed what Roger Reina preached after watching Williams lose at the World Championships: Williams was talented, Williams was tough, but Williams could be beat.

Wrestling was not a science, just like betting was far from an exact one, it was arena where records, rules and men were destined to be broken and it was foolish to believe in absolutes, all one could really count on was time and its passing, which is why Nakamura is now sponsored by a former Penn alumni, why he left his cushy comforts of home at the urging of his wife and took his one shot at the Olympics months before the Olympic Trials.

As a result of such events the air in the OTC room was a bit more congested and Williams wasn't the only 163-pounder drinking from the OTC well. And, hell, if one couldn't see the odds changing after hearing Nakamura's quest then they were small-minded and thought just like those who drifted into the Bellagio and Sands and Sundowners gaming rooms and pored over stats and lines, rules and numbers, circumstance and chance, but never had the guts to take one themselves.

Despite his exhaustion, despite the doubts on his face that were easy to decipher, Nakamura picked himself off the practice mat and went for some more training, more lifting, more cardio because this was the only way to put the odds in his favor.

One never learned anything about a wrestler until he was tired, and Nakamura knew it, he knew what the moment called for, he knew he had to be hard, he had to cut off the part of him that wanted to quit, that wanted to walk away from the mat, find a quiet corner and be by himself, where no one was cheering for or against him, where no pressure existed, where he didn't have to continue fighting, where he didn't have to be a champion. Nakamura knew about this place of peace and solitude, but he decided that he wanted nothing to do with it, he didn't want to hide out in the locker room, he didn't want to relax in the stands, that he wanted to be a participant and not an observer, a doer and not a dreamer, that he wanted to be out on the mats where the action was, where the juice was, where he could ride the edge of victory and defeat because Nakamura had once watched the battle in the arena wondering silently to himself, wondering why he wasn't out there, why the crowd wasn't cheering for or against him, wondering whether he had it in him to be the U.S. Olympian, so he took the challenge and now he was back in the thick of wrestling's eternal inner struggle and he knew he had to be hard and not give in to fatigue, not worry about his scorched lungs, because he would rather pass out from exhaustion, fall face-down right here on the mat, than be sitting in the stands silently relieved of never having to face the gauntlet that the mat, the sport presented himself.

**

"There's a flip side to that coin."

-ROBERT DENIRO, HEAT

As Nakamura recanted his life story one wanted to believe in him and side in his favor, was ready to dismiss his competition and discredit anyone who stood in his way. But then Nakamura disappeared after training, the passion of his words subsided and shortly thereafter Joe Williams, the baddest 163-pound motherfucker in the U.S., came into the OTC wrestling room for a late workout. As he tore apart another practice partner, one remembered that Williams was also raised by a single mother, that he had rode the school bus early in the morning and arrived home late at night, and that he had worked for years to reach the top spot he was now in. And one was quickly reminded that neutrality was to be exercised when forecasting the outcome of such contests, because emotional speeches would have nothing to do with it.

The Olympic team would be settled by cold, hard ambition and pure talent. Not who had the better story, who was more valiant and worthy in the Lord's eye, who thumped harder on the good book. This deal came down to who was more prepared to seize the moment, who would be the cut-throat executioner on the mat in Indy.

As the facts were, Nakamura was in a race against time. While Nakamura was in corporate board rooms, Williams was sweating in the Hawkeye wrestling room. Williams was the U.S. national champ three years running and he treated the prestigious Midlands Invitational like a j.v. tournament, winning it ten times. There was sound reasoning why Williams was the odds-on Olympic favorite. He was so athletically talented international wrestlers nicknamed him "The Freak." He had arms like a condor and while listed at 163-pounds, he looked like he cut 20 just to make weight. There wasn't any way an opponent's coach could tell his wrestler that they had the physical edge when pitted against Williams and it would be hard to trust a coach who said he had the mental one as well. Williams only lost once in high school (if you count being disqualified for slamming an opponent while leading 12-2 a loss), he didn't really get touched in college and he had a body that layered muscles on top of muscles; thick veins and bulges in his back, bumps of flesh on top of his biceps and rips along his abdomen. And Williams knew how good he was. He had to. Any wrestler in the country, who was going to win big, had to. And Williams knew.

He knew he could get away with winning close matches, with only taking down his competition a couple times, because he had done it on enough occasions to make his coaches wonder if he felt challenged at all. Williams knew he could beat former NCAA champs Casey Cunningham out of Central Michigan, Donny Pritzlaff from Wisconsin, Joe Heskett from Iowa State or any other American at the weight. He had done it before. He would do it again. But there was a glitch in Williams and the top coaches in the country readily admit to it. He didn't attack all the time and after all these years Quintroy

Harrell, William's grade school coach, proved to be quite the prophet; the only person that can beat Joe Williams is himself.

Maybe if Williams yelled every time he slammed an opponent or screamed after each victory or drew more attention to himself when he wasn't on the mat, would he not give off the impression that everything was so easy for him, that he didn't run, drill, spend hours in the weight room building muscle and grueling moments in the sauna trimming it down, maybe if Williams opened up, got angry, showed emotion, maybe then it would look like he was actually trying hard.

But Williams never lets on, competing with an aggressive coolness, plotting for the right time to strike, seldom changing his nonchalant expression. When he moves his opponents, he is nearly impossible to stop and nothing appears out of reach of his considerable grasp. If his talent were measured in dollars, he would be one of the richest in the world, but, at times, he squanders his assets by refusing to take risks. "I don't think I've ever seen Joe Williams put out more than 75 percent of his talent," Bobby Douglas said. "Ten percent more and he might be unbeatable. Joe is limited because he only uses one setup at a time, as good as he is, he could be a *whooooole* lot better."

Many people felt this is why Williams lost to Slay, and this is why Nakamura felt he could beat him. Like Slay, Nakamura was a horse, predicated on power and pump, and much of his training involving the weight room where he built himself to be explosively quick. He had practiced judo throws since he was knee-high and if Williams was being passive or waiting around for the right shot, Nakamura could upset him with one toss to the back; no wrestler was exempt from the unstable laws of competition.

"Joe and I don't engage," Nakamura said. "I don't pretend to be his best friend and neither does he." Nakamura didn't come to Colorado Springs to make new friends and when he spoke of Williams he was all balls and bravado, 'I've got something in store for him!' His plan was to surprise Williams at U.S. Nationals or the Olympic Trials, but one afternoon on the practice mat this plot is foiled.

Jackson blows a whistle and instructs the wrestlers to rotate partners. Nakamura, within ten feet of Williams, looks for anyone but him, twisting and turning to solicit other athletes as if his head were on a swivel, but like a game of musical chairs Nakamura has run out of options, Jackson is set to start the drill and he and Williams are the only two without partners. Jackson points Nakamura to Williams and Williams waits as Nakamura reluctantly walks over because he does not want to expose his skills during the drill. The whistle blows but Nakamura doesn't attempt a maneuver and when the two wrestlers separate, he is disturbed by the sequence while Williams seemed to give it no more thought than he did to which sock to put on first in the morning.

Heartfelt stories were for screenplays and movies, tear-jerkers produced on a studio budget and wrapped in an eight-week shoot. Judging by the way Williams went about his business in the OTC room, ignoring all the competitors around him, it was obvious that he could care less whether Nakamura was a saint or an orphan, anymore than Nakamura would feel sorry for him. *The Silent Gladiators* is a story of Romans, not a PG-13 flick.

*"A man so popular, he could travel the world for months
without ever checking into a hotel."*

-RICK REILY, SPORTS ILLUSTRATED

The Schultz Memorial
XIV

He would have made the team. He would have won a medal. He
would have put on a show. Dave Schultz was favored to do all these
things in the summer of 1996, but Schultz never made it to the Atlanta
Olympics. Months before the Olympic Trials, Schultz was shot and
killed by wrestling sponsor John Du Pont's property in western
Pennsylvania.

Du Pont, great-grandson of E.I. Du Pont, had a net worth of nearly
a quarter of a billion dollars, and was funding Schultz's travel and
training expenses. USA Wrestling, a non-profit organization, relies
on private donors whether they like it or not; the livelihood of their
wrestlers depend on it. With a lack of overwhelming revenue, with
numerous Olympic hopefuls to fund, USA Wrestling was faced with
no other choice. This meant dealing with powerful egos and eccentric
personalities, most of the time it was a positive relationship, but with
Du Pont it was a tender exchange.

It was widely known throughout the wrestling world that Du Pont's
sanity was questionable but it was also known that he was exactly
the kind of supporter that could help the USA team reach its goals,

which is the reason he can be found in pictures of U.S. national teams, standing among American coaches and athletes.

Schultz's death left a void in the American wrestling community. He was the only American to win the Tiblisi Tournament two times, which some observers consider to be a tougher tournament than the World Championships. He won both the Olympics and World Championships and was a seven-time world level medalist. As terrific of a competitor as Schultz was, those who knew him talk about his qualities as a person. Schultz was an ambassador of the sport who spoke fluent Russian and over his career made dozens of visits to the Soviet Union where he was widely respected for his competitive spirit.

The tournament that runs in his name routinely fields world and Olympic medalists, but it is the absence of the Russian athletes, who were unable to obtain visas to enter the country, that weakened the 2004 field considerably.

Outside it's a frigid 20 degrees, leaving the windows of the cars parked in the OTC lot caked with frost; the gloomy weather heightened by the gun-metal gray Colorado sky. The Schultz, originally held at the nearby Fort Carson military base hanger, was moved to a small gym on the OTC complex where blue, red and neon colors swirl together, creating a swell of energy from the mass of bodies that circle the mats. Wrestlers of all shapes, sizes and nationality run laps, dipping in and out of their wrestling stance before sprinting off to the outside, eventually dispersing like water spiraling down a drain as the clock inches toward the nine a.m. start, leaving only the Japanese team in the middle, hopping back and forth to pulsating techno beats.

The air in the gym is bone chilling; the athletes due to compete continue moving to not lose their sweat, alternately checking bracket sheets posted on the side walls. The first match of a wrestling tournament is typically the toughest for the body to prepare for, which is significantly amplified by the high elevation, so the wrestlers sprint back and forth in the hallways, trying to blow out their lungs and get their bodies used to the strain it will have to cope with in just six minutes of action.

Stephen Abas is alone in the warm-up area, separated from the stands by a metal railing, with his arms folded behind him, hand over wrist, perusing the scene like a bored graveyard shift security guard making his customary survelliance checks.

Abas starts the tournament against a U.S. Marine who is capable, in shape, and who one knows just by his affiliation that he is disciplined, hard-working and intense. The Marine has nothing to lose. Abas could be having a bad day, he could be cocky or better yet, hardly awake. The Marine could surprise Abas and toss him to the mat. Perhaps the Marine doesn't even know who Stephen Abas is and can just call it like he sees it. Abas is slim, slight and has dark circles around his eyes that indicate a hard day's night; at this hour of the morning he appears hardly cognizant. If this were the case, if Abas had spent the prior evening with Jack Daniels rather than resting in his dorm room bed, than he is in a disadvantage because wrestlers cannot rely on a substitution. Abas has to step into the circle alone. The stout Marine awaits. Wrestling is nothing but six minutes of opportunity.

But a minute into the match it is clear that the Marine has drawn a very short straw. Abas doesn't touch alcohol several weeks before competition, and on the mat he is not slight, he is not slender, he is in his element, a dimension he has nearly mastered and the Marine is the one who is pummeled. Because this is not a Muscle Beach beauty contest where the strongest appearance wins, this is a wrestling mat, a circle that Abas has spent much of his life within, where he can dance around opponents, toy and manipulate them as part of his technical flow, a circle where this Marine really has no chance; it's a 6-0 deficit in the very first minute.

During the break, Abas walks to his corner and cracks a shark's grin. Kevin Jackson is there but has nothing to say. He expects domination. Business is business. An ass-whuppin is an ass-whuppin. Abas is still grinning as he walks back to the center.

The match seems as scripted as the battles of an unrivaled kung-fu movie hero. The protagonist knows he is going to win. The audience knows he's going to win. Even the opponent seems to be waiting for him to win. Anything the Marine brings, Abas can handle. He snakes his foot around his opponent's leg and tosses him to the mat in one motion. Coming off the mat Abas is hardly sweating. Shortly thereafter, he is just like he was before the match: calm.

Not all drew from this relaxed trait. There are many wrestlers who were fueled by some deep inner anger like a Method Actor prepping

a wrestling match, sheer athleticism can be negated, withheld and
lapsed by position, force and grit.

Fullhart clasps on Lawal's neck with his heavy hands, weakening it
moment by moment like body shots from a boxer until there is little
length left. Suddenly Lawal's stance is not as steady, his movements
not nearly as swift. Lawal fakes in and out, searching for openings,
dodging, evading, shifting his position but this will not last long. Not
at this level. Not with Fullhart.

"Keep the heat on him!" Fullhart's coach Mike Duroe yells from the
corner. "Keep the heat on him!"

This violent courtship goes on for a minute before Fullhart bulldozes
Lawal out of bounds, toppling over his legs and smothering him for the
takedown."F*CK!" Lawal yells and the frustration has set in. Now on
top, Fullhart clamps onto to Lawal's wrist and clenches his other arm
around Lawal's waist, trapping his arm to his stomach and working
him into a tilt. Lawal is at Fullhart's mercy at this point, giving up
points with each passing moment. Lawal looks to his corner helplessly
and with his one free hand, motions with his palm open to his training
partner Daniel Cormier. "What do I do?" Lawal's lips read.

Cormier, sitting on one of two coaches' chairs with his elbows
resting on his knees, continues checking the scoreboard to his right
as the points pile on. After stepping into the circle, the coach can bark
instructions, teammates can shout encouragement, but in the end, one
can't run and they sure as hell can't hide. Cormier shrugs. He can do
nothing. The match is a technical blowout for Fullhart.

When it's over Lawal stands up and throws his mouthpiece. As it
roams toward his corner, he rips off the tape that wrapped his forehead
and tosses that too. He slumps down against a concrete wall where he
sits sullen and dejected for a half-hour. Sweat trickles off his forehead
and peppers his charcoal grey t-shirt as he bites his lip and stares into
space. Like a peacock that had its feathers plucked, Lawal's cockiness
is no longer present, replaced by silent frustration.

Many of the college competitors and OTC resident athletes have
been eliminated and banished to the stands like schoolboys sent to
the corner for detention. This disappointing finish for athletes funded
by the USOC is not forgiven by Olympic coach Kevin Jackson who
is sipping coffee at the scorer's table. But until his team is finalized,
Jackson can only watch these contests with the clinical detachment

for a scene. These ones could be found in the corners o[...]
slapping their faces, muttering to themselves, playing the [...]
Times Square nut job and when they walk out on their stag[...]
ready to perform.

Any casual observer who walks into a wrestling tourname[...]
to pick the thoroughbreds out. Wrestlers wear singlets; un[...]
the barest necessity possible. If it were a horserace and one w[...]
solely on physical appearance, it would be easy to pick the[...]
T.J. Williams is long, lean, physically controlled and much lik[...]
ranked older brother Joe, he looks like a professional athlet[...]
He steps on the mat, cut up like a *Sin City* assassin with all [...]
white attire: dark socks and shoes, white athletic tape wrappe[...]
each bridge, pale headgear, black singlet. Waiting on the o[...]
of the circle is a wrestler who is poor of build, tattooed, lack[...]
definition and begins the bout jumping and faking all awkwa[...]
movements like some kind of drunken matador.

Williams waits patiently like any respectable killer on the n[...]
his hand rested on his knee, still and emotionless, unflinching [...]
seen enough. Blasting through on a double-leg, Williams bur[...]
him clear off the surface and into the metal railing, head meeti[...]
knocking the contraption back a few feet and leaving his victi[...]
and confused. Williams makes his way to the center as his o[...]
does a slow sit-up, starry-eyed, and needs time to process such[...]
information as his full name, phone number and date of birt[...]
athletic trainer. Soon thereafter, Williams cradles him, head [...]
from a standing position, runs him to his back and pins him [...]
pancake; and to think that Williams opponent actually paid mo[...]
this.

Mohammed Lawal spent the early rounds of the tournament [...]
his competition with powerful double-leg attacks, hitting six o[...]
each match, even bringing one brute to tears. But in the sem[...]
Lawal wasn't facing an average competitor from a small [...]
college, Lawal was revisiting a rivaly that captivates NCAA [...]
Iowa versus Oklahoma State, Hawkeye versus Cowboy, pow[...]
pressure versus athleticism and technique.

If Lawal and Fullhart ran the 40-yard dash, Lawal would [...]
Fullhart. If they played basketball, Fullhart might get dunked o[...]

his position requires. While a national team wrestler takes a lead in a match, Jackson offered no reaction, neither approving nor disapproving the outcome.

On the other side of the arena Sergei Beloglazov is in the middle of a controversial match. As a national team coach, unless competing against a foreign competitor, Beloglazov is not supposed to show favor or flex his influence, but Beloglazov cannot let it slide in this particular bout. "You guys know rules," Beloglazov replies to a referee, offering the rulebook like a waiter with a menu. "It's bad call." He returns to his seat and crosses his arm, shaking his head. "Ref has no idea."

Later on that day, at least one USA Wrestling employee questions why Beloglazov even disputed the referee's decision. "What the hell does Beloglazov think he's doing? He can't be out there throwing his weight around. How do you think that looks on us? He's supposed to be neutral."

***

Tables line three sides of the surface. A waist-high metal fence separates the finalists from the rest of the competitors, a fence that many former NCAA All-Americans and OTC resident athletes were not able to cross with their performance in the tournament. The grandstands have been moved out for the championship finals, the money matches where the top three placers earn several hundred dollar meal checks, but the gym has no more than a 150 fans, less than one would typically find at a middle school tournament. And in many ways its pathetic.

Grown men. Paltry income. Unable to part with fading glory. Gambling what stake they have, wrestling for what destiny would give, commiserating in mess halls and discussing one another on the side of the mats, but this is what they do. This is who they are. They are silent gladiators no matter how loud they yell after victory because their accomplishments remain unspoken to the rest.

Ron Groves, 32, a former Iowa St. wrestler who trains full-time in Colorado Springs, sometimes questioned his own pursuit. "You're always trying to come up with reasons why you do this on a continual basis. There's no fame or fortune in it. I do it because I believe that wrestling is a natural mental state for men to be in. It's a state of struggle and conflict. Life without struggle is artificial, that to me does not make sense. Wrestling has no politics, no advanced weaponry and it demonstrates the basic conflict and struggle that the human spirit is made up of. It's humanity at its most basic form."

Many of the athletes in the gym have gotten to know each other through training camps, coaching jobs and competitions and just like the fraternity of wrestlers gathered around, the meeting of Stephen Abas and Jeremy Hunter is nothing new. They had once battled for the NCAA title before thousands of fans, their match broadcast over ESPN. But this encounter would not have the same promotional perks and each wrestler's motivation is beyond NCAA domination.

It's a fierce game of cat and mouse, each lightweight probing for openings, each action bringing an equal and opposite reaction. Abas attempts a half-shot and Hunter, ready, sprawls down, keeping his head up. Never fully committing, Abas slowly backs off, but just when Hunter appears to be safe, rising from his knees, Abas springs in and slithers behind for the first point. The more time ticks away, the more Hunter is forced to press the action, playing into Abas' hands. Hunter attacks aggressively, liberally shooting at Abas legs. Leading by three, Abas bobs and weaves, dodging his attempts, then freezes in his stance as Hunter closes in. At the last moment, Abas fakes, momentarily stunting Hunter before circling again.

Abas wins.

Hunter loses.

Time, atmosphere, nor experience changes the result. For Hunter, Abas has been a roadblock since they met in the NCAA finals in 1999. During the gap in years, Hunter has improved. He worked on technique. He logged countless hours in the gym, but Abas is still better. For Hunter the defeat can do no good. He was beaten, beaten again by the only man in his weight he has not defeated and somehow he must not let this get to him. Somehow, to be the U.S. Olympian, Hunter must continue believing. For Abas, the victory only strengthens his vice grip on the top spot. He can only be surer of his destiny, more confident in his skills, more adamant that he will be in Athens.

As one official holds each competitor's wrist, a second ref places a silver medal around Hunter's neck, who swiftly removes it as if it were a noose. Hunter will not accept this. Hunter does not wrestle for second place. Then Abas, whose face is as expressionless as his defeated counterpart, has his hand raised. He too removes the medal. He doesn't smile, he doesn't wave, he doesn't celebrate; Abas expected nothing less. This is not what they are after.

Few, if any wrestlers let the medals linger around their necks. It's as if they believe the shine would taint them, blind them to their goals, make them proud or, even worse, content. Their eye is on the Olympics and to get there, wins at The Schultz are expected.

***

Kerry McCoy is America's top-ranked heavyweight, but he is nowhere to be seen. Open wrestling is not a professional league where athletes compete for select teams with an organized schedule. There is no a contract that states McCoy must face off against Steve Mocco three times a year to keep television executives happy. McCoy was not obligated to compete at any tournament other than the U.S. Nationals to qualify for the Olympic Trials. From a marketing standpoint, there can hardly be a loyal fan base that follows a wrestler around the country, appearing in various cities for events or autograph shows. If a wrestling fan were to want to track McCoy down, they would be advised to go to Lehigh University in Pennsylvania where he trains and coaches college athletes.

U.S. top wrestlers largely avoid one another, waiting until something was on the line to compete, and tactically they are better off for it even if the sport wasn't. So U.S. fans will can only wonder about next big thing in the American heavyweight ranks; American wrestling's fans greatest entertainment is also American wrestler's greatest vice.

Kerry McCoy succeeded at Longwood High School in Middle Island, N.Y. and was dominant at Penn State, winning Big Ten and NCAA titles competing in the toughest conference in the county. After graduation, he defeated 1999 World Champion Stephen Neal to take the U.S. Olympic heavyweight spot in 2000, won three straight national open titles and generally dismissed his U.S. competition.

But McCoy was the anti-bully, the type of gentle giant who was always smiling and was known for his voracity to devour intellectual material. He was patient when he spoke and his knack for planning and logical thinking was praised by those who interacted with him. When McCoy, an African-American, showed up at social functions he was always well-dressed, displaying the proper etiquette and articulation that had many impressed with his potential as a businessman. "He's a real gentleman," Sonny Greenhalgh, wrestling chairmen of the NYAC said. "I always tell Kerry that if he lived in New York he would become president of the New York Athletic Club."

McCoy earned a bachelors degree in marketing at Penn St. and while he wasn't adverse to having a good time, he was a straight-edge athlete. He didn't drink. He didn't smoke. He never touched a drop of rotgut. He never saw a reason for boozing but that didn't stop him from carousing late at night with his friends often as the designated driver nor did it hurt McCoy's reputation as a ladies man. "He had a real charm with the women." Greenhlagh said. "They just followed him around."

A night owl who liked to stay up and toy with his electronics, Greg Strobel, McCoy's coaching partner at Lehigh, would often trade emails with McCoy when he got to work in the morning and McCoy hadn't even gotten to bed yet. His coaches also knew that McCoy could be found wandering around local malls on wrestling trips rummaging through Best Buy and other electronic stores on the hunt for cutting edge gadgets.

McCoy was six-foot-two, but his bulky back and legs made him appear bigger. He had a tattoo of a Japanese character on one shoulder that was interpreted: 'To Dominate,' and one with the five Olympic rings that he inked for motivation after failing to make the U.S. Olympic team in 1996. McCoy did not have the burly frame of most heavyweights; he was all-sculpted muscle. His thighs were large enough to make any NFL fullback jealous, to the point where they were disproportionate with the rest of his body.

He won 131 of 132 matches in his final three years at Penn St. and was twice crowned NCAA champ. He developed a rivalry with Stephen Neal from Cal-State Bakersfield, and it carried over to the national open level, where they battled over 20 times. Strobel first followed McCoy's career in 1991, and the Lehigh coach was immediately struck by how much he hated to lose. When he graduated, Strobel sold McCoy on the idea of coaching at Lehigh where he could assist with the program and continue training. McCoy took the job, bought a house in Bethlehem, Pennsylvania and split his training time between there and the OTC where an apartment was afforded to him through the resident athlete program.

McCoy would shadow Strobel while coaching as an assistant at Lehigh, in addition to handling alumni relations work and running the university's wrestling club, but many times their conversations would turn to McCoy's Christian religious beliefs and the two coaches would discuss the foundation of their philosophies. But American wrestling fans are not debating McCoy's personal qualities at The Schultz tournament, nor are they giving McCoy credit for beating the world champion Neal years prior. He is not being recognized as a five-time U.S. national champion or as the former leader of the NCAA athlete advisory committee. Nobody cares if McCoy is an honorary citizen away from the mat. All of McCoy's accomplishments are overshadowed by people's hunger for change, an excitement for a new face, and the speculation of how Mocco and McCoy would match up.

Steve Mocco is restless. He shifts one foot then the other, slapping his knees, arms and face as he prepares for the championship match. As the moment counts down, he picks up the intensity and all heads tilt in his direction.

Mocco attempts successive judo foot sweeps, but the German heavyweight isn't having it, confidently fending off each attack, never letting Mocco penetrate past the hands. Beloglazov, seated at the scorer's table on the other side of the arena, watches intently. A question is posed to him: *Will Mocco or McCoy make the Olympic team?* Beloglazov leaned back and tried to weigh his answer with objectivity.

Beloglazov liked Mocco. He liked the way he nodded respectfully and eagerly bent his ear toward instruction. He liked the way that he embraced the brutal contact of the sport and was not much for talking about it. He liked that he was at The Schultz, like a Russian, getting competition wherever he could. Beloglazov felt Mocco filled the void of things McCoy lacked. "Right now I say Mocco," Beloglazov says. "McCoy lazy, Mocco has good character."

Just as the words escape Beloglazov's mouth a whistle blows and the crowd cheers. Mocco has just pinned the German. Getting up, the hulking heavyweight exults, pumping his meaty fist. Then, arresting himself in mid-celebration, his expression changes to blank, he shuffles over and helps his opponent to his feet. Then Mocco runs off, his face nearly as red as the blood running down his forehead, shifting and cutting through the crowd of departing spectators, bounding out of the gym like he has a plane to catch.

"Be water. If you pour water into a cup, it takes the shape of a cup. If you pour it into a teapot, it takes the shape of a teapot. Be fluid. The best style is no style because styles can be figured out. And when you have no style, they can't figure you out."

-BRUCE LEE

Californication
VX

In a state filled with great athletes, one that has produced more combined Olympians than any other, the sport of wrestling is no different. Like many of the state's prep teams, the 1995 California Junior National Team was loaded with talent, going on to produce four individual NCAA champions; a total of eight championships among them. When Eric Guerrero and Stephen Abas would train with each other after national team practices, teammates would sit and watch with the coaches as the two prodigies drilled with unwavering focus. Guerrero went on to win junior nationals while Abas finished fourth after losing in the semi's to Pennsylvania prep Teague Moore.

Manuel Guerrero, Eric's father, was one of six brothers and began wrestling as a sophomore in 1958 at Cocoran High in Kings County, near Fresno. His younger brothers, Armen and Fred, also competed. When they qualified for the sectional tournament, the entire family attended. The youngest, Gene, was the only Guerrero who got to compete at the state and his siblings were on hand to watch him make it to the finals, before losing to a wrestler from Madera. When the Guerrero's were finished competing at the College of Sequoias, they remained close to the sport and made the California state tournament a family affair, attending every year since its inception.

The state tourney eventually moved to the University of the Pacific in Stockton and currently takes place in Bakersfield. Like the old Indiana High School State basketball championship, the California Interscholastic Federation has only one division. The crowds annually reach 7,000 for the championship finals and college recruiters flock to the arena.

The atmosphere is amplified for the athletes once they are called to the UOP warm-up tunnel, a winding concrete hallway that leads to the arena floor of ten mats, where thousands of fans are sitting on top of the action as competitors wait side-by-side for their bout to be called, shuffling forth with the completion of every few matches, the adrenaline and noise intensifying with each step. "Eric grew up in the warm-up tunnel with the Palomino boys," Gene Guerrero, Eric's uncle, recalls. "Those boys grew up playing in that tournament."

There were many elements feeding into Guerrero's success. He began working out with the California junior national team in sixth grade and during the summer, future NCAA champions Adam Tirapelle, Otto Olson and Stephen Abas would come to work out in San Jose for weeks at a time. As a freshman competing for Independence High, Guerrero's coaches were already picking tougher tournaments in which to groom him. His workout partners, Tony Gomez and Ricky Palomino, would eventually become CIF state champions. Trainers were careful not to let other teammates join the practice group that included a local high school state champ and a junior college state champ. "There was blood flying during practices," Gene Guerrero said. "These kids were just letting it fly."

When Guerrero reached the CIF state tournament at UOP as a freshman, the electric atmosphere did not intimidate him. His father who closely followed the sport, his uncle who coached him and all of his family was there. Guerrero was ready to do what had never been done before, he was ready to take California state four times. He reached the semi-finals before being defeated; eventually placing third but the sincerity of his quest never dawned on his coaches until they found the precocious 14-year-old slumped in a corner, just beyond the mat in tears after losing. "I'll never be able to win it four times," he said. Eric Guerrero never lost in another California state tournament.

At the same time, across the San Francisco Bay Area, another standout wrestling family was forming. Greg Gascon, the oldest of the Abas's brothers, was a hyperactive high school freshman with a propensity for getting into trouble. Given a choice of wrestling or detention by school administrators, Gascon chose wrestling. His younger brothers followed him to practices at the Wan-Tu-Wazuri Club at Oakland Tech High, where the mats had holes and kids were consistently spraining their ankles. "It was a ghetto-style club," Gerry Abas recalled. "It was not uncommon for guys to wander into the practice room with beer on their breath, trying to spar with us."

High school coach Ashley Sherman became a mentor to the Abas brothers whose parents were divorced and father was largely absent from their live; wrestling quickly became the family sport. "It was an escape," Gerry Abas said. "There was a calm to it that did not exist in other parts of our lives."

The three Abas brothers, Gerry, Norman and Stephen, began competing at the same time and for Stephen coming home from a tournament with a medal around his neck was a way to gain respect from his older siblings.

Genetically, the Abas's were thin, quick and rarely overpowered to their opponents, but they had a mean streak and toughness that came from their mother Mary Alice Bennett. Gerry was a break dancer in high school, which helped him develop the flexibility and footwork that allowed him to form a low-level attacking style he had first seen watching John Smith on TV competing at the Olympics. They were awed by how opponents were unsure of how to react to Smith and the sport turned into an art form for the brothers. They experimented with moves, one day creating the Abas roll, an escape maneuver where one wrestler dives through his opponent's leg while the opponent is still holding his own, creating an entanglement of limbs and a scramble for position where once all looked lost for the defensive wrestler.

Gascon, the oldest brother from a different father, earned All-American honors at New Mexico University before it dropped the program. Gerry watched him compete while in high school and picked up enough skill to earn a scholarship to Fresno State. His biggest surprise came when he was at a western regional competing for Fresno

State and he called back to California on a payphone in the middle of a Wyoming winter storm to find out that his younger brother Stephen had placed in the California state tournament as a freshman. Gerry, who had been passing on technique to Stephen the way he had been passing down clothes, became emotional as he realized his younger brother's infinite potential. By the time he was a sophomore at James Logan High in Union City, Stephen Abas was ready to compete in college. After winning three state titles and breaking national prep takedown records, he signed with Fresno State.

After placing fourth at the NCAA's as a freshman, Stephen Abas never lost another NCAA tournament. Communication became strained between Gerry and his younger brother who had always been under his guidance, but was now doing it his own way. Gerry, a three-time NCAA runner-up, knew there would come a point where people did not see Stephen as his protégé. "Things changed after Stephen won an NCAA title," Gerry said. "He was developing into his own man. Initially, I didn't know how to deal with it, but eventually I accepted his individuality. He was ready to go on his own and he took it to another level. He was a junior world champion, that's how he wanted to express himself."

By their sophomore year in college, Abas and Guerrero were already kings of NCAA wrestling. Meanwhile, Jamill Kelly, another member of the '95 California Junior National Team, was training in obscurity.

***

Lassen College is located in Susanville, California, near the Oregon border. It is a remote, high-plains desert town surrounded by mountains. There is a casino, a prison, a college and not much else. The population is listed just under 10,000, but it is widely known that the township includes local prison inmates into its census for tax benefits.

Lassen Community College is a place for the grade-weary and probation-stricken athletes or, in the case of Kelly, the overlooked. Introduced to the sport by his older cousin, Kelly used to hang around the wrestling room as a youth watching practice. When he arrived at Atwater High in California's central valley as a four-foot-eleven, 95-pound freshman, he was too small for his first love, basketball, so his football coaches told him to go out for the other winter sport. Other than two varsity matches, Kelly competed at the J.V. level his entire first year. As a sophomore, he was ranked in the state, but failed to qualify out of the rugged San Joaquin Section Tournament. He began to run and lift and bug his coaches for videotapes and wrestling books; sitting in the back of the van on the way to tournaments dissecting wrestling technique. His coach, Paul Bristow, would tell him: "Jamill, you know more about your opponents than they do."

As a senior, Kelly split matches with top-ranked Tony Gomez from Independence in the regular season, but lost to him at the state tournament by a point. Gomez won state; Kelly fell to fourth and was lightly recruited after a disappointing finish. He chose the J.C. route and before leaving Atwater and heading north to Susanville, Bristow warned him, "Don't screw this up Jamill, this is your shot."

Kelly didn't screw it up. He took advantage. He did what he had to do. After placing second at junior college nationals as a freshman, Kelly took a red-shirt year and competed at open tournaments around the country. At Midlands in Chicago, he defeated the Oklahoma State starter and the Cowboy coaches took notice. He transferred to OSU, joining Guerrero who was already an NCAA champion, but when Kelly cracked the OSU lineup, he still didn't have the ultimate confidence in himself and many disappointments followed. He entered the NCAA tournament as the top-seeded but lost to Michael Lightner, a southpaw from rival Oklahoma University and was defeated in the consolation wrestle-backs as well; both matches decided by a point. Years later, Kelly still looks back on his NCAA defeats, wondering what would have been different if he had scored those overtime points.

He no longer resembled the skinny Atwater freshman who knew more about his opponent than they knew about themselves. He now competed at 145-pounds and was a portrait of physical symmetry and despite failing to earn All-American honors in college, Kelly's fortunes changed at the 2003 World Team trials, where he tore through a gauntlet of four former NCAA champs. After defeating Tony Davis in the first round, then Bill Zadick and 2000 Olympic bronze medalist Lincoln McIlravy, Kelly took out Chris Bono in the finals.

Nearly a decade after making the junior national team, Abas, Guerrero and Kelly reunited on the U.S. World Team that competed in New York, each, however, finished with crushing defeats.

Guerrero had to be forced off the mat by Jackson after a controversial loss and was found doubled over in pain in a corridor of Madison Square Garden, inconsolable after defeat. Abas, after knocking off the former Russian Olympic champ, suffered the most disturbing loss of his career. The night before the world championships Abas saw his draw and only worried about advancing through his stacked pool competition. The next day he approached his first bout with the Olympic champ thinking it was the world championship match and after a narrow victory, Abas celebrated with the crowd, but in reality he hadn't accomplished anything. The following day, Abas was emotionally deflated and was beaten in his first match. Kelly, who entered world's with a lingering rib injury, was knocked out of the tournament by a Cuban wrestler.

"Joyful in difficulty, the people forget about their death."

-I CHING, THE ART OF WAR

The Cut
XVI

Its two days before U.S. Nationals and the tapering of body weight has begun. The weight-cutting period is when wrestlers, like animals, become irascible. As their stomachs grumble, they jog around the mat in ritual of commitment. As their bodies lose mass with each minute they continue to push forward. Covered with clothes and shrouded by a hooded sweatshirt, Yoshi Nakamura's face hangs over the handlebars and looks down to the floor of the OTC wrestling room; his identity undetected from the backside. Sweat pours off his head, forming tiny puddles on the cold concrete surface as the agonizing procedure whittles down to its last days.

Nakamura, like Abas, Guerrero and Kelly, like Sanderson , Lawal and Fullhart, Mocco and McCoy, like every other elite wrestler preparing around the country, will take all necessary measures to make the cut. A sauna is inside the men's locker room. Exercise bikes are lined along the entrance of the practice facility. Sparring partners are scattered along the walls if needed. Nakamura, bundled up like an eskimo, pedals incessantly on one of the Aerodyne machines, churning his legs and ripping his arms back and forth until the wind from the bicycle wheel whistles throughout the facility. He works at a steady pace and then for five to ten seconds, whips into a frenzy before slowing again.

As time passes, the room begins to fill with athletes until there is little space left on the mats. The speakers blast the pulse-pounding music of Aerosmith; the volume ratcheted so high, it's hard to think straight. The wrestling room has turned into a locker room: bags and soaked workout clothes, running shoes and damp towels patching the surroundings. Tall, short and powerful wrestlers are scattered across the mats wearing the universal look of the sport during these moments: Cheekbones jutting out, eyes sunk back in their skulls, black rings lined around the eye sockets; physical characteristics normally associated with sleep deprivation.

They circle in sweat tops and down jackets, as the heater pumps warm air at a steady flow. Some are simply picking up one foot and putting it in front of the other, sloshing around the mats, heads down, mouths agape, despising every moment.

Throughout the day, wrestlers funnel in and out of the room to run, spar and skip rope, doing just enough to get under the weight, nothing more. Some move slowly after their workouts to sustain a steady sweat as they head into the locker room for a date with the digital scale. There is little talking during these moments, all movements kept to a minimum, each athlete preoccupied with their body weight and while they might nod at passing competitors or slap hands in greeting, there is only one priority.

The scale controls them at this point, the scale will give them the verdict, will tell them whether they can rest or keep running, drink or keep spitting, sit against the wall or head back in the sauna. After shedding sopping-wet clothes, pushing the reset button and waiting for the zero to appear, they step on and watch their body weight be exacted down to a tenth of a pound. It's not healthy, it's not right, it's just routine.

When they first arrived they were in good shape, but as time passed and training progressed, as they rose each morning and sweated every day, putting their bodies through the rituals of the sport, they got in wrestling shape. Breaking it down, building it up, then breaking it down again. The body and mood changing shape like the cycle of the seasons. The ritual of cutting weight like the shedding of leaves in the fall. First falling slowly and steadily, then as the process whittled down, coming off in bunches. This is the final step of the cycle.

"It's not luck-there's probably no such thing as luck, and if there is you can't depend on it. All you can do is play the percentages, play your best game, and when the critical bet comes-in every money game there is always a critical bet-you hold your stomach tight and push hard. That's the clutch. And that's where you're born loser loses."

-BERT GORDON, THE HUSTLER

VEGA$
XVII

Just off The Strip... Away from the cash-guzzling slot machines and smoke-filled casinos, away from the broken dreams and pirate themes, away from the sizzle and sin that defines this city, is a side road where rows of marquee resorts and tourist attractions are replaced by motels with fading stucco and liquor store corners teeming with criminal intentions. The old Vegas, the one absent in the infomercials, is where the Las Vegas Convention Center sits; a pink trimmed mega-complex with numerous showrooms spacious enough to fit several airplanes in and where the toughest wrestlers in America have congregated.

People arrived by car and air from every corner of the country to this transient town and the wrestling crowd was no different. There would be three days of action before heading home with something to remember or something to regret.

The stakes are high in Vegas. The winners of U.S. National's will have a bye through the mini-tournament portion of the Olympic Trials and would be the heavy favorite to be the Olympian come May. Those who lose are thrown back into the fray, having to brawl through the mini-tournament just to reach the championship final round in

Indianapolis where they would then have to win best-of-three against a well rested national champ. It was a daunting task for any competitor and a prospect no one wanted to face down the road.

Inside a banquet room of the convention center, shirtless wrestlers form lines leading to registration tables and weigh-in scales. It was a familiar scene, the room is on edge: wary eyes, tense bodies, last minute jogging and spitting and jump roping and plastic sweat suits that were illegal but who was really checking.

The room held the smell of athletic manure: sweaty gym clothes and anatomies cordoned off in a small area that could benefit from the use of a couple air-conditioning fans. The wrestlers' arms were branded with black marker, signifying their classification. One competitor was said to have lost 25 pounds. Another resembled a Holocaust victim. In this nondescript room, world class athletes chugged Pedialyte and Gatorade and devoured energy bars and cold pasta. The lot was indistinguishable at this point. While there were contenders and pretenders, NCAA Champions and also-rans, have and have-nots stripped to their shorts, lost of any college program identity, every wrestler in the room looked more or less the same.

They were thirsty.

They were hungry.

They wanted to weigh-in.

"CAEL SANDERSON!" a tournament official hollers out. *"CAEL SANDERSON!"* After the third call, Sanderson makes his way to the front of the room with his hand raised in the air. Nearly everyone in the room looks over toward Sanderson, a vacuum seems to have sucked out the noise. He makes little effort to draw attention, quietly excusing himself as he moves through clustered groups with his head down, but it's inescapable. He is taller than most of them, he competes with the best of them and he makes more money than all of them.

In college Sanderson was untouchable. He wasn't plagued by mental breakdowns. He was impervious to serious injury. He never had to learn from an NCAA defeat. So in this room, among his peers, jealously could be natural for some, but Sanderson seems to be wrestling this off as well.

As he moves through this rough crowd he displays no air of entitlement, no words of braggadocio, no absorbent demands of a VIP. Sanderson just wants to grab his weigh-in card and fall back line with the rest of the platoon. The room draws quieter as he shifts through the crowd. Some are envious, some in awe, some not. When Sanderson settles in the back, the commotion resumes.

***

Through a set of double-doors at the entrance of the convention center, past the ticket counters and into the heart of the building, a blitz of merchandise tables line the backside of the portable steel bleachers. To the right, just a short walk away, all the tournament entries are warming up. Top ranked 134-pounder Eric Guerrero and a training partner drill hard and fast, occasionally bumping into other groups. Guerrero, sporting a thick beard and jet-black long hair, appears like he just returned from a packing trip in the mountains. Religiously focused, Guerrero is oblivious to the action that surrounds him. He doesn't look up to catch a glance of a friend or foe. He doesn't see who's watching from the stands. He doesn't take sporadic breaks to catch his breath. Eric Guerrero just drills.

By the end of the weekend Guerrero will be crowned national champion of his weight like the two years prior. He expects this result and the cocksure look on his face suggests as much. But while Guerrero was the top-ranked wrestler in the country, he was afforded no personal locker room, no pre-match press conference, no discernable privileges that would distinguish him from his competitors. However, if one looked closer at his movements, his foot speed, his ruthless intensity, it is apparent that he is not just some face in a crowd.

Eventually, Guerrero would float through his weight bracket, picking apart three separate opponents as quickly and bloodlessly as the toughest six minutes in sport would allow. Then, and only then, when on the mat, on the surface of substance, would it become clear that at 134-pounds Guerrero had no U.S. peers. In the U.S. Nationals program, his biography is a long scroll of championships, spanning high school to college to several years on the open level. Like any list one can crunch the numbers and see the patterns: Guerrero spends one year figuring out his level of competition (placing fourth in the high school state tournament as a freshman; fifth at NCAA's; third at 2000 Olympic Trials) before he dominates the field, which leads one to the conclusion that Eric Guerrero will not lose to another American this year.

Spectators and coaches stand shoulder to shoulder, observing the scene from behind waist-high metal barriers, resting their arms on top with bracket sheets rolled in hand like racetrack bettors. From here, they can see a connecting row of mats that extend across the concrete surface of the showroom. They can see the good, bad and the ugly of what U.S. wrestling had to offer.

Anyone can sign up.

It was as if the sport did not have the financial luxury of turning anyone away. There was no qualification process. The tournament took only $35 to enter. But it is not a place for the weak, nor a worthy gamble for a drifter wondering how far a fistful of dollars will take him. This is a tournament that demands years of training and world-class talent to dominate and it's a harsh reality that seems to be lost on one competitor who looks horribly out of place. He sprawls and attacks the surface as if it's his own opponent. Then he gets up and stares bug-eyed into the gallery like a WWF villain; repeating the act a few more times before draping a silver and black Oakland Raiders towel around his neck. It hangs off his shoulders like a cape as he walks through an opening in the fence and is soon lost in the sea of the thick, ever-shifting crowd. False bravado may work at the local pub or schoolyard, but at the American wrestling's national championship, it won't last so long. He will be dealt with.

"GOOD MORNING LADIES AND GENTLEMAN! WELCOME TO THE U.S. NATIONAL TOURNAMENT!...JAMILL KELLY REPORT TO MAT TWO!" As the arena announcer offers introductions, competitors anxiously shed warm-ups and prepare for mat assignments. There is little time between names being called and the wrestlers walking out, so competitors dart through crowds and the maze of mats with apprehension. In the far corner of the building Kelly is expressionless as he takes down his opponent who is the reigning NCAA Division III national champ.

Few fans are in Kelly's corner, but wrestling legend John Smith is. His face is a picture of calm mirroring Kelly's whose bored with his early competition. Wearing a bright orange polo shirt, Smith refuses to yell or even encourage at this point, he is a spectator, appearing almost neutral as he squats behind an OSU assistant who mans the coaching chair.

To lose this match is not an option; Kelly is a pro and his first opponent is to be dismissed. He was trained to beat the best and this is just a warm-up for the bigger matches, the bigger names, the bigger games. Smith observes quietly, expecting nothing but absolute victory. Between periods he comes over and gives a pat on the back to Kelly, but he says nothing.

Throughout the building, fans push and sway toward the elite. They flock to Stephen Abas mat but while the bout has just started, the outcome is predetermined. Abas will win. The other American will lose. There is hardly any fighting it. The fans know this but they watch anyway, because they aren't observing a struggle between two competitors colliding head-to-head, they're watching Abas hoping to witness a flurry of action they've never seen before. During a ceasefire, Abas senses the crowd's eyes upon him, but he doesn't look up. Not once did Abas look up. To do so would have been acknowledging the satisfaction of a temporary thing, one that was not present during his daily training routine, one that was non-existent as he came in and out of the practice room to work on the finer points of his movements, conditioning, and goals. To look up would have suggested Abas was competing for the attention that followed athletes of his caliber but, in the sport of his choice, was rarely there. To reveal, to in some way confide that it was one of his motivations, would get him no closer to the mats he wanted to be on, under the lights he wanted to shine in, so not once does Abas look up. After the ref raised his hand he walked off silently.

In the first few rounds, the tallied score between the U.S.'s top-ranked wrestlers and their counterparts was 200 to 11. Abas didn't have a tough match until the quarterfinals; Guerrero wasn't challenged until the semis. They are absolute in victory and unemotional in triumph and while they kept opponents in check, others scrape by.

Melvin Douglas' mother is cheering twenty feet away, watching next to a pack of spectators who are lined five deep just to get a closer look of her son, her boy, who is a grown man. They cram along the railing to watch a former champion of the world, master of his domain, but who, at this moment, is far from dominant, if anything, Melvin Douglas is just trying to survive. "You can do it Melvin!" Karen Douglas yells. "He's too old for this. He'll do it, he'll do it, yes, yes he's always been good."

She is convincing herself, just like Douglas is trying to convince himself. He's locked in a tight match against an opponent who wouldn't have presented a challenge in earlier years and he needs to walk back to the center at the rate of a senior citizen in order to preserve energy. He lies down and directs the trainers to his knee, but he is visibly straining in the lungs.

The ref eventually raises Douglas' hand in victory, but he exits wearing the universal look of defeat. Head down, shaking his head disapprovingly, silently cursing himself. At this level, his performance will not last long. Every round brings a tougher foe and this wasn't the work of a U.S. national champion. Later on this won't cut it and Melvin Douglas knows it.

***

Steve Mocco's father Joe is never far behind his son at wrestling tournaments. As he lumbers through the procession of fans gripping Steve's gym bag, some offer words of encouragement, and he acknowledges them with a warm smile, but he pushes forth towards the reason he is here, to watch his son wrestle.

As a crowd gathers, video cameras flip on. Mocco removes his thick sweater and uses it to wipe sweat off his shoulders. He toes the ground with each foot and moves onto the mat. Relentless off the whistle, Mocco leg-trips his opponent, flipping and rolling him on his side like a roped calf and pinning him in under a minute flat.

When the fight was over and Steve returned from wherever he ran off to, the Mocco family could be found in the back of the arena, a faint cry from the matches and whistles. They would sit together, father, son, brother and sister, and relax. The father traveled to nearly all of Steve's competitions in a van where he prepared Italian meals in between Steve's matches and it's easy to see where the talented heavyweight got his breadth of shoulders, blue-grey eyes, and unwavering gaze. "Steve's all the time about business," Sonny Greenhlagh of the New York Athletic Club said. "I don't even remember him looking at women, it would conflict with the wrestling, he's totally focused. Even when he trained at the NYAC in junior high, his coaches knew he wanted to be the best wrestler in the world."

Steve was not the only success story in the Mocco family. The older brother Joe was an Eastern League champ from Brown University and eventually became a lawyer, another brother is a doctor and Mocco's sister is nationally ranked in judo. All of Mocco's siblings, especially the father, were supportive of his athletic pursuit. "To this day I can't tell you what his father does for a living," Greenhlagh said. "It's almost like nothing else interests him but seeing his kid win. I think his father thrived on his wins. But they're all pushing Steve to be Olympic champion."

***

The brackets shrank and the overflow crowd liquidated with the passing hour, the picture of elite becoming clearer as the quarterfinalists file in just before seven p.m. Teague Moore, formerly of Oklahoma St. and Sammie Henson, the 2000 Olympic silver medalist at the 126-pound weight, were the two wrestlers considered to have the best shot at defeating Abas and they battle for the right to do so on mat one.

Henson's physique evokes images of a lightweight Mr. Olympia. He is ripped from head to toe, which isn't very high up, five-feet four inches total, but he's imposing nonetheless, possessing a key element to any obsessive compulsive wrestler's workout routine, Henson is the type of man who seems to enjoy pain.

Henson was a family guy, married with four children, and one could quote him to say just as much, but he was truly an action junkie, charged by the type of kinetic, restless energy that had to be released or he wouldn't know what to do with himself.It was not the muscle bound Hercules physical specimens, it was not the perfectly shaped *Men's Fitness* magazine cover types, it was the scrappers, the ones who had nothing to lose, the ones who competed over anything, who had a constant chip on their shoulder, who went about seizing whatever life wouldn't give them, these were the men to be feared. In crime, in society, on the circular mats in the gladiator arena, it was men like Henson who presented the most dangerous opponent.

Typical of his nature, Henson attacks with the aggression of a man fighting for his life, clubbing Moore repeatedly across the neck. A break in the action leaves Moore on the mat with trainers tending to his leg while Henson waits with his arms up in disgust, implying with few subtleties that Moore is stalling.

Henson earns a lead he will not relinquish but Moore will not let his defeat go unchecked. From the top position he begins grinding his forearm across Henson's jaw, raping and scraping him across the face as if he were checking the strength of his Henson's nose with a billyclub. Henson, hardly the type to walk away from a cheapshot, is livid. When the match ends, he bucks Moore off his back and shoves him as soon as he can reach his feet. The ref restrains Henson who, blood rushing to his face, storms off like a mini-hurricane.

As the sun rose in the desert Saturday morning, more than half the tournament had folded, cashed out after two defeats. The undefeated were set to square off in the semi-finals. Stephen Abas, with his hands locked behind his back, waits to compete with the patience of an obedient schoolboy for the bell to ring. As the bleacher seats begin to fill for the semi-final round, Abas holds his blood rag overhead and, with the referee's nod, slips it back in between his singlet.

Across the mat Jeremy Hunter shifts about, trying to remain loose in a drafty, spacious event center. Hunter, positioned in a low stance, is dead-set on not giving up an early takedown, but soon thereafter Hunter falls to the mat anyway. Abas wraps his legs and turns him for two more points as Hunter, on his stomach, glances over at the score clock. Already down 3-0, he cannot hide the look of resigned defeat. Hunter knows his coaches would say that a match is never over and to never give up. Hunter knows he is capable of a great comeback as he was once an NCAA champion. Hunter knows all of these things and he also seems to grasp that he is not going to beat Abas on this day, but that won't stop him from trying.

Hunter shoots two straight leg attacks but he elevates too high in his stance and Abas just drops right in, picks of his balance, scoring again. After the win, Abas hustles off, hair flopping, taking a spot next to his older brother Gerry. He pulls a hooded sweater over his head while never taking an eye off the mat, appearing to allow himself no more reflection of his semi-final triumph than a climber would after several steps in the ascent of Mt. Everest.

In the crowd, between bouts, top-ranked competitors could be found spying on future opponents while attempting to remain incognito. Abas watches Sammie Henson come onto the mat the same way Henson walked into a wrestling room, on his toes, lurching forward, turning his head this way and that, sizing up the surroundings with the trigger impulse of desperado one insult away from a gunfight.

Abas knows Henson well. He knew him four years ago when he was an NCAA titlist trying to make the Olympic team but wasn't quite ready and Henson made sure of it; dismantling him at the Olympic Trials in Dallas. Henson went on to take silver in Sydney after a controversial one-point loss in the gold medal match, a defeat that he is on a blood hunt to get back. The Olmypic loss could be the only reason Henson drew himself out of retirement, out of a coaching job and back into the solitary confinement of a wrestling room because he wants more, he wants it all, Sammie Henson wants the gold medal. When Abas watches Henson smash his opponent as Abas knew he would, their rematch is set.

As the session ends, Teague Moore, the former OSU star, sits on the back of a moving cart behind the bleachers in a corner of the building. He's still wearing warm-ups and is shortly removed from placing third in the nation with a victory in the consolation finals. Moore is young, fit and his physique is in untouchable condition, but his face is sullen and his demeanor gloomy as he gazes across the floor in far-off thought. He is not hurt. He is not injured. Moore is the third best wrestler in America.

But it didn't mean a thing. Only the championship finalists were where they wanted to be, heading back to their hotels for a meal and rest before the evening competition, their worldly ambition still intact.

Third place is not what Moore came for. Third place leaves Moore in the mini-tournament. Third place is a long way from Athens.

***

"People who sit down with me are expecting to lose and goddammit, I don't want to disappoint them."

-JOHNNY CHAN, POKER PLAYER

Thirty-five minutes before one of the biggest matches of his life, Stephen Abas lay on a single mat next to Eric Gurrero behind the east bleachers. Roughly fifty spectators, women, children, wrestlers young and old, have gathered around, talking quietly amongst themselves as they watch the two engage.

The California kids grew up together on the freestyle circuit and became close friends on junior and national cadet teams. As their careers paralleled one another, they developed a natural bond that would take them to the highest echelon of amateur wrestling. Now they are both aiming to win another national title.

Abas gets up, slow and serene and begins to move around. His coach, Dennis Dellido, comes up from behind and bear hugs him, pats him on the chest and says a few words only they will know.

On the other side of the building, his opponent Sammie Henson, is slumped against a concrete wall, between a ladies restroom and a snack stand, flanked by a training partner. He wears a black Superman t-shirt; his right eye is purple and swollen from battle. He rubs his head and face like he's deciding whether to shave and stares around looking for something. He appears exhausted after only having six competition matches heading into the tournament and defeating the number two and three seeds just to make it to the finals. Now he faces Abas, who he handled at the 2000 Olympic Trials, but the tables have clearly turned. Henson, 33, is four years older. Abas, 26, is four years better.

Fans file in from every corner as the rest of the finalists begin last-minute preparations. Behind the north-end bleachers, Guerrero's opponent, Mike Zadick, out of the University of Iowa, is bouncing around, loosening his limbs. Zadick is easy to spot in this crowd, looking as country as *Cash*, sporting a thick, dark beard, wool mountain hiking socks and a lipstick red Great Falls, Montana wrestling sweater that pays homage to his hometown. Like most Iowa products, Zadick is full of unruly energy, stalking around next to a sponsor's tent, which the Hawkeyes used as campground between matches, as Terry Brands watches a few feet away.

In the main seating area, the announcer table sits to the left, surrounded by bleachers and a media section. Camera crews and photographers line the side of the elevated competition platform. Above the north stands, a gigantic USA Wrestling banner hangs from the ceiling. Four mats are all that remain.

Each major American wrestling tournament is a reunion of sorts, evidenced by the walkways and seats filled with wrestlers past and present. The NCAA Division I Championships, Cadet and Junior

Nationals and the U.S. Open Championship bring many of the same faces; before the finals the announcer introduces each former world or Olympic team member in attendance.

Gold medalists Gable, Smith, Brands and Jackson hear their names called once again. Melvin Douglas, nonchalant as ever hours after competing, limps his way down the catwalk to an applauding crowd as others follow. As they line up, there are short men, tall men, gigantic men, graying, balding, imposing. Some are doctors, some are businessman, but all ultimately defined as wrestlers. Look a little closer at the chipped teeth, the rough edges, the battered ears that are clues to their past, each gladiator like an ancient Greek relic from a lost sport that had washed onto a remote Mediterranean beach. Less polish, less shine, fractured, but enduring, becoming rarer with each passing year, somehow surviving like the sport itself. Wrestling does this at major tournaments because this is what they have to show. No great arenas to call there own. No mainstream American popularity. Wrestling endures, if not much else.

As nightfall descends upon the Western landscape, the stars of the sport come out; Henson wears blue, Abas is in red. Abas takes Henson down within 20 seconds. Another score makes it 2-0. The hard-charging Henson is charging now, but his power is pointless, as Abas keeps scoring when the opening appears. Late in the second period it's over. As they follow each other off the mat, Abas is escorted by a media entourage while Henson trails off in isolation.

The following three weights go quickly, Eric Guerrero, Jamill Kelly and Joe Williams were the victorious names, and then all the attention and ambivalence in the arena centers on one wrestler.

Was Cael Sanderson really training?

Was Sanderson really prepared?

Did the Iowa St. legend really want to continue wrestling?

The questions were as inescapable as the white-hot lights that radiated from a hospital emergency room, the answers surely to be exposed in the forthcoming six minutes as the pressure and expectations of the crowd were ready to cut into Sanderson's defeat like the scalpel of a tramu surgeon, the fall of another All-American wrestling hero to be added to the pile of body bags of former champions headed to the morgue.

Sanderson, wearing sponsored white wrestling shoes that accentuated his pale skin, bounces lightly atop the wrestling surface. He is graceful as a lone figure swaying across the mat, but the previous months have been conflicting for the former Iowa St. star. Olympic coach Kevin Jackson was convinced that Sanderson wanted to quit the sport, which was backed by rumors that he had not been training at his regular blistering pace. The void in his conditioning was easily noticeable to Cody, the older brother who knew him best, nor did it go unwarranted by the man across the surface looking to exploit it.

Lee Fullhart, veins slithering across his forearms, face grimacing with contempt, stalks around his side of the mat like a brooding beast, whipping up a silent furor within. Months back, Fullhart said he could defeat Sanderson but one would hear these words and wouldn't understand how he could feel this way. How could he? Fullhart had been defeated by Sanderson more than seven times over the past three years and had only won once. Fullhart was a logical man. He knew the score. Defeat-after-defeat, year-after-year, does not reassure belief. But Fullhart didn't accept these thoughts. Fullhart believed in work. Fullhart believed in his plan. Fullhart believed he was going to win and it was quite clear from watching the Iowa product beforehand, the way he eyed the former Iowa St. wrestler before the ref unleashed him, that he had his own ideas about Sanderson's invincibility.

Off the whistle, Sanderson swoops down on Fullhart's ankles, who counters by grabbing Sanderson's leg and a vicious battle for position ends in a stalemate. Sanderson jumps to an early two-point lead, but his stamina is evaporating faster than the precious seconds of the clock and Fullhart is not stopping, managing a reversal and gut wrench to go up one point at the break. In their corners, both wrestlers lean over and rest their hands on their knees as their coaches furiously bark into their ears.

In college, Sanderson earned the reputation of a wrestler who never let up, setting a pace that no NCAA challenger could hang with, but years later there's been a drop-off in his preparation. Back in action, Sanderson lunges at the legs, but Fullhart lowers and crushes the once-open gap by running through Sanderson, head in the ribs, bulldozing him out of the circle. No takedown is scored, but Sanderson is slow to emerge from the pile. Fullhart, sensing weakness as surely as a predator senses fear, pours it on. Sanderson goes for another half-shot but its not quick or powerful, swift or fluid and when the lack of hard training shows its ugly, exhausted, pitiful face, Fullhart is there to take advantage, plowing Sanderson like he envisioned in his workouts. Fullhart knew he couldn't be baited into a shootout with Sanderson that favored technical superiority. Fullhart is a grinder, a masher, he wants his opponents to feel at every moment as if they were suffocating. Fullhart knows this. Fullhart knows himself. Fullhart knows this is the only way.

As the bout wears on, as Sanderson's defeat looks more and more certain, Kevin Jackson sits back and watches, not expecting a comeback, but looking for clues that go beyond conditioning, technique and mat awareness. Jackson had a trained eye for the sport and he knew both Fullhart and Sanderson well. He offered both athletes advice and had pushed each through workouts at the OTC. He knew their strengths, weaknesses and how each could be beat. And from Jackson's vantage point, from eyes that had achieved the golden standard of sport, it was at a point break in the contest where the U.S. Olympic coach witnessed something he has never seen from the former Cyclone star: Kevin Jackson saw Cael Sanderson quit; hard work beats talent when talent doesn't work hard. Fullhart 5-2.

As Fullhart walked off, his parents ran up and hugged him, but he was too winded to fully embrace and could only grip his elated mother with one arm as he headed to a room to be drug-tested like the other finalists after their matches.

***

Clearly Steve Mocco had what McCoy didn't. McCoy was nice, polite, and pleasant to be around. Mocco was brooding, powerful and had the type of aura that made people look twice. All this led many in the stands to wonder if Mocco might break McCoy, might pummel him to the surface, might whoop his ass in front of the entire Las Vegas Convention Center, in some sorry excuse for an event arena that was normally reserved for sales conventions and car shows and yes, surely this would be the end of it. McCoy would retire right there and then, exit the arena with his head bowed, feeling worthless for not living up to his national heavyweight title, his reputation, his dominance in the U.S. he had worked years to build, surely McCoy was going to get beat in Vegas, and one ashy-faced, mercenary-eyed, bear of a man by the name of Steve Mocco was going to play executioner.

Dressed in black, Mocco takes off his shirt with the sudden temper of a man before a backyard brawl, scowling viciously as he screws his feet into the mat. McCoy, seven years his senior, is stately and confident as he walks up the steps of the platform with his coach following closely behind. Steady as a scientist, McCoy extracts his red sweater and places it on the carpet before gently setting his reading glasses on top. He looks across the mat, sizes up the task at hand, then slaps each of his powerful legs, fingers his singlet and moves onto the surface nodding his head.

As the two heavyweights gravitate toward the center, an electricity of anticipation circulates through the stands as the American fans have been looking for a match like this, the sport needed a match like this and if USA Wrestling were a professional sports league and were attempting to sell its stake to an investor, some media mogul or wealthy entrepreneur, and that person were sitting mat side gauging whether the sport was a sound business investment, then USA Wrestling would be advised to showcase its principal assets, its athletes, and these two heavyweights in particular, because they would know what professional boxing knows and that is that people like giants, people like to see giants fight each other and Mocco and McCoy would be the perfect match up to sell the sport, to market it mainstream, to seal the colossal deal and the big shot mogul would be enticed by the two giants, would edge to the front of his VIP seat and chew harder on the Cuban cigar in his mouth and get chills as Mocco and McCoy shake hands, step back and wait for the whistle to blow.

Because surely these two bruisers, who intimidate many of men by presence alone, were ready to sink their teeth into each other, were ready to paw and fight and club and slam one another to the mat and the conqueror would roar after brutally pounding the other into submission and the mogul sitting mat side would have his financial handlers on his Blackberry before the match had even ended and say what only powerful men such as these could say, yes the man would say, *"GET IT DONE!!"* And soon thereafter the necessary legal paperwork would be drafted, handled and signed by representative lawyers and wrestling would be sold and ready for the big-time. Mocco, McCoy and others would be on the cover of magazines and endorsing products in commercials, would be highly-paid and well-

known and wrestling would be a major draw across the county…
*and…and…*this did not happen.

The glorious battle on the mat never took place, each competitor wrestled not to make a mistake and the media tycoon was fictional. Even if such a powerful man were sitting mat-side he surely would have declined the offer based on the lack of true entertainment, the void of continuous high-wire action that could be found at the NCAA tournament, at The Border Brawl between Iowa and Minnesota, at wrestling meets across Russia and Iran, but not at this heavyweight contest that was flat as an open can of soda pop and couldn't be pitched to the average fan because people wanted action, violence, even some good ol' fashioned American arrogance, anything but a scoreless first period, a stalemate, a bailout in the clinch position. Because now the tycoon was a reluctant tycoon who would be forced to say, *"Thanks, but no thanks."* to his wrestling hosts and would be walking out of the Las Vegas Convention Center like the rest of the wrestling fans were right now because outside, in the city of sin, there were far more entertaining things to do, things that put a shot of adrenaline through the blood, things that got the heart racing, hell, the people exiting the arena would rather throw their money away than watch two giants hold back and that's exactly what they were going to do.

McCoy won. Mocco lost. Nobody cared.

After the stands had emptied, the seven national champions were brought together for a group photo. The constant beeping of a reversing moving truck wails from the other side of the building. Workers were stacking, loading and carting off equipment from the tournament, carrying with it a weekend's worth of sweat and blood, wins and losses, the site of triumphs and failures just items on the back of a U-haul trailer speeding down the Las Vegas Expressway.

U.S. wrestlers have no great arena to return to, no Lambeau Field, no Yankee Stadium or Boston Garden. No site to point to their kids in the future and say: 'This is where I was crowned champion wrestler of the whole United States son.' Wrestlers were gypsies. They carried few belongings and were capable of adapting to whatever environment they found themselves in.

Not that any of the U.S. champions cared. They were right where they wanted to be. Stephen Abas, Eric Guerrero and Jamill Kelly kneeled down on one knee in the first row. Joe Williams, Lee Fullhart, Daniel Cormier and Kerry McCoy stood in the back, clutching plate-sized wooden national champion plaques. They have struck this proud pose before at Cadet and Junior Nationals, at high school state meets and after climbing the ladder at the NCAA tournament. Abas did it three times at Fresno State, Guerrero the same for Oklahoma State; McCoy twice for Penn St.; Williams three times and Fullhart once for Iowa; Cormier as a junior college national champ and Kelly after making the World Team. But this one, this championship was different, putting one foot in Greece and only two victories-three matches max-at the Olympic Trials, from making the final, monumental step toward Athens.

After the photo-op, there are hugs, smiles and slaps on the back all around. Rich Bender, USA Wrestling's Executive Director, personally congratulates all the winners, glad-handling like a seasoned diplomat. Guerrero signs a kid's poster. A teenage girl asks to have a photo with McCoy. Fullhart, in what seemed like the first time ever, wore a constant smile.

Right now they look good, real good, like champions. Best in the nation, top-flight shape, two wins, just two, from reaching a lifelong dream. But questions remain. Will the champion's photo be the same on May 23 in Indy? Who would be replaced? Who will be missing? And there was another lingering inquiry, one that loomed larger than any athlete in the photo, that concerned a man whose success was in many ways tied to USA Wrestling's fortunes as well, but it was a question like the others, one that would yield no answer at the moment, one that only time would tell.

At 10:35 p.m., Cael Sanderson, finally leaving the convention center, was slumped dejectedly in the back seat of a town car waiting at a red light, staring out at the million bright lights of Las Vegas. On the mat he had been shockingly vulnerable and his face said as much.

When the stoplight turned green, Cody Sanderson hung a left on Paradise Road and sped off into the desert night, carrying with him the biggest name in the sport who now, Olympic dream tilting in the balance, faced his toughest test less than two months away.

"There's not enough oversight at USA Wrestling, anything worth a damn has oversight. Even the President of the United States has someone to critically answer to. You cannot have an agency run with a lifetime contract. They can't sit in a position for hell and ever. USA Wrestling doesn't have oversight because there's not enough money at stake. There would be a lot more changes if more money was coming through. The athletes are wrestling for pennies. Leadership at USA Wrestling has not been looked at critically. The leadership goes out to get the money, they pay us nothing and they expect the athletes to work 90 hours a week for charity. There not doing enough. With USA Wrestling there's no money involved. If athletes were being paid, if there was money funneling through the agency, the sponsors, the endorsers would constantly be rethinking the direction for the program. Not even the President of the United States has a lifetime contract."*

-NATIONALLY-RANKED U.S. WRESTLER

Rocky Mountain Qualifier
XVIII

Traveling north on U.S. Interstate 25, through Denver, past Boulder and just beyond Fort Collins, the scenery begins to change. The landscape, once littered with billboards and clustered with traffic, breaks open. Roadside advertisements are replaced by the tracks of the Southern Pacific Railroad and an endless stream of telephone poles are the few signs of civilization. The view is flat and wide in one of America's great divides. Where the city ends and the country begins, where Colorado becomes Wyoming, is where the cowboys call home.

Roughly a three-hour drive from the OTC, this is the road of the Olympic long shots. Truck drivers, roamers of the West, are welcomed to Laramie by signs offering steak and egg dinners for $9.95 and motel rooms for not much more. Pickup truck after pickup truck move up and down Main St. where the University of Wyoming school logo, a cowboy riding a bucking bronco, is plastered on storefront windows and the back of flatbed Fords. Just off the dusty streets of downtown, the state's only university sits off to the left.

The athletic parking lot is empty. On the other side of the arena, Wyoming football players trudge into the locker room to dress for spring ball. A chilling wind sweeps across the lot, through the dead grass, carrying up and into the states 100-mile views.

Off in the distance, on a field in the middle of fraternity row, an intercollegiate lacrosse match is taking place. Fraternity brothers sit on rooftops and patios swigging cheap beer while hammering the opposing team with a stream of clever insults. Students, just relieved of Friday classes, crowd the sidelines, huddling together to shield themselves from the biting cold. Just around the corner in the athletic complex, it's a ghost town. For a sport which is losing collegiate programs by the year, this is a bad omen. An invitation to the Olympic Trials is up for grabs and seven spots were reserved for the winners of each weight, but several hours before weigh-ins, the sport of wrestling seems to have been abandoned by every soul in the world.

Inside the War Memorial Field House, a dull consciousness permeates throughout. From the handful of men cutting weight across the misaligned mats, to the top of the steep, high-rising seats, the energy is lacking.

Through a side door and at the entrance of the locker room, a former world champion sits dehydrated on a bench with his back to a set of faded yellow lockers. His upper-body is still powerful, but his stomach protrudes with extra skin. A couple strips of white athletic tape are visible beneath a knee pad, lingering traces of an injury sustained at the U.S. Nationals. At the age of 40, Melvin Douglas is making one last Olympic run.

Alone.

Desolate.

Dismal.

Bleak.

Like a lonely cowboy in search of a gunfight, Douglas arrived to Laramie with a purpose of qualifying for the Olympic Trials, but what he found was hardly worth the effort. Four hours before weigh-ins, he is stripped to his shorts. Sweat glistens off his body, having just stepped out of the sauna around the corner. Douglas looks up briefly, sleepy-eyed at two high school competitors before going on with his business. Douglas has been places where they are likely to never go. He has battled in front of large Eastern European crowds and faced Iranians in the Middle East, but these experiences held little currency at the moment. The reality was Douglas was just like the other wrestlers in the gym. He had no endorsement contract. He was not making money off this deal. He was a wrestler in America and that meant a former world champ would compete in the same venues as schoolboys.

It is hard to imagine wrestling to be that potent of a drug that it can drag a two-time Olympian to this far-off place, to mill about in a creaky old locker room with a ragged brown carpet that's seen better days, lounging among wrestlers half his age; a thousand miles from his family, a far cry from the athletic pinnacles of Atlanta and Sydney, a world away from Athens.

It was hard to reason why any of them were pushing on. Why Yoshi Nakamura would ditch financial stability and the comforts of home for dorm rooms and two-a-days, sore muscles and ice bags, frustrations and bits of improvements for the fulfilling of a promise. Why Marcus Mollica, a two-time NCAA champ would leave a coaching position at Harvard to train at the OTC. There was former All-American Yero Washington, who walked away from similar circumstances at Columbia University. Douglas was just like the rest of them. The sport had become so much of the way they lived. It had shaped their bodies and introduced them to lifelong friends. It put their names in the paper and gave them an identity. And when it came time for Douglas and others to walk away from competition, it was like a part of him had died. To deny the sport, to write it off just because others weren't watching it, was in a way denying their very existence; the lack of popularity made it no less valiant in the wrestlers' minds.

For some, training was their fix. For others, it was the euphoric feeling of accomplishment that they struggled to find in other areas of life. Each had questioned whether to go on. It came after college when the sport no longer paid for an education, when continuing to train no longer seemed viable. But in the end, for this group of wrestlers and many others, it was too much of a habit, too hard to kick; the sport lingered like the love of an old girlfriend that never quite went away.

At 7:30 p.m., several clans of wrestlers move across the hall and into a side gym where registration and skin check took place. As weigh-in time draws closer, athletes walk down the stairs, one by one, drawing blank stares from table workers, tournament officials and competitors alike.

The OTC sent a mini-van full of wrestlers. Air Force has entered several competitors. So has the U.S. Army. Eventually, like three gangs claiming the same turf, they will fight for all the top spots. Sergei Beloglazov, surveying the scene from a plastic seat on the second floor balcony, is disappointed. "In Russia there would be 120 guys here, it would be crazy. I thought this was qualifier for Olympic trials."

It is.

It was.

USA Wrestling accepts it.

***

Although amateur wrestling has strong participation in U.S. high schools, it is declining at the collegiate level from 400 NCAA programs in the 1970s to a shallow 230 programs in 2004. Each year, additional institutions pull the plug on wrestling and it is often the first program to be cut, the choice of least resistance for the athletic department. With few exceptions, wrestling didn't bring in revenue and it also lacked a NCAA female equivalent. For athletic directors faced with yearly budget cuts and one shot to shoot with, college wrestling was a sitting duck.

The sport's leaders point the finger at Title IX for most of its problems. Passed in 1979, Title IX demanded that the percentage of female participants in a university's athletic program reflect the percentage of female students attending the institution. Schools scrambled to become compliant by adding new female teams, scrapping men's programs, or both; Title IX became NCAA wrestling's grim reaper.

A new opponent emerged that must have perplexed the leaders of the wrestling community. The coaches of the sport, men who were NCAA, world and Olympic champions, who were experts in the physical laws, cycles of training, and how to push the human body to the limit, found themselves in the same position they always told their wrestling protégés to avoid: the position of vulnerability and of being at the complete mercy of others.

Title IX attacked the sport with alarming results. Programs crumbled under the pressure of economic and judiciary laws, attacking the sport, not on the familiar mats in the arena, but in courtrooms and boardrooms where physical expertise was of no use. Title IX was particularly elusive because its effect on wrestling was an indirect result of its actions. Title IX was not out to destroy the sport and when enacted, there was no apparent conflict of interest. While its aims were noble, give women an opportunity equal to that of men in athletic participation, its interpretation was lethal. The wrestling community was so clearly caught off balance that there was no opportunity to adjust, fight out and somehow scramble to a favorable position.

Football, the central and often defining sport of college athletic programs, took the lion's share of the male scholarships, with upwards of 85 athletes on a roster. No female sport exists to offset footballs numbers, so athletic departments had to balance an equal accumulation of male and female sports that fit within the budget of the school. The balancing act of remaining under the athletic budget and satisfying proportionality requirements of Title IX often left wrestling the odd sport out.

University of Minnesota wrestling coach J. Robinson, an outspoken critic of the current interpretation of Title IX, claims the law has been hijacked by left-wing feminists. "The law was never intended for how it is used today," Robinson said. "It was intended for an equal opportunity for women entering law and medical schools. Title IX activists will claim that they haven't had enough time. That's bullshit. They will point to the success of the world soccer championship in 1998. But do you know that they won one in the eighties and tried to start a league and guess what happened to it? It went belly-up. And what happens to the WNBA every year? They lose money. And who supports them? The NBA. So what do women want protection in? Things they can't compete in."

Coach Robinson does not want women's sports to cease to exist, but in a NCAA world where resources and budgets are tight, taking away from men's programs, Title IX threatens Robinson's livelihood.

**

Early Saturday morning, a snow drift falls lazily to the pavement of the Wyoming athletic parking lot that is half-full of minivans and trucks. Inside the War Memorial Fieldhouse, the arena is slowly springing to life. Country music blares from overhead speakers as laconic ranchers dressed in blue jeans, spit-polished boots and shiny rodeo belt buckles prepare to watch their offspring compete.

Jon Trenge, a hulking 211-pound collegiate star out of Lehigh who resembled Clark Kent when wearing glasses, is going through his pre-match routine. Many of the young wrestlers and their dads didn't know Trenge by name but they gauge his physical movements, they take note of his powerful build and they figure he had something to offer their children. So fathers and sons, ten in all, sidle over to Trenge and ask, "Would you mind showing that again?" The young wrestlers bashfully introduce themselves and Trenge obliges.

Playing the part of gracious technician, Trenge asks a youth competitor his name and walks him through the execution of the move. For Trenge and his wrestling peers are traveling pitchmen of the sport, showcasing their skills at tournaments and demonstrating later at camp clinics. With a passage of knowledge, the seed is planted. This is how the sport survives.

The arena falls silent as a young girl sings the national anthem. With the exception of a few competitors shuffling back and forth, there is stillness freezing the arena as if someone were reciting a eulogy. The girl finishes. The crowd applauds. The action begins.

Melvin Douglas walks off the mat, berating himself after the 3-2 loss to Trenge who is eighteen years his junior, which eliminates any purpose of Douglas' trek to Wyoming. He had traveled from Arizona, leaving his family for the weekend, he had cut amounts of weight that would make anyone uncomfortable and the best finish the former world champ could muster was third place in a tournament full of youths, amateurs and a handful of American hopefuls. But he did not storm off and catch the first ride out of town. He did not throw his headgear or curse the ref. Instead, Melvin Douglas stuck around.

He spent the remainder of the day dispatching lesser contenders, but Douglas could not hide his boredom. He would talk to his coach while holding his opponent in a front headlock, stop leg shots by the palm of his hand, holding off challengers like a master does to a hyper puppy. When he needed to, Douglas would score with a quick combo attack, but his matches were useless and he appeared disinterested, choosing to mingle with the crowd and trade stories to whoever was around.

Several weeks earlier Douglas was at the national tournament, telling reporters that his Olympic ambition was a mission to show that old people can still get it done and while the reporters laughed and scribbled into their notebooks, a couple rounds later Douglas ran into Daniel Cormier, the nation's top-ranked wrestler out of Stillwater, Oklahoma and the ending didn't fulfill his visionquest. Cormier, a 5-foot-11 inch, 211-pound replica of what Douglas once was: young, powerful and explosive. During their bout, Douglas worked into an under hook throwing position and as he was locked and ready to throw Cormier, his powerful leg went from a tree stump to a wet noodle in one action; Cormier pinned Douglas after he fell faintly to the ground like a running back tearing an ACL in the open field. His loss in Wyoming could not bode for greater glory especially at a tournament that didn't exactly rouse the local masses to attend.

There is little fanfare for the championship matches. No clamor of the announcer reading off the finalists accomplishments. No spotlight under a singular mat. The tournament organizers ran the bouts all the way through with the urgency of a group trying to make it home in time to catch the six o'clock news.

An Olympic Trials bid is up for grabs and a fight for it is about to take place. Two competitors, long shots to clinch an Olympic spot, are directed to the center mat and they quickly split to opposing sides. On one end is a former NCAA runner-up who once competed before tens of thousands, on the other is an OTC resident athlete.

Clint Mussner, a hard-knocks wrestler from Cuyahoga Falls, Ohio, has the type of resume that once had entire gyms view him as a marquee attraction: He was a three-time state wrestling champ at national power Walsh Jesuit, an Asics and Junior National All-American and was consistently in the running for the NCAA title at Penn State. Mussner has taken time off since competing in college and as a result, a wrestler who never achieved his level of success is about to hurt him. Mussner works himself into a fury beforehand. He slaps his arms and legs awake. He clenches and moves about like an actor building for a dramatic moment, but on the mat, Tony DeAnza whips him.

Like a victim caught in a black widow's web, Mussner shifts and fakes and does all he can to escape but DeAnza has caught him on his back, in a predicament as comfortable as kidney stones and a short time later his loss will be certain. Sucking the power and energy right out of him, DeAnza turns him three consecutive times before pinning him cold. Mussner's still lying on the mat while DeAnza, adrenaline rushing, nods with an assassin's certainty in the center, waiting to shake hands.

Homegrown
XIX

Not much happens around Decorah, Iowa, especially during winters that can drop to -37 degrees below. It's located in Iowa's Winneshiek County, roughly twenty miles south of the Minnesota border, just west of Wisconsin and Illinois and as close as one can get to the middle of nowhere.

The city was named after Chief Waukon Decorah who cooperated with whites during the Black Hawk War and whose people were subsequently forced out of Wisconsin and Northeast Iowa. Modern-day Decorah residents watches travelers come and go with the Nordic Fest, a celebration of music, food and dancing that lit up the town every July. Tourist groups visited the Vesterheim Norwegian-American museum, the largest in the country devoted to the immigrant group, but the population, which hasn't cracked 10,000, is not headed for a boom anytime soon. While there are the staples of American small towns, JC Penney, Wal-Mart and Hallmark stores, many Decorah residents venture to other commercial centers in the tri-state area to do their shopping.

Local nightlife options consist of The Corner Bar, The Haymarket and Roscoe's, a popular hangout for local Luther College students, but downtown Decorah was not exactly the Sunset Strip. On the surface, it would be no stretch to say that a teenager could get bored as heck in Decorah and might be inclined to seek escape as soon as they learned the basic fundamentals of hitchhiking. They could reach Chicago is less than half a day or drift down south to the college town of Lawrence, Kansas, anything to avoid the prospect of growing up in an area that was dotted with densly populated towns and high school senior classes of 30 graduates. For any kid who had the big-city blues, a setting like Decorah would be just the excuse to knot their life's belongings into a bandanna and hop the first freighter that came by the tracks to escape a part of the country that seemed to be just miles and miles of miles and miles.

But maybe one might not feel this way if they grew up with three brothers and large fields to play in and rivers to fish and plenty of land to hunt. Not unless they were the type of person who loved proving people wrong and had tons of time to invest into a sport like cross-country where logging hundreds of miles a roadwork a month was mandatory or wrestling where dedicating yourself into the practice room was as much of a requirement for success as making weight. If you were this type of person, if you were Lee Fullhart, then Decorah was the place for you.

The upper Iowa river flowed through town so you could get one of your three brothers Bill, Bob, or Howard, or just take all three down to fish streams filled with trout. You could run along the hills of a wide-open landscape building your endurance for cross-country and when the winters dropped to freezing ass cold it was just fine with you because the wrestling season was heating up. The sport was always a hotbed in Iowa and over the years Decorah High put out three or four NCAA champs alone. Since your older brothers did it, then you did it, and your entire family supported the whole thing; that's the way it worked with the Fullhart's.

In fact, your dad was recalled by your old high school coach as being a quiet, reserved guy unless he got onto the topic of his kids wrestling and then, and really only then, Ron Fullhart was able to talk your ear off. He could tell you about his oldest sons Howard and Bill who just missed out on winning the state tournament, both were runner-ups, and Bob who took state as a senior. Then there was Lee, who after placing fifth as a freshman, decided he never wanted to be anywhere but on the top of the victory stand and that's exactly what he did; winning three individual state titles. But you weren't going to get those words out of Lee. No, Lee, the third youngest, was all about action and proving others wrong. People who didn't think he could run cross-country successfully, but that's what he did. Those who thought Lee was too ambitious when he said he was going to be an Olympian while in high school, but that's what he was going to do. Yeah, Ron could have told you that. To this day, he and his wife Linda were still backing Lee's wrestling and to this day Lee hadn't really changed. He still didn't talk much. He was still competing. And he was still proving people wrong.

Fullhart acted the same way after beating Cael Sanderson at Nationals than he did after winning three Iowa state tournaments. He expected to do it, he was going to get it done, he just wouldn't be much for telling someone about it. Lee was pretty much the shining image of his father, give or take thirty pounds and twenty odd years or so: sturdy, dependable and rumored to have a real sense of humor once people got past a certain point with him.

But one couldn't call up Lee Fullhart and ask him questions about this type of thing because as his father Ron put it, "He doesn't think much of publicity." Unless of course Lee got around the kids in the wrestling room where he was always communicating and staying after practice to assist. Lee had a big heart for children, and he probably got that from his folks too, considering they had five kids (one girl and four boys) before deciding to adopt three more boys. It took a good two, three years to get to know Lee and if one didn't have that amount of time on their hands to do so, then they would have to settle for the superficial first impression.

Fullhart was the type who looked prepared even in his photos, but not in the sense that he was trying to look stylish. His hair was never slicked with gel or combed with a perfect part in the middle. His face wasn't shaved to clean-cut presentable. He wore a beard like a woodsman and everything in his manner pointed to resolute awareness of what he wanted. His chin was low, his focus straight and he had clever eyes that watched people the way a cat did; always ready for the next step. There was no glint in his eye that offered clues to a special charm. There wasn't anything ambiguous in his manner. He wouldn't have much of a career as an actor.

Lee Fullhart was the type of straight forward person one would feel comfortable loaning their car to after one conversation. Other than that, a person might be inclined to say that Fullhart hadn't much a personality at all. They could ask around, but that didn't produce a good crop of information either. The saying on Fullhart was universal.

He liked the outdoors.

He liked to wrestle.

He loved to prove people wrong.

There wasn't any dramatic moment in Fullhart's existence that led him to pursue the sport. He wasn't beaten by his parents. He wasn't abandoned on the side of the road. He wasn't slighted in his youth. He was not the type of adolescent who would dye his hair or pierce his ear in defiance. He never ran away from home or rebelled against local authority. He was not lost in a world of ambition and choices; there was never any sense that he didn't know who he was. Fullhart had pretty much been the same his whole life and wrestling, in the words of his younger brother Bob, "had pretty much been his whole life."

Fullhart fit the mold of the typical Iowa youth competitor. He baled hay in the summer, wrestled in the winter and worked his tail off year-round; the Fullhart's were no strangers to it. Ron Fullhart had to quit playing baseball as a high school freshman so he could support his family and when he took up football at a college in northern Missouri he still had pay his way through school. Lee's mother Linda Fullhart was an all-state basketball player before knee injuries cut her career short and after Ron stopped teaching at the local school they opened a meat locker which they ran for 20 years.

For their sons growing up, Saturday and Sunday mornings were spent at the Hesper Locker, the local meat manufacturer. And while the four Fullhart boys had to stretch a bit to get to Decorah High from where they lived, about 15 to 20 minutes depending on how fast your tires burn, their commute to work was nothing to complain about. They got out of bed, threw some clothes on, walked out the back door and got right to it. The Hesper Locker was located behind the house and the family worked as a team. Local farmers would bring in their animals and the Fullhart's would manufacture the rest: killing the animal, packaging it, making sausage and such. Depended on the time of year and how much work was needed, two brothers would work each shift while the other two were off, but their place in the company pecking order was always defined. "Our dad was always the leader of the group," Bob Fullhart said. "We did what he told us."

That ethic was handed down at an early age, gaining a mentality from their parents that when they set their minds to something, they were going to accomplish it. After placing fifth in the Iowa state tournament as a freshman, Lee told his coach in an even tone, "I'm going to be on the top of that stand next year." And that was that.

"Emotion wasn't a part of it," Roger Williams, Fullhart's high school coach said. "Lee expected to do it. He just hated losing, he just couldn't accept losing."

***

"The surprising thing about the match at Nationals was the last shot," Kevin Jackson says. "That last shot was amazing because I saw Cael quit. I've never seen him quit. People start talking about playing favorites. I don't really care who wins. I want whoever's gonna be the world champ, let the cream rise to the top. Cael thinks about quitting everyday, too much pressure. Nobody knows what going undefeated through college did to him, because none of us has done it. He's not nearly as good as he wants to be, and recently he hasn't got any better. Nobody's gonna get better working out with their college team. They need to be in Colorado Springs or they're not going to improve, but it's hard when you have a family and kids or a career."

Jackson respected the athletes who came to the OTC to train everyday but weren't top prospects for the Olympic team. "Look at a guy like Ron Groves who if he didn't get hurt would have made the Trials. Or Jason Kutz who never was an All-American in college and has been on the national team the last few years. Or David Rechual who goes hard with everybody." But Jackson reserved the most honor for Fullhart, who had finally broken through after four years of defeat to Sanderson. "He's just stayed the course and kept improving. Cael beat him by six and seven last year at the world team trials, Lee Fullhart kept believing in himself. He's a beast."

Weeks out from the Olympic Trials, both Sanderson and Fullhart are back at the OTC room. They do their best to avoid one another, working out on opposite ends of the mat. Fullhart walks over to a practice dummy that weighs 80-pounds. Tom Brands holds it like a place kick holder and Fullhart lines up a few feet away and begins teeing off, hitting double legs attacks; after a couple dozen he is finished. Brands looks at the dummy and then, as if imagining a face of a past opponent, stands up and kicks it in the head, before walking over to Fullhart who is slumped against the wall.

Sanderson climbs on the exercise bike and begins a sprint workout with Jackson pushing him through. Fullhart, with an ice pad wrapped behind his neck and his shirt stuck to his skin like saran wrap, finally looks over at Sanderson on the exercise bike whose pants of exhaustion are too loud to ignore. Seeing this, Fullhart walks through the connecting door to the weight room where a young strength coach awaited his arrival. He proceeds to the squat rack, performing the clean and jerk exercise.

"Up!!" the trainer yells.

"AAH!!"

"Up!!"

"AAH!!

Fullhart struggles with the fifth repetition, unable to life it past halfway in two quick attempts.

"Get it Lee!" Yoshi Nakamura yells in-between his bench press sets. *"Get it!"*

Fullhart gets it and moves over to the next workout. He straps on a weighted vest for shoulder dips. Then pull-ups. Then push-ups. Then stair steppers with steel dumbbells gripped in his hand. Fullhart closes his eyes as if afraid to see, perspiration dampening his beard, lowering into a squat position as four donut weights bend each side of the barbell. A German wrestling coach watches with admiration a few feet back; hard work translates in any language.

***

"I don't train for Cael Sanderson..."

Lee Fullhart could say it while sitting on a chair outside the OTC wrestling room, he could say it in the cafeteria when his body was clean of sweat, but Fullhart could not say it on the surface of battle where it was as if everything human had been removed from him and he morphed into the mechanic fighting machine that earned him the nickname of Drago from Rocky IV. Yes, Fullhart could say it but anyone who watched him train over the last several months knew it was bullshit.

When Fullhart went into his corner during the finals of the U.S. Nationals against Sanderson, Tom Brands, another Conan of the mat, shouted instructions into his ear and Fullhart nodded in such a robotic way that one wondered if he had gone off the deep end, if the sport had become too much for him and that Brands must have told him: *'KILL! KILL! KILL!'* because Fullhart nodded like all emotion had evaporated and only a hard murderous shell was left.

But visit with Fullhart and one senses none of this. He is soft spoken and easygoing, which contradicted the screams of exhaustion he let out when training. One can pick up on his incredible discipline and self-control, Fullhart measured his words like he was fighting not to let them out and his high-pitched voice seemed misplaced on such a broad-shouldered brute. Like Sanderson, language seemed useless with Fullhart; it was not how he truly communicated.

Fullhart rarely appeared hurried away from the wrestling room, one never sees him sprinting to the computer lab or cafeteria. After practice, he walked with his head high and his steps slow, his days work completed. He would sit in the mess hall, freshly showered but sporting bruises, cuts and fresh bandages that were already spotted with blood and eat quietly by himself. His hair is short and even around the sides, a style for minimal distractions. Fullhart doesn't smile in photos, he doesn't really smile much at all and if he does it comes out with a regimented reluctance. He is not a skirt-chaser. Female wrestlers at the OTC felt comfortable around him and considered him a friend and he had the type of single-minded focused that was tailored for the sport; one can imagine him thinking about wrestling even if he was locked in a room with the Los Angeles Laker girls.

Fullhart's increased certitude had more fans doubting Sanderson could comeback to take the U.S. spot. For the past several weeks, since his defeat of the reigning national champ, there has been a new shine around Fullhart; he has been afforded a new level of respect in the OTC wrestling room. Sanderson is not here, he left to train in Ames, but he is a looming presence even in his absence. Every time a wrestler looks at Fullhart they think of Sanderson. Every time he pushes through a workout. Every time he walks into a weight room. And despite his words, Fullhart trains for Sanderson, Fullhart had beaten Sanderson and Fullhart was going to beat Cael Sanderson at the Olympic Trials, but asking him this would not yield as much, all one had to do was watch Fullhart work and let his silence speak.

Throughout these hallways Fullhart's intensity never took a day off. There seemed to be little outside of the sport that he wished to accomplish, that he was going to go through the rest of his life in some kind of silent purpose. That Fullhart would be the type in his later stages of life to wave at his country neighbors when they passed, but if pressed they wouldn't have much to say about him, that even though they have lived next to him for several years, they hadn't shared more than a few sentences and that while he didn't seem suspicious nor troubled, he just wasn't the type to discuss much. But like a farmer of the highest work ethic, Fullhart could be relied upon to be found in the same place day by passing day, cultivating the only thing he ever held interest in.

One can picture a destiny like this for Fullhart, a life of quiet isolation, of memories locked within, not one of a middle-aged man struggling with his mortality and seeking ways to relive his glory days. There was a quiet dignity in the way he went about his business, Fullhart was Iowa through and through, so much so that if he were to end up in a fast times city like L.A., mixing into the Hollywood scene, Fullhart would appear like some sort of alien and would be out of place in a town of glitz and glamour, of show and tell, and one can imagine him wandering through star-stamped streets with questioning eyes and would soon return to his home state with his gathered opinion of a life that could never be his. Fullhart would probably shake his head and tuck the experience away like a postcard buried in the bottom drawer of a bedroom dresser and be back on the farm the day after he returned from California, working, digging, cultivating the only thing he had ever known.

> *"I often regret that I have spoken;*
> *never that I have been silent."*

-PUBLILIUS SYRUS, ROMAN AUTHOR 1ST CENTURY B.C.

Heber
XX

Cael Sanderson grew up in Heber City, which ate up more than half of the 18,000-plus population of Wasatch County, Utah. Founded by English emigrants who were members of the Mormon Church and named after apostle Heber C. Kimball, the city consists of dairy farms, cattle ranches, and is a bedroom community for nearby Provo and Park City. More than 70 percent of the households were married couples and most of the high school kids in town worked at the gas stations and fast food chains along Main Street.

Sanderson attended Wasatch High with his three brothers Cody, Cole and Cyler, and competed for the wrestling team coached by his father Steve. He inherited his father's six-foot height and his low-key disposition as well. Sanderson's father is an easygoing man in conversation, and he didn't seem to take his son's athletic success too seriously. He was not an Iowa type. He talked about how wrestling was just a game and he repeated it enough times in conversations that one knew he wasn't feigning humility. He found humor in a story of the time Dan Gable came to Utah to run a wrestling camp with Cael.

Gable, although long retired from competitive wrestling, woke on the morning of the camp for a workout and asked Cael if he would like to join. Cael brushed Gable off, telling him he didn't feel like practicing and Gable, who was known to train seven days a week, was stunned that a wrestler as talented as Sanderson was going to skip a workout. "Cael did it just to see how he would react," his father said with a lighthearted laugh. "The concept of missing a workout didn't make sense to Gable."

While Steve Sanderson had competed at Brigham Young University, he didn't even claim the genetic credit for his children's success. "You know his mother was the real athlete in the family," Steve Sanderson said. "She rode horses growing up on a ranch and she could have competed in any sport if she had the opportunity." Nor did he understand or agree with the Hawkeye mentality. When Cael was bearing down on breaking Gable's college record, his father was quick to take him aside and show him the video of Gable's last match. "All the attention doesn't have to be like this son, it doesn't have to be like this."

The rest of the family was just as protective. It was not uncommon to see Sanderson working out with his younger brother Cyler at the OTC and Cody, the oldest, was always by Cael's side at tournaments, Robin to his Batman, shorter in stature but unwavering in loyalty, shielding him from the media, pumping him up for matches, taking over the role of their father who used to tell them before competition, "You came here to fight, now go fight!"

And Cael certainly did.

He would go and fight and rarely lose because he was fast and slick and had grown up with two older brothers in the practice room that had split him in two. Cody, the oldest, would take him with technique and Cole would bruise him with his powerful attack and the result after all those years of tournaments and camps and living room wrestling matches that left holes in the walls of their home was a six-foot-one, 185-pound maverick of a wrestler who was fast as the fastest lightweight, tough as any heavyweight and who was never afraid to lose.

Growing up Sanderson never had to worry about defeat, because his father never stressed this point. He never told his kids that he wouldn't buy them dinner if they didn't win. He never made them feel their self-worth depended on it. Steve Sanderson made it a game, which is all it was from his take, not an issue of life or death, not in the way any of those guys from the University of Iowa did. "Sometimes I don't understand the mentalities of Gable and Brands," Steve Sanderson said. "Wrestling is just a game, play it as well as you can."

But, nonetheless, the Sanderson's lives revolved around the sport. "Wrestling has kept us close," Cael said. "My brothers and I always go to one another with their problems. We depend on each other for support, they're everything to me." Cael couldn't ever recall taking a family vacation that didn't involve wrestling. One of those trips was down to the Arizona St. camp where Bobby Douglas was turning the Sun Devils into a national powerhouse. After watching the four Sanderson boys, noticing their skill, competitiveness and especially the third youngest's speed, Douglas sidled up alongside their father and told him he would be recruiting his boys to college one day. And years later that day came. Douglas, now at Iowa St., would hold true to his word, plucking Cody out of Wasatch High and his three siblings soon followed. Cody would be a multiple All-American and Cole would have his share of success, but it was the third Sanderson brother that would link the esteemed coach back with his own competitive rival.

"In 1970 Bill Farrell and Bill Wick decided to put Dan Gable on the world team despite the fact that I beat him repeatedly. I was ready to pack my bags and leave the camp but they insisted I wrestled the matches. The coaches said they wanted us to wrestle again in a best of three wrestling match-up when I had already won the first two. *Was it racism?* To me it was racism. I told them where they could go and what they could do with themselves in some strong language. I was going to leave but my teammates convinced me to stay. We must have wrestled 15 times and they finally put me on the team. Four days later I competed in the World Championships but I was already spent, I had left my best performance in the practice room. Gable and his parents, to their credit, stepped up and said the situation wasn't right. But I'm still pissed off with Farrell and Zwick about it, even though were friends to this day."

***

Sanderson majored in graphic design at Iowa St. and is a fan of cartoonist Gary Larson from The Far Side. Like Larson, Sanderson was drawn to the subject of nature. It was an environment he grew up with Heber City as well as Ames, both places supporting his desire to fish, hunt and relax on the river. One of Sanderson's strongest memories involves catching a 22-pound Arctic Char in Alaska and there are Elmer Fudd-like stories of him going on recruiting trips for Iowa St., driving his Toyota Camry across the Great Plains in search of wrestling talent and after coming upon a field of rabbits, stopping to hunt and not returning for two days.

He loved to disappear and drive outside of Ames and be on the river in fifteen minutes, which would come in handy during his college years because his feats made him a wanted man in the wrestling world. Cameras and reporters and interviews for ESPN and generally Sanderson would oblige, not out of wanting the attention but from loyalty to a sport that needed it, but sometimes he turned into an escape artist, ducking into hallways and vanishing through arena tunnels and generally offered just as much in interviews, divulging nothing as a part of his master plan.

"I had to keep it simple and direct," Sanderson said of his college career. "Giving boring media interviews was part of that." And those statements were as plain as the man behind them. He met his wife at a local pizza parlor. He attended church with regularity. And one wondered if Sanderson ever stepped on flowers or walked on the neighbor's grass or did anything but appear as square as Ned Flanders. But this could not be his totality because Sanderson was a daredevil on the mat, attacking without restraint, twisting and flipping into dangerous positions with not a care for hell, as unafraid of losing as Evil Knievel was of crashing, and just because Sanderson didn't tear up bars or joyride in stolen cars didn't mean he didn't possess the same rebellious gene.

Sanderson never conformed to the rules of the sport. While Gable overwhelmed opponents and Smith took the sport to a new low-level, Sanderson's style was unique as well. He was always on the attack, closing the gap on his competitor, then he would slide, smooth as a sweet talker, to pick off the ankle and lay his opponent down to the mat.

Sanderson offered hints of a different personality, having the same sly half-cocked grin as any crook who got away with it, but publicly he would confess nothing. As a result, the pull of his personality was even stronger. Fans were drawn to him, wanted to understand and unlock his secret simply for the reason that he had accomplished what no other American wrestler had and possessed everything a modern pro athlete wanted (adulation, success, endorsements) but seemed to desire little of it. How he won and won and never had the itch to brag. How he could be considered one the world's toughest men but was capable of drifting in and out of a unknowing crowd with no tattoos, no macho air of violence, no signs that pointed at such a distinction.

Douglas began an eight-year Olympic plan the day Sanderson set foot on the Iowa St. campus. "We started it his freshman year," Douglas said. "He had to get a certain amount of freestyle matches in the off-season and a certain number before the Olympic Trials based on the evaluations we used the collegiate season. We set a target of twenty days training at Colorado Springs."

But Sanderson had not met the number of competition matches that Douglas set forth and he had taken time off to get married to his fiancée Kelly Minard. He also missed the world championships twice over three years due to factors out of his control and Douglas also hadn't counted on Sanderson's desire to waver, the external pressure to be perfect and the obsessiveness that had him thinking about opponents even on vacation with his wife and family. All of which reached a breaking point one afternoon in the OTC wrestling room when Olympic Coach Kevin Jackson scheduled a private workout for Sanderson with heavyweight Mike Faust.

Sanderson and Faust went through minutes of drilling before Jackson instructed them to compete in live conditions. Faust took down Sanderson repeatedly, scoring on double-legs and spin-behinds and basically handling America's top talent. Faust, a nationally ranked heavyweight, didn't claim any merit from his practice battle. "He was off, you could tell," Faust said. "He was getting frustrated." Sanderson continued to be scored upon by Faust to the point that he stormed out of the room cursing. He went to cool off in the locker room, but like any wrestler whose body is not doing what they tell it, Sanderson couldn't take the frustration and continued cussing as Jackson tried to coax him back into the wrestling room.

Wrestling was a closely knit group and Lee Fullhart had to hear of Sanderson's weak point in the OTC, gathering in this information the way a tracker traced a footprint, and one could count on what the Iowa blueblood was going to do with it; it only drove Fullhart further in his training. While Sanderson had beaten Fullhart numerous times over the past three years and he was not the athlete that Sanderson was, Fullhart was not concerned with these factors, because wrestling was not about blazing 40-yard dashes or 50-inch vertical leaps, it concerned mind power chiefly, and if there ever was a coach who was a sports psychologist it was Dan Gable. And Fullhart's mind was full of Gable's approach and the Brands brothers' thoughts and while this hard-ass mentality was injected into to all Iowa wrestlers, Gable had more than a casual stake in the Fullhart vs. Sanderson rivalry because anyone who with half a cauliflower ear knew that Gable had never gotten over his lone college defeat and he still wanted to win just as badly as a coach, twisting and gyrating on the sideline while on crutches with a bum hip at one point in his career, and not being able to create a wrestler to beat Sanderson was surely going to be among his worst regrets.

The athlete that had broken Gable's record was going to be faced with a wrestler that was a Gable clone. Years back, the legendary coach must have seen something in the Decorah High product that separated him from other homegrown recruits, probably taking stock in Fullhart's parents as he was known to do when judging athletes, seeing Fullhart's mother Linda, a husky former all-state basketball player and his father Ron, a quiet, unemotional, hardworking man, and Gable quickly deciding that Fullhart was Hawkeye tough.

In Iowa City, Gable and the Brands brothers had built the perfect wrestler to combat speed, the perfect beast to crush indecision, the perfect challenger to block Sanderson's pursuit of Olympic gold. While the Brands were coaching Fullhart now, Gable recruited Fullhart and was still in on the action because he was still a competitor as a coach and wanted an Iowa wrestler to beat the sports current star. There was a hint of jealously in Fullhart as well. "I fight the crowd every match because he is the guy everyone wants to win," Fullhart said after winning the national title. "But I've done everything right to prepare for this."

And he certainly had. Fullhart resigned from his coaching job at

Tennessee-Chattanooga to train in Colorado Springs, leaving his dogs, his house and uprooting his life. The investment Fullhart made was singular and amount of work put in was a tremendous emotional risk for any athlete. As a former Iowa coach said of the depression that some former Hawkeyes felt after failing to win an NCAA title, "You wondered if something was wrong with you."

One had to specualte how the loser of Sanderson vs. Fullhart would recover: Would Sanderson be written off as a college star that didn't have the guts for the international sport? Would he be labeled a coward for failing to win what every coach thought he was capable of? Where would Fullhart go if he lost at the Olympic Trials? Would he have the stomach to train another four years?

As the story of Sanderson storming out of the OTC wrestling room circulated and the subsequent pounding he took at Nationals sunk in, as rumors persisted that Sanderson would soon be finished with the sport, it was quite apparent that this was Fullhart's one chance to beat Sanderson, this was Gable's only chance to beat Sanderson, this was Iowa's last chance to beat Sanderson. All of which led any rational mind to predict one conclusion: Lee Fullhart trained for Cael Sanderson, Lee Fullhart beat Cael Sanderson and Fullhart was going to beat Sanderson at the Olympic Trials.

As American wrestling's reluctant star waned in commitment to the sport, it was hard to imagine him having the strength or endurance to weather the forthcoming Iowa storm.

"A coward dies a thousand deaths, a hero only one."

-WILLIAM SHAKESPEARE

Ambition's Curse
XXI

As the Olympic Trials were closing in, the O.T.C. wrestling room was getting more cramped with personal rivals. Paranoia pervaded the mats, as every day Abas and Henson, Sanderson and Fullhart, Mocco and McCoy were just a few of the counterparts forced to share the same space.

They passed each other in the weight room. They ate in the same cafeteria. They worked on the same mats. And there was a feeling around the facility of time disappearing, of pressure choking the atmosphere, the nervous edge of an opportunity that wouldn't present itself again.

It was hard to grasp that many truly believed they were going to be America's Olympian, athletes like Nick Preston, a multiple All-American out of Ohio St., but who was now on the fringe of Olympic hopefuls. Many of these athletes spoke of winning Olympic gold medal with the assurance of a man who had finally found the one woman he was going to marry, reciting their destinies with such a strong belief that one couldn't imagine them ever being in love with someone else. But one also had to speculate about the intoxicating effects of a fool in love, how it made logical thoughts melt in the breath of passionate voices, how it made every dream feel like it was coming true and that the Olympic gold medal was surely their fate and all the heartbreak losses that preceded it never existed. The men of the mats spoke with this kind of assurance, not knowing, not caring that every Olympic hopeful in their weight, every Olympian around the world had fell for the same golden lady Madonna.

In Athens she would make her pick, in the gladiator arena he would be chosen. He would rise above the others, he would prove himself more valiant, more honorable, more worthy than the rest. This is the glory the Games would yield. But before reaching these hallowed gates, they had to be battle-tested. If the Olympics are the destiny, the Trials are their passageway.

"Pressure...changes everything pressure. Some people you squeeze em' they focus, others fold. Can you summon your talent at will? Can you deliver on a deadline?"

-AL PACINO, THE DEVIL'S ADVOCATE

One Dream-One Weekend-One Shot
XXII

Indianapolis, Indiana: In the amateur sports capital of the country, in a professional football team's arena, final preparations for the 2004 U.S. Olympic Wrestling Trials are taking place. Outside, it's a steam bath, the kind of day that leaves clothes sticking to backs. Inside, other than the yellow-jacketed security guards, the corridors of the massive RCA Dome are deserted.

Through a single door in the hallway, past several rows of half-filled media seats, University of Minnesota head coach J. Robinson sits at a table on the far left of the podium, with Dan Gable and Bobby Douglas seated side by side on the opposite end. Robinson used to coach with Gable at Iowa, but left after a power struggle over the control of his successful wrestling camps, feeling that Gable didn't back him and sided with the university's position; while the conflict between the two was long resolved, they are cool with each other during the news conference, trading no words.

After answering several questions from the media, Robinson exits stage left, disappearing behind the backdrop of a plastic sponsorship decal. Then Douglas takes his turn as the voice of reason for the sport, speaking in low serious tones. Gable nods slowly as he restlessly waits to talk, his hands concealed behind curtains that drape over the podium.

Despite coaching rival colleges, each man is a strong ambassador of the sport and seeming unified in the quest to increase its participation in the U.S., but Gable's name transcends that of Douglas' as his Iowa teams of yesteryear crushed NCAA opposition for decades. Thirty-four years earlier, Douglas and Gable had a different relationship. Gable was a sophomore at Iowa St. when Douglas was brought over from Oklahoma St. as an assistant. By his own account, Douglas' job description was to prepare Gable for the Olympics, to bring him up to the level of Douglas, who had represented the U.S. in the two prior Olympics. Douglas remembers a Gable who lacked speed and quickness. He remembers a Gable who forced his upper-body technique. Douglas, a Greco-Roman wrestler well-versed in throws, remembers a vast disparity in their workouts, and would recall at a later date, of, *'Owning Gable'* on the mat.

"Gable was my workout partner," Douglas said. "In the entire three years we worked out together he scored two, maybe three points. You couldn't count the points I scored. I owned the day when we were on the mat, *I was Gable's master.*"

But these recollections remained concealed during the press conference. The thought of Douglas having once gotten the better of Gable is foreign to the national press, who knows Gable as the one American wrestler who reached household-name status. In these circles, Gable is king. His influence still lingers and is felt in the attention his presence commands in the room. Journalists drop their pens and focus in. Video cameramen peer into their lens. It comes as no surprise to learn that Gable is a regular request for speaking engagements as his voice is distinct and resonant throughout. As his words flow, the room listens intently. Obligated, he mentions sponsors, casually checking down at prepared notes, but as the subject moves from the marketing pitch to the athletes, his tone and passion rise as if he were giving a pre-match speech to his wrestlers.

"I'm looking for athletes to lay it on the line," Gable said. "At Nationals I wasn't impressed. Some people trying to win as easy as possible. Others coming from behind are not going as hard. As I leave here Sunday night, I would hope that everybody leaves it on the mat and see who the best is. This sport needs a good showing, America needs a good showing."

Kevin Jackson stood in the back of the room taking in the words and when Gable finished, he and Kerry McCoy replaced the coaches on the platform. "I disagree with Coach Gable," Jackson says with a laugh to diffuse the statement. "I felt the best guys won. He might've been talking directly to me. He might have been saying, 'Coach Jackson you need to get these guys a little more aggressive.' Gable's been around the block a few times more than me, so his view could be different. When he's around he motivates the athletes, they seem to work a little bit harder. So I'm more than happy to have him involved as much as he wants to be involved. He's got an open-door policy."

A reporter refers to Sanderson's loss to Fullhart at Nationals as unexpected. "You could call it a rare loss," Jackson said. "He went undefeated in college, but he lost a couple times on the senior circuit his junior and senior years. He handled the loss well, but it's never a good thing to have to go through the mini-tournament, a guy could get injured or upset."

Kerry McCoy, wearing a baseball cap backwards, exudes the nonchalance of someone who experienced this atmosphere before. "I see myself winning the Trials. I concentrate on positive reinforcement. I don't get caught up in how it's going to go, who it is or who it's gonna be. I have a faceless opponent. It's something I picked up a long time ago. My greatest opponent is myself. I focus on myself, ready for all comers. My strengths in my areas are better than strength in your areas."

The RCA Dome, normally reserved for the NFL's Indianapolis Colts, is nearly converted. The turf has been removed and stashed out of sight, revealing a dark gray concrete floor. On the surface, a massive curtain cuts across the second deck of seats, hovering a few feet above the 50-yard line. Four elevated wrestling mats are on one side, four warm-up mats on the other. Mid-afternoon light filters through the giant white bubble roof, dipping and dimming under Mother Nature's control. Electricity buzzes from above the rafters, killing the steady silence of event workers completing last minute duties for a tournament four years in the making. One meticulously wipes down the hand railing while others huddle for a meeting in the middle of the platform. The mats, chest height, are clean and glistening. The score clocks in each corner are turned on; triple zeros dot each box.

Two rows of press tables extend down the side of the platform. Assigned seats are designated with placards from the largest media outlets in the country, *Sports Illustrated*, *The New York Times* and *The Chicago Sun-Times*, parallel the competition surface. On the top of the tables, twenty-two TVs, each tuned in unison to ESPN, are strategically set along the two rows. Everything is in place.

Not a seat taken.

Not a whistle blown.

Everyone is undefeated.

Primed and ready, the competitors wind down the last hours to weigh-ins. Nick Preston jogs around the arena in blue warm-ups. Unshaven, his hard face is cast downward. After two laps, he stops and disappears into a tunnel under section 124. Another former college star, Minnesota upper weight Damion Hahn, walks in and cases the arena with his coach. Hahn looks at the workers, the mats, the silent void of it all knowing a day later it will all be so different.

Seats will fill.

Crowds will roar.

Hearts will race.

Gladiators will rise.

Others will fall.

And Hahn will be in the thick of it all.

This is the calm before the storm. Five years earlier, Hahn was a high school man-child, ruling his peers like a schoolyard bully held back for two years. Hahn was bigger, better, stronger, becoming one of the most sought-after recruits in prep wrestling history. Now, after fulfilling the hype with back-to-back NCAA titles for the Golden Gophers, he is at the highest level of the American sport. But Hahn and all others going through the mini-tournament have their work cut out for them.

Forty-five minutes before stepping on the digital scales, the U.S.

185-pound national champions in freestyle and Greco sit next to one another in the first row, passing the time with small talk. One wears a jogging suit, the other waits in his singlet, resting his feet atop the railing that separates the arena floor from the stands. They are two of the best from the Midwest: Lee Fullhart from Decorah, Iowa tops in freestyle, Brad Vering from Howells, Nebraska No. 1 in Greco, each as much a representative of their home states that can be found.

They are the privileged ones who earned two days of rest while the others will fend for their sporting lives in the mini-tournament. All that remains between accomplishing their goals is winning two out of three on Sunday. After four years of tournaments, practices, weight lifting sessions, wins, losses, injuries and setbacks, each wrestler sits, sure of destinies that would be realized less than 48 hours away.

For the athletes in the arena, the risks were known and taken years earlier. As they step on the weigh-in scales, bodies taut and cut to a fine edge, they are pushing four years of investment to the center of an all-in gamble. This was the place where it all would be justified or where it would all fall apart.

When they are released from weigh-ins, a sense of closure fills the air. There will be no more cutting weight. No more day-in, day-out preparation to make the U.S. team. All that is left to do is wrestle. Relief is written on many of their faces as small groups walk out into the humid Indiana evening. Many join family and friends for dinner in nearby restaurants while others retreat to hotels.

At the press conference earlier in the day, a wrestling apparel sponsor introduced the official Olympic uniforms. Red and light blue singlet's with Olympic rings and a wreath logo plastered across the chest; tiny stars cutting down the side of the leg that hung hollow from a silver metal clothes rack. But who will wear these uniforms? Who has what it takes? Who will walk into the Athens Olympic stadium wearing the red, white and blue?

These and other four-year-old questions would be answered by the end of the weekend. As Kevin Jackson settled in to watch his team form, he understood the unpredictable nature of the event: "At this point anything can happen."

"Don't let it end like this, tell them I said something."

-LAST WORDS OF PANCHO VILLA, 1877-1923

The Trials
XXIII

Spectators slowly emerge from the arena tunnels beneath the first and second deck, spilling down the stairs to front row seats as the sounds of Tom Petty fill the RCA Dome.

Behind the veil of the massive curtain, more than a hundred wrestlers are waking their bodies. Real estate is hard to come by in the warm-up area, some jog around the outside, others drill moves in the middle; one competitor rides a stationary bike alongside four connected wrestling mats. They are the same ones who competed at the Schultz and Sunkist tournaments, the same athletes who battled in Las Vegas and New York, ghosts of NCAA Championships past, honored in the hallways and trophy cases of their alma maters, imbedded in event programs across the country.

In the media lounge, there were multiple-page dossiers prepared by USA Wrestling's staff that broke down the careers of these athletes. Reporters who had never covered wrestling had highlighters ready in hand, circling those with the finest stats: 3x NCAA titlists, 4x high school state champions, achievements that solidified their standing at various stages of their careers. But whatever accomplishments divided them in the past, whatever differing characteristics they held, meant nothing at the moment; they now converged for a singular pursuit.

Melvin Douglas cruises through the curtains, clutching the straps of his black backpack. Two feet onto the warm-up mats, he abruptly stops to scan the scene. Douglas has seen this all before, twice in fact. Had trained for it, lived it, conquered it. He slaloms through a maze of activity and stops to talk with Dominic Black. Four years earlier at the Olympic Trials in Dallas, they found each other in the finals with a trip to Sydney on the line. Douglas prevailed in two matches and became America's Olympian. But time has changed things.

Black is in his mid-30s, Douglas is 40, and neither is a top seed; Douglas, considered the more dangerous of the two, is hampered by a injured knee and out-of-shape physique. Amid the swell of action, their conversation carries on for a few minutes; an obvious respect had formed long ago between the two. Earlier in the week, Douglas praised Black as one of his biggest challengers to making his third Olympic team. But it was fools talk. It was a talk of a man who wanted to believe his invincibility, who wanted to think that he could walk wounded through the jungle and escape his prey. It was the talk of a man whose time was coming. In the swirl of young and powerful bodies on the warm-up mats it was unlikely that either Black or Douglas would get their wish.

"WELCOME TO THE TWO THOUSAND AND FOUR U.S. OLYMPIC TRIALS!"

The athletes stop their warm-ups, halting in mid-step to search for the American flag, finding the image of one on the Jumbotron screen in the second deck. Following the national anthem, they linger in the warm-up area until they are herded into a tunnel, which allows just enough space to shake out nervous energy and walk along the carpet, 15 paces at best, before their number is called. Then they emerge from behind the curtains like actors in a play, each as distinctive characters, only the action, the event, the drama was real.

"Let's go Sammie!" Sammie Henson arrives with the intent of making quick work of the opposition, whomever and wherever it is. He rushed in full energy, running to the first mat, arms charging forward, wasting little time with the proceedings, hurriedly shaking hands with the ref as if in a rush to get his hands on someone to unleash

his fury, the aggression he worked so hard to build. It could be anyone at this moment, faceless, bloodless, didn't matter, Henson was locked in his pursuit like a mini-tornado that sweeps across a barren Midwest town, rocking weak foundations, destroying the poorly built, leaving no hope to whatever it passed.

Henson's opponent, ranked among the top ten in the country, holds solid defense until Henson bulls him to the surface, pinning him in just over a minute.

With the completion of each bout, the athletes exit down the side of the mats, just below the breadth of the crowd. The winners are escorted into the media pen for interviews while the defeated cut to the outside, too frustrated, too emotional, too lost for words, passing through the proceedings, stares never wavering until they reach the solitude of the other side of the curtain, the backside of the dome where only the credentialed could go, to find an empty corner where nobody can bother them.

On each mat, one rises as another falls. Eric Akin, a runner-up in the last two Olympic Trials, walks off head bowed, chin glued to his chest after a loss. Iowa State's Nate Gallick takes out the U.S. Army's Jason Kutz in a detached fashion. Everywhere, years of work shattered like antiques crashing onto a hardwood floor. After losing to Eric Larkin, Bill Zadick of Iowa lays face down on the surface, clutching his head like a wide receiver who dropped the game-winning touchdown pass. Zadick dissapears to the back of the arena, sweat perspiring off a physique that is all but useless now. For months, years on end, he had driven it to be a champion, but now it gleamed in the harsh light of defeat like some muscle car stranded on the side of a country road, out of fuel, with no destination in sight.

Yoshi Nakamura walks off the mat silently, proceeding behind the curtains slowly and stiffly, looking down to the ground as if sick to his stomach. He sits down and stares in the direction of the Donny Pritzlaff, the opponent who just defeated him, who is already preparing for his next battle. A man approaches Nakamura with words of encouragement, but they carry little weight at the moment. For many engaged in this pursuit, there is no next time.

Reality checks are issued with each defeat. Jon Trenge knocks off Dominic Black, who wanders through the exit area silently muttering *'Jesus Christ,'* as he passes. Later in the day, Black would retire.

Time. There is no running from it. No avoiding it. No denying its inevitability. It's racing *right now* and eventually it catches everyone. On the wrestling mats of the RCA Dome, Tim Hartung, 28, plays the young executioner of Melvin Douglas's career. With each takedown Hartung completed, with each tick off the clock, the end drew closer, more realistic, sobering any thoughts of Douglas making a third Olympic team and there was nothing dramatic or poetic about the way his career ended.

It. Just. Did.

***

Olympic wrestling is not an old man's sport, nor one conquered by youth. The last collegiate wrestler to make the American freestyle team was John Smith in 1988 and the opportunity lies somewhere after college and before the mid-thirties. With the wear and tear on bodies, with families taking precedent over training, with the annual influx of fresh talent from the collegiate ranks, the day would have to be seized.

Jeremy Hunter and Matt Azevedo, both several years out of school but having not yet reached their thirties, crush Olympic hopes. Hunter faces Mike Mena, once the only undefeated four-time state champion in Illinois high school history, a former Iowa standout and now an Indiana assistant coach. In their previous four matches the two had split, but this time Azevedo rocked Mena 7-1. Afterwards, Mena sounded like a man who was moving on. "It's been a way of life for me," he said. "It's been a great experience all around."

Tim Derlan, a Penn State assistant coach hopes to put on a show for friends and family in attendance but Jeremy Hunter, a former PSU NCAA champion dictated from the outset, never allows the elder Derlan to make a move, shutting him out.

The Olympics is not a realistic pursuit for many NCAA standouts either. Teague Moore, short, buffed and wild-haired, pounded Michigan State All-American Nick Simmons. This was the difference between college all-star and Olympic contender.

Like the Civil War pitted brother against brother, the sport forces friends to become foes. Doug Schwab and Jared Lawrence are training partners in Minneapolis. They practiced together, dined together, traveled across the country together. But now the sport they are devoted to calls for them to detach and go to their opposing corners and gear up to explode, tangle and manipulate each other. So this is what Lawrence and Schwab do. They explode, they tangle, they manipulate each other's limbs, grinding for every point until Lawrence is victorious, but not satisfied. "He's a friend of mine," Lawrence said with a pained look. "He's the last guy I wanted to wrestle. It's a lose-lose situation. You feel bad afterwards either way. We have real close matches in practice. It comes down to who is better that day."

As the stakes get higher, as more bodies are eliminated, the outcome of who will emerge becomes clearer and, as a result, the matches get closer, the competition tighter and the chance for controversy greater. The fans have come to life; the stands rip and roar with every bout. They know these athletes' stories. They understand their sacrifices. Contenders separate from pretenders. Survival of the fittest has begun.

Chris Bono's finished second to career nemesis Lincoln McIlravy at the 2000 Olympic Trials and many American coaches felt that his best chance at making the Olympic team was in 2004. He would be of prime age, athletically peaked, and his season leading up to this point hardly changed those thoughts. He had defeated the 2000 Olympic gold medalist, Ali Reza Dabir, to qualify the U.S. weight class for the Olympics. He had beat reigning world champ Irbek Farniev of Russia. He had worked closely with the U.S. coaches, many of whom believed it was his time. But Jared Lawrence just knocked him out of contention.

In this tournament one slip, one miss-step changes fortunes instantly, leaving the fallen left to wonder what if? What if Bono, not Jamill Kelly, had scored the final point at the U.S. Nationals and Bono, instead of Kelly, could sit out the mini-tournament? What if his grip hadn't broken against Lawrence in the clinch? What if the weight classes weren't slashed from 10 to 7 halfway through this Olympic cycle, jamming Bono in with eight former NCAA champs? *What if?* But these thoughts were meaningless. At the moment, as Bono walked off scanning the crowd unemotionally, the pain was the only thing that was real.

One competitor summed up the feelings of the defeated. "I blew it when I had the lead," Ryan Lewis of Minnesota said. "It will bother me for the rest of my life."

"In ancient times skillful warriors first made themselves invincible, and then watched for vulnerability in their opponents." -MASTER SUN, THE ART OF WAR

Fans head for the exits just after noon, by the end of the hour the stands are deserted. As ushers pick up trash along the aisles, two wrestlers also go to work. In the backside of the dome, on the second mat in the warm-up zone, they drill anonymously. The rip of masking tape slices through the air, resonating in the upper reaches of the building. Construction equipment, stacks of chairs and tables are scattered on the perimeter of the field. The scoreboard reads 1:04 p.m.

In preparation for a six-minute go, the national champ begins running in place. His partner, tall, athletic and rangy, bounces around. After finishing an interview, Tom Brands, 1996 Olympic Champion, gives tactical instructions to his athlete. Then he walks over and does the same to his workout partner.

With a blow of the whistle, a flurry ensues. His partner circles side to side on the attack in a manner that was not his own, before shooting low on the stalking counterpart. In ten-second bursts, he moves in and out as the other mechanically pursues. Brands watches in a corner with the film crew as one hunts the ankles and the other, in anticipation, pounces quickly on top. The champion moves forward with a vigilante's intent, guarding each foot with a hand down on each step while the other attempts to counter his opponent's unforgiving style.

The 185-pound U.S. National wrestling champion only expects one opponent to emerge from the mini-tournament and his training partner is wrestling accordingly. During a breather, he removes his white, long-sleeve shirt and warm-up pants before returning to work. He continues the simulation for a half-hour before vanishing from the scene. Less than 36 hours remain.

One hour later, Cael Sanderson competes in a fishbowl. Fifteen photographers line the side of the mats. Six video cameras follow his every move. It's 7-0 at the break against a three-time college All-American but somehow, in the crush and glare of media expectations, Sanderson is not doing enough.

Flashbulbs pop with every motion, capturing Sanderson's dissection of another wrestler. Afterwards, he walks slowly along the path that leads to the interview area, stopping several feet away. The athletes are given a five-minute breather before they are required to speak with the press, but Sanderson forces the hand, wanting to get it over with.

"Does anybody have any questions?" he asks. Reporters turn and scramble for position behind the metal barrier. Notebooks flip open and tape recorders turn on. Light illuminates off Sanderson's perspiring face as several microphones strike out at his mouth.

"Gotta take it one match at a time," Sanderson says, fiddling with the bottom of his hooded sweater. "The main thing is I gotta have fun and work hard." His answers are self-deprecating, cliché' riddled and evasive. Like a bashful homecoming king forced to go through with the proceedings, Sanderson is uncomfortable with his status. As questions are thrown his way, he bites his lip and his uneasy expression never changes. Wrestling is what he enjoys, the rest he accepts as some painful chore that arrived in the baggage of his talent.

One national reporter walks off in disgust. "That sucks!" The journalist says to no one in particular. "These guys want coverage for their sport and this is the type of B.S. they give!"

For all the technical grace and skill in the elite levels of the sport, wrestling, in its purest form, is brutal and Mo Lawal never strays far from it. Trailing Aaron Simpson, Lawal attacks on a double-leg and as he's done all year, keeps driving his opponent off the surface. Reporters scatter as Simpson crashed in the well between the two mats, clipping two photographers.

"Ohhhaaahh!!" The crowd leaves its seats as Lawal hops back on the mat. The referees check with one another before awarding him a point. Simpson untangles himself from the pile, climbs to the surface and rushes straight for Lawal in a scenario that could easily be mistaken for the Ultimate Fighting Championship. Simpson is a portrait of unrestrained rage and as he closes in on Lawal, appears ready and willing to throw a punch, but his senses restrain him and he veers off instead, refusing to shake Lawal's outstretched hand.

One would imagine that officials from USA Wrestling, an organization that prides itself on the promotion of a family sport, cringed at the sight of what could be termed, *'unsportsmanlike'* conduct by Lawal. But family values were hardly the hot stock in the entertainment world and maybe Lawal knew something USA Wrestling didn't because while some fans like Lawal and some hate him, they all watch to see what he would do next.

Once again the center of the crowd's attention, Lawal hits a running double and bulrushes Simpson to the ground for the decisive points. He gets up and bounces back to the center flexing his arms and chest like the Wolverine, beaming at the row of press photographers, one of whom is still being tended to by a trainer. Afterwards, Lawal praised Simpson's talent, but refused to make excuses.

"He'd do the same thing to me. This is wres-lin, you tryin to hurt sum-ba-dey," Lawal said in his Texas-Oklahoma twang. "You hurt people to win, that's part of the sport."

Bill Zadick and Chris Bono, formerly of Iowa and Iowa St., were preparing to battle for whatever consolation scraps the tournament had left. They enter the tunnel with stubborn faces, Olympic aspirations already dashed, walking out to fight with lesser purpose, if any, in sight. Amid this setting, age-old conflicts resurfaced and tensions ran high in a half-empty arena.

Bono and Zadick begin pushing and jabbing each other in the face. The ref intervenes, briefly halting the fracas but when the action resumes, Zadick charges forward, upper cutting Bono with his forearm and chaos ensues. The two wrestlers charge at one another. Tom Brands rushes on the mat to restrain Bono. Bobby Douglas comes from behind to halt Zadick. Perhaps not knowing who it is, Zadick pushes Douglas down to the mat. Seeing this, Bono untangles himself from Brands, rushes across several feet and double-legs Zadick.

A crowd gravitates like a high school cafeteria fight and fans tilt to the edge of the bleachers to get a closer look; some running down to the arena floor. Two policemen break apart a live re-enactment of a WWF Royal Rumble, all that was missing was chairs being smashed over heads. But as both athletes sprint to the back of the arena, with Brands, Douglas, the coppers and half the crowd chasing after, it was apparent that the action was far from scripted as each wrestler had enough testosterone shooting through him that if they were to cross each other at a bar in Ames or ran into each other on the streets of Iowa City, it would be hard to believe either would be able to hold their intentions back. Fifteen minutes later, Zadick, the eternal Hawkeye, is still steaming as he circles the warm-up area alone while Bono, the loyal Cyclone, is nowhere to be found; college rivalries die hard.

Several consolation matches follow, where Steve Mocco waits like a caged animal to face Kellen Fluckinger. As he bounces behind the blue curtains, several young boys watch the heavyweight interact with his personal coach. Neither of his Iowa coaches, Tom Brands or Jim Zalesky, are by his side, but Mocco's brother is, clutching his gym bag as he watches the matches taking place. He is the same Steve Mocco, but he might as well have been on a scrap heap. No one looked at him with the same hopeful eyes after his loss to Tolly Thompson.

As he steps on to face his opponent, Tommy Rowlands, the Ohio State heavyweight NCAA champion steps off. It used to be Rowlands versus Mocco that was the talk of the sport. The athletic Buckeye bruiser vs. the Hawkeye heavyweight, but since then, Mocco took a year off from college, Rowlands dropped a weight class and their rivalry ceased. Now it's Mocco running his opponent off the mat. While Mocco stops, Fluckinger continues and the momentum carries him into the photographer's well between the two mats. Immediately, Mocco turns to apologize, but he doesn't appear too remorseful. While he dominates the consolation bout, there is little satisfaction that can be taken from it. Mocco looks slow. Out of shape. Disengaged. This was not how it was supposed to be.

Many theorized that Mocco would be battling McCoy in a heavyweight rivalry that the sport had longed for ever since Stephen Neal left for the NFL. At Sunkist, he beamed out of the arena, leaving the wrestling world buzzing the clash that lay ahead. In Russia, he proved himself against international competition and at the Schultz, his Olympic prospects only grew after pinning a talented German. Each time Mocco was unable to accept tournament prize money because of his amateur status as an NCAA athlete, but the payoff was going to come down the road when he was supposed to make the U.S. team. But now that he reached the end of it, Mocco was just another face in the exiting crowd. Not even the kids stuck around to watch that.

***

Earlier in the day, former NCAA champion Teague Moore, dramatically claimed himself to be the best wrestler in the world after beating Jeremy Hunter and was one step closer to achieving that as he scored first on Sammie Henson in the finals of the mini-tournament.

As they fall to the mat, Henson's shoe rips off and Moore grabs it and without looking back, whips it behind him, tossing it clear off the platform in disgust. Then Moore toes the line and stares straight ahead as if the behavior were normal. Observers watching the match laugh at the exchange but Henson does not find any humor in it and he turns to the ref to complain.

Moore came here to beat Henson and pay him back for U.S. Nationals. A month earlier in Vegas, Moore lost his cool against the veteran Henson. But now, when it truly mattered, Moore is superior. He is confident, he has a strut, he is poised, absolute; victory is certain. When the action resumes he builds his lead to three with less than a minute remaining.

Then the inexplicable happens. Henson's indomitable will takes over. Improbably, unrealistically, he has something left. Henson arches Moore over for two points and the crowd, stunned, begins to roar. Moore flails his arms and legs to escape, but is helpless. At this point, it's over!

Henson executes a two point tilt-and-hold, then two more. With each score, Henson's Olympic glory stays alive. With each point, Moore's fall's apart. The clock, once Henson's enemy, solidifies his advancement as it halts at zero. Henson gets up and beams toward the crowd with outstretched arms as if waiting for a hug to certify his greatness. Then he turns to Moore who is disconsolate and needs assistance leaving the mat. The techno beats race faster and faster as Henson grabs the back of Moore's head and gently knocks it with his. One minute Moore was on the verge of greatness, the next-devastated, crying, hardly able to walk, ready to retire; twenty-nine seconds the difference between Athens and agony.

Later in the evening, Moore, at the age of 28, declared himself to be done. "No more, this is it," Moore said, fighting through tears. "I don't know what happened out there. I looked up when there were 35 seconds left and told myself to hold position and be smart. After that, it was like swimming in mud. Next thing I know, it's over. Someday when I see God, I'm going to ask him why this kept happening to me."

***

There is renewed energy circulating in the RCA Dome as the second round of the championship tournament is set to resume. The lights are brighter, almost fluorescent. An NBC contraption, resembling a giant fishing pole with a camera at the end, is being set-up next to the mats as immaculately dressed National Guardsmen, shoes shining like mirrors, parade flags into the arena.

Stephen Abas circles the mat, Sammie Henson warms up with his partner. Eric Guerrero works in par-terre, Mike Zadick works on his own. Jamill Kelly drills, Jared Lawrence works alone. Joe Williams stretches, Joe Heskett runs. Tim Hartung talks with coaches, Cormier runs sprints. McCoy is joking and relaxed, Thompson jogs slowly across the surface.

Sanderson enters the arena with a gym bag slung around his shoulder. Fullhart is already through with his warm-up and is stretching on the second mat. The matches were set. An Olympic berth was up for grabs. It was down to two. Only one would survive.

A win bought entrance into the most elite athletic fraternity on the planet, a loss leaving a terrible sinking feeling, an emptiness that could not be replaced for another four years, if ever. The crowd senses it. The coaches understand it. The competitors live it.

This is it.

In the brief moment he has to himself before competing, Stephen Abas finds a small area between the mats and the fans. His grey sweatshirt covers the top half of his red stars and white stripes singlet. He shakes his arms loosely and stretches out his fingers before clasping them behind his back. There is an air of calm in his movements, in the way he surveys the four mats and the packed seats, as if he had envisioned himself at this point years back. As he casually sizes up the surroundings, sucking his mouthpiece in and out, his expression seems to say, *'So this is where it's going to go down.'*

As he makes his way onto the mat, Sammie Henson, the wrestler who knocked him out of the Olympic running in 2000, follows. Four years earlier, Henson throttled Abas on his way to making the Olympic team, but Abas is no longer in college and Henson is no longer in his twenties and the 2000 Olympian doesn't resemble the energetic competitor he was the day before. His steps are slower, his movements measured, less sure. He attacks with a vigilante's intent, but this hardly mattered, Abas will have none of it. He keeps picking off the charging Henson, just like he did in their previous match earlier in the day, just like he did at U.S. Nationals. When Henson finally gets a hold of him, Abas defends too fast for Henson to score. It's 4-1 with two minutes to go.

But then Henson gets on top and turns Abas in the same critical point where he left Moore in shambles a day earlier. Henson had the experience, the energy, the will of three men and he began to attack with such a vicious intensity that one wondered if he needed counseling, if he had crossed over to the other side for good. Henson was always like this, talking, moving, squeezing something out of whatever was in front of him and he rarely looked relaxed, yes, this was the Sammie Henson of old, a 126-pound ball of fury, and now Henson was attacking hard, the score was 4-3 and the crowd wants it, feels it, awakens with the sense that Henson could do it again, half-rising from their seats, lurching forward with the anticipation of what was surely to happen next because they had witnessed Henson break another young bull the day before.

But Abas is not Moore and hardly got caught up in their match the day before, sitting in the stands smiling and laughing with the arrogant assurance of a Wall Street inside trader, someone who knew something that would guarantee success that others couldn't, but Abas' secret was a belief, a knowledge that he was better than Moore, better than Henson, better than any U.S. wrestler that weighed 126-pounds. So Abas just dismisses it, the crowd, the cheers, the surging momentum of Henson with a stubborn, swift reversal takedown that squashed any notion of Henson's comeback because Abas was the new man of the weight.

The referee raises Abas' right hand as casually as a handshake, but its significance is as life-changing as an earthquake. He walks toward his corner, lightly tapping his chest before his coach Dennis Dellido climbs up to embrace him. When Abas reaches the media pen he is still wearing his mouthpiece. His straight hair slopes down, halting at his eyebrows. Blood trickles from his nose. His face is bruised. But pleasure overrides pain in this case, Stephen Abas is smiling.

As he leaves the scene where another athlete is surrounded by cameras, Dellido clutches him by the shoulder and they walk to the back of the arena away from the mats and commotion. Away from Eric Guerrero who is already leading his encounter with Mike Zadick, for his win, too, was inevitable. When they reach the warm-up mats, Abas watches Guerrero on the overhead arena screen clench his fist as the newest Olympic team member. He watches Guerrero walk along the carpet carrying a small American flag ocassionally signing autographs. He didn't hear Guerrero tell reporters, "The goal is a gold medal," because Abas already knew, it was his target as well.

Meanwhile, Jared Lawrence whips by Jamill Kelly to score from the clinch position. After wrestling defensively in the first match, now Lawrence doesn't flinch.

Kelly shoots in on Lawrence and contorts his leg, edging to turn the corner but Lawrence breaks Kelly's grip and spins behind to take a 2-1 lead. Minnesota fans rise to their feet. Seven seconds left and Kelly is quickly on the legs again. Lawrence counters, shoving Kelly out of bounds, knocking him on his ass. Lawrence is so focused that moments after the whistle blows, Lawrence is still crouched in his stance, still as a statue, staring at the sitting Kelly. Back in the center with two seconds remaining, Kelly doesn't even bother to attack; there will be six more minutes for that.

Shortly thereafter, Joe Williams beats Joe Heskett to clinch his Olympic berth; another battle between the wrestlers from the Iowa schools won by the Hawkeyes, but it is the following showdown that reserves the Dome's loudest cheers, which splits the audience into differing sides; Fullhart receives a loud ovation, Sanderson a louder one.

"And now the champion in red LEEEEEEE FULHART!! And the challenger in blue CAELLLLL SANDERSON!!"

In the first bout Sanderson attacks right away, scoring a quick takedown. Fullhart aims to contain Sanderson's bobbing and weaving movements. He wants to latch on to Sanderson's head, pierce the back of his neck with pressure and suck the energy out of it so when the second period comes, Sanderson's stamina is gone he will be trapped within a circle and forced to deal with Fullhart head on. This is what Fullhart seeks. That is his strategy. This is the only way he could win.

But Sanderson is too good, too ready for this. He deftly moves side-to-side, refusing to be boxed in, picking off Fullhart's ankles like a sharpshooter and winning solidly.

In the second match of the best of three, Sanderson is out of character on the mat, complaining to the referee over a call and when he and Fullhart go out of bounds, instead of letting up, he gives Fullhart an extra shove on the chest. A growing agitation seeps through as he swats Fullhart aside, visibly frustrated at his ways that constrict his movement and reduce the sport to a battle of attrition. The meeting turns into a slugfest as Sanderson gets the early lead, but Fullhart ties it up quickly.

Twenty of Fullhart's family members and friends sit in the arena's upper section, tilting and shifting with each of his movements. With 53 seconds left, one yells out against Sanderson's stalling.

"Come on let's wrestle!"

Sanderson is slowing, the relentless pace taxing his stamina. He doesn't react as quickly to Fullhart's attacks and his killer instinct isn't there. Every tick on the clock sways momentum to Fullhart, whose singlet appears to have changed color, from royal blue to midnight with the aide of nonstop perspiration.

As if instructing city traffic, Brands screams for Fullhart to keep pressuring. Sanderson is not dodging the heat as much as fighting it head on. Fullhart scores with forty seconds left. The second period ends with the score locked at two. In overtime, Fullhart clings to Sanderson as a boxer does to prevent an opponent from being able to throw a punch; neither is able to score as the extra period ends.

In Sanderson's corner, Bobby Douglas was furious over the politics of the match and drew a quick parallel to his own situation in 1970 when he and Gable were trying out for the world championship team and wrestled off in a best of three series. Douglas defeated Gable in two straight matches but was forced by the Olympic coaches to wrestle again, fifteen times in Douglas' estimation, which left him depleted at the world championships and years later Douglas felt he was battling the same forces of Gable as a coach. "Dan Gable wants Fullhart on the team, the people from Iowa want Fullhart on the team," Douglas said. "The officials from USA wrestling want Fullhart on the team."

Fullhart and Sanderson head to the center of the mat at the end of overtime, the score tied 2-2. The referee holds them by the clutch of his wrist and looks to the scorer's table. Then Fullhart's right hand is thrust into the air. Fans explode from their seats. Music screams out of the speakers. Brands clears a passage way as Fullhart exits nodding his head dramatically as the music and arena roars. He jogs out of their view confidently, the robust crowd willing him forward.

Sanderson moves slowly through the commotion, hands on hips, with a look of pained exhaustion. The sustained roar ensues as he cuts straight across the warm-up mats and disappears into a far tunnel with Cody and Douglas following closely behind. As the Cyclone disappears into an arena tunnel, the Hawkeye looks off in the other direction and keeps jogging in place, keeps moving and stretching like he can't wait an hour before the final bout, like he couldn't wait to get his hands on Sanderson, like he could go on forever.

Meanwhile, Cael Sanderson was cracking. Earlier in the year when he was wavering back and forth with his desire to continue wrestling, Douglas gave him as much space and support he needed, but with one match remaining, there is no time to ponder whether he wants to continue on.

"Get ready to go out and fight!" Cody instructed to Cael. "Don't play his game! You're out there thinking too much! Frustrate him! Lower your forehead and tie him up!"

"I don't know what I'm doing here!" Cael yelled at his brother.

Douglas stood nearby, furious over the officiating. He felt that Fullhart was being awarded for pushing him off the mat, while Sanderson was being discriminated for using technique. He was concerned that Sanderson didn't want to compete anymore and much like Douglas at World Team camp in 1970, Sanderson was ready to walk out.

"I insist that you wrestle!" Douglas told Sanderson.

"Forget it!" Sanderson said, and for a moment he decided to go home.

"You will have to live with quitting for the rest of your life," Douglas yelled back to Sanderson.

"I don't know what I'm doing here!"

"If you don't wrestle America will lose the gold medal and it will be the biggest mistake of your life!"

Douglas was worried about Gable influencing the officiating, Cody was concerned that too much time was passing between their last match. In the tunnel of the RCA Dome, both coaches knew that Cael Sanderson had reached his lowest point and Lee Fullhart was intent on breaking it.

***

In the arena fans let out massive roars. Meanwhile, on the other side of the curtain, in the secluded athlete warm-up area, emotions are fragile. A wrestler sobs after defeat while another, one win away from clinching an Olympic berth, sits in a metal chair discussing strategy with his coach. Seated nearby is Joe Heskett, the second best 163-pounder in America, possibly one of the top wrestlers in the world, who has nothing to prepare for after losing his second match to Joe Williams.

In the past three Olympic Trials under the same format, the National Champions who earned a bye to the championship finals won nearly 90 percent of the matches, but never was this edge more evident than at 211-pounds.

After putting Douglas into retirement and giving Tommy Rowlands another four years to think about it, Tim Hartung headed into the finals of the championship tournament with momentum, but now he faced Daniel Cormier, who is neither as old as Douglas nor young as Rowlands. With the energy of youth and power of man, Cormier is the next level. After resting during the weekend, Cormier was ready for whomever emerged from the tournament and after four matches in two days Hartung was sapped of strength, weary and ineffective, the mini-tournament taking its toll. Cormier tightens the vice, turning Hartung in a gut wrench as his family from Oklahoma and Louisiana cheer loudly from the second deck. Tasting blood, Cormier wastes little time in the second period, bowling over Hartung and sticking his back to the mat.

Cormier sprints to the corner and embraces John Smith as he's the third former OSU Cowboy to make the team, putting a final stamp on the shift of amateur wrestling power from Iowa to Oklahoma St.

Afterwards, Hartung walks past barefoot with his shirt slung over his shoulder, unnoticed by the media crowd that was drawn to him the day before. While Hartung is speechless, Cormier's words pour out as fast as the sweat from his pores. "Right now is the big payoff, I love wrestling, it's been my life since I was nine years old. Back then, it was mostly talent. Coach Smith taught me how to train, how to wrestle as hard as I can. NCAA titles are good but we're on the highest level in the country. I was all-state Louisiana football, I led the team in tackles with 160, but you gotta count on people too much."

As Cormier keeps talking, Kerry McCoy keeps scoring. For several of the weight classes, it doesn't seem to matter. It could have been this moment or the next and the results would be the same, champions find a way to win. At heavyweight, this mental edge is clear. Over their careers, McCoy has owned Thompson, defeating him all fifteen times they've met and this bout is no different. Beforehand, McCoy looked like he was preparing for a pick up basketball game, smiling and joking with others, and he looked even more at ease on the mat where he anticipates any move Thompson attempts.

After his win, McCoy begins to clap along with the crowd. He climbs over a railing and runs up the steps and as he rises closer to his destination the crowd rises as well, as if his presence jolts them from their seats and brings whistles from their mouths. Nearing the second-level exit, McCoy cuts left and embraces his mother, just like he had done after his second title at the NCAA's his senior year and after the 2000 Trials.

Shielded by curtains, Jared Lawrence and Jamill Kelly shift nervously as they await the completion of the match between Greco-Roman wrestlers Dennis Hall and Brandon Paulson. Kelly, America's top-ranked 145-pounder, slaps his legs. Lawrence taps his hip and adjusts the black kneepad on his left leg. His faded grey Minnesota workout shirt is patched with sweat and his eyebrows are arched in focus. As both competitors mimic one-another's movements, pacing nearly step-for-step, the outlines of their bodies are visible through the drapes and they are strongly aware of each other's movements as prior encounters cross each of their minds. It was how they justified each past win and defeat and how they let it shape their confidence heading into the current match-up that would be the real battle.

Here Kelly is at the edge of glory, one match between him and what he always wanted, and an eerie feeling begins to cloud his thoughts. It was here, in Indy, where he had made the tournament run of his career in 2003, taking out three higher-seeded wrestlers in stunning fashion. A year later, Lawrence was doing the same: shutting down Bono, edging Schwab and outlasting Larkin. The similarities were hard to escape, even harder to deny, so Kelly let go of these thoughts, resigned to the fact that there was nothing left to do but compete.

As the final two 145-pound Olympic candidates wait, Hall and Paulson keep going through first and second overtimes as the remaining wrestlers halt their warm-ups. The fans urge the wrestlers forward, the action picks up but the chants fade as seventeen minutes pass on the score clock and no points are scored. Suddenly, Hall snaps Paulson down, slides by and topples over his 2000 Olympic roommate just outside the circle.

"AAAAAAAHHH!!"

There is nothing but a constant roar. Hall scores the final points and then races across the mat, practically floating off the stage. Stumbling on the landing, he is undeterred, cutting through the photographer section and embracing coaches, cameramen, everyone in sight. When he hops back onto the platform, Hall finds Paulson on his knees, crying inconsolably.

As the arena continues to cheer, Lawrence and Kelly push through the curtains and toward their futures; only one will walk off an Olympian. The second period starts in the clinch. "Alright here we go," the announcer says with urgency and Kelly swiftly hip tosses Lawrence, sending him flying to the mat for three points. With all the lead he needed, Kelly wrestles defensively the rest of the match and clinches his spot on the U.S. team.

***

20,000 eyes fixate on the entrance of the arena. Like weary travelers at an airport baggage claim, the emotionally taxed crowd looks down at the curtain wondering which Cael Sanderson would emerge: weathered, damaged, or if at all. But whatever doubt Sanderson was feeling in the tunnel after his second match evaporates because Sanderson is now ready to fight.

He and Fullhart embrace, battling for what each feels is rightfully his. The past four years are irrelevant; Fullhart is not the national champion and Sanderson is no longer college's undefeated wrestler. The only thing that matters is the next six minutes on the clock and who is tough enough to own them.

Midway through the first period, as the crowd is still settling in for one final epic bout, Fullhart blocks two consecutive shots and goes on the attack, but as if Fullhart wants to control Sanderson too much, he gets too aggressive in his pursuit, extending his reach, and ends up stretched out on the mat like a ballplayer sliding in a bag. For the split-second that Fullhart has no mobility, Sanderson swiftly takes what comes to him, exposing Fullhart's back to score two quick, cheap tilts.

Back on their feet, Fullhart chases and Sanderson dodges. Venomous boos rain down, charging Sanderson with stalling. There is time for Fullhart to overcome the deficit but then something falls in Sanderson's favor: Fullhart's blood. Athletic trainers hastily shove two pieces of cotton into each of Fullhart's nostrils while another mummy wraps his forehead. Fullhart's family members, who were rising and falling with each series of attacks like a slow, uncoordinated wave, are now bending over their seats in the upper row as if ready to throw up.

Up by four, Sanderson refuses to make a move he doesn't have to and while they continue to boo Sanderson and had the right to do so, it didn't matter. Fullhart's blood has dissipated but nothing can stop the bleeding of time off the score clock that will soon signal death to Fullhart's Olympic hopes. As it withers from triple to double digits, Fullhart continues to charge at Sanderson and Brands continues to yell, *"Leeeee!! Shuck him off to the side! Leeeee!!"* But the Iowa coach's voice is desperate for a reason.

He has his lungs.

He will not wilt.

He is the Olympian.

Afterwards, a red film has seeped through Fullhart's wounds and his bandage forehead makes him resemble a soldier hit with shrapnel. As he trudges through a large group of media personnel, they see the gash below Fullhart's swollen and beaten left eye, his damp hair going every which way, his mashed-up forehead that looks like it had been grinded with sandpaper, the journalists see all of this and say nothing.

Fullhart would have fought Sanderson to the grave if he had to, he would have gone whatever distance it took, and if anyone had the moxie to ask him at the moment, it would be an easy prediction to say that Fullhart would have traded the result of that match for five years of his life, for a chunk of his future, for anything the sporting gods were willing to bargain because for anyone who ever knew a bit about this sport could tell you, wrestling gets inside of the mind, it layers itself into the veins, the blood, the heart and every fiber of muscle in the body and right now Fullhart's was reeling in shock and part of it would never recover from this defeat. But there was no more time to wear Sanderson out. No more matches to execute a plan. No more workouts to get an edge. Lee Fullhart had emptied himself in the arena, there was nothing left to give and because of this, he walks through with his head held high.

Moment's later the reporters are back at it, scurrying to find Sanderson in a state of exhaustion and relief. The vital fluid that leaked from his ear has dried up, crisscrossing his right cheek like two tiny intersecting riverbeds on a forest map. "The match wasn't pretty, but I guess it doesn't need to be right now," Sanderson says. "I just had to get on the team."

In the arena, officials begin introducing the 2004 U.S. Olympic Wrestling Team and its coaches. Each member is brought out one-by-one to a backdrop of patriotic music playing on repeat. Each athlete wears navy blue warm-ups with Athens logos across the breast of the jacket. Each climbs the steps and walks onto the center mat. Dennis Hall comes out first, Kerry McCoy last; in between, sixteen other Olympians are showcased to the crowd.

Tom Brands, with his jaw clenched tight, steps out of formation and walks over to shake Sanderson's hand before returning to his spot. Still reeling from Fullhart's loss, Brands stares straight ahead, eyes cast downward, hands clasped in front, paralyzed in defeat. He grinded his teeth and the disappointment on his face was the same as if he were Fullhart's own father. Sanderson nods and accepts his congratulations but holds his place in line and shows no emotion; what happened at Nationals in Vegas, would stay in Vegas.

The ceremony ends and the athletes come off the mat as Bruce

Springsteen's, *'Born in the USA'* plays over the sound sytem. The teams are brought together for a group photo. Shuttled over to a corner next to a popcorn stand, they line up in three rows as spectators take photographs. The four members of the first women's Olympic wrestling team smile in the first row, clutching small American flags. Abas, Guerrero, Williams, Cormier and Kelly kneel behind them. Sanderson clenches his jaw like a reluctant adolescent forced to take pictures with a school uniform on. McCoy smiles without a hitch.

The members of the freestyle, women's and Greco-Roman Olympic wrestling teams couldn't be any more different. There is the long shot from California's Central Valley; a once in a lifetime talent from the mountains of Utah; a gold-medal hopeful from inner-city Chicago; athletes representing towns in Louisiana and New York, Nebraska and Wyoming; a high school math teacher from Colorado; an Olympic medalist from Minnesota; a women's wrestler awaiting entrance into Yale, another from a tiny fishing community in Alaska; member of the U.S. Army; Caucasian, African-American, Asian and Mexican, but all Americans, and now, all Olympians.

They return to the mats, kneeling down to sign large white posters. Grown-ups smile as they shake hands with the Olympians, the national press hang on their every word, young and old watch with admiration. As they continue autograph posters, t-shirts and event programs, the defeated were nowhere to be found. They were afterthoughts. The team is set. The process has begun.

At 8:07 p.m., wrestling mats are being folded, curtains packed and removed from the RCA Dome. A steady hum of computer keys was the only sound in the media lounge. Sanderson, the lone athlete in the interview room, expresses relief to a small group of writers. Shortly thereafter, he is escorted by two volunteer workers, flanked on each side, into the locker room where behind closed doors each Olympian was immediately drug-tested.

After the proceedings, groups file out of the arena and head to a nearby hotel. Stephen Abas, U.S. Olympian, walks beneath the shadow of the overhead train tracks with the anonymity of a solemn waiter who just clocked out after a late shift, crossing the walkway with a gym bag over his shoulder and slipping through the lobby entrance just before the rains come down. And indeed, they stormed the city, washing away the heat and the tension that hung in the air, cooling the pavement of the downtown streets that were all but deserted.

With all challengers swept off by defeat, seven American freestyle wrestlers remained. They are Olympians now and would be treated as such. A banquet in their honor is held in the ballroom of a swank Indianapolis hotel. Tables encircle a checkered ballroom floor. The lights are dimmed just so. Cameras pop and flash as the Olympic team, still in warm-ups, is presented with plaques in front of a standing, applauding crowd.

As the evening drew later and the music and dancing stopped, the crowd thinned until no one is left but hotel maintenance workers on clean-up duty. Groups of wrestlers walked around the corner and gathered at The Slippery Noodle, the oldest bar in Indiana, for one last call.

Competitive rivals, Jared Lawrence, Eric Larkin and Jamill Kelly congregated in different sections of the joint. A blues band wailed in the background. Cigarette smoke filled the air. At two a.m., as patrons spilled into the warm Midwest night, Larkin and Lawrence went their separate ways. Jamill Kelly was headed back to Stillwater, his greatest journey lying ahead.

"Excellence is not a singular act, but a habit."

-ARISTOTLE

Olympic Training Camp
XXIV

July temperatures have reached the mid-90s in Colorado Springs and 32 days remain until the opening ceremonies. The grounds of the training center are immaculate. Flowers bloom at the entrance. The lawn is cut and lined with the precision of a major league outfield. There is the expectancy of the spring season, the hope of renewal, as change circulates throughout the complex. Banners of various athletes are attached to the light poles throughout the facility; McCoy's hangs at the entrance, Sanderson's is near the recreational gym. Day by day, more visitors are descending upon the grounds as the Games approach.

As the wrestlers head into their second training camp, the coaches set the goal of getting the conditioning back to the level it was at the Olympic Trials. They aim to build a strong base and provide various drills to test their athletes' mental prowess. Jackson wants to simulate Olympic conditions, keeping the team guessing what will happen during their workouts.

The camp was originally scheduled to take place in Florida, but to eliminate distractions the Olympic coaching staff of Jackson, Bobby Douglas, Zeke Jones, Tom Brands and John Smith chose against it.

So instead of warm Florida breezes and sandy beaches, the wrestlers are packed into a wrestling room with a low ceiling and padded walls, rubber mats and training devices, hard work instead of lazy days.

The Olympians are not alone in the room. NCAA wrestlers, who would usually be relaxing after a grueling NCAA season with just 12 units in the spring quarter and weight lifting and practice only three times a week, are packed into a room with the rest of the Olympians and their training partners. Iowa and Oklahoma St. have the most NCAA wrestling representatives in the room. But there has been another shift, another telling sign that the balance of power in amateur wrestling has transferred from Iowa City to Stillwater.

After his disappointing finish at the Trials, Mocco and his family met with Iowa coaches and asked for a scholarship release from the program. Iowa coach Jim Zalesky granted Mocco's request as he had promised to do so when Mocco signed with the Hawkeyes out of Blair Academy. Gable tried to set up a meeting with Mocco to discuss his decision, but it was too late, he was already fielding offers from other schools. Lehigh University initially pushed hard to obtain Mocco and set up a one-day interview, but the heavyweight's visit in Bethlehem didn't go as well as planned.

"I'm not so sure they Mocco and McCoy liked each other," Sonny Greenhalgh, wrestling Chairman of the NYAC, said. "He went out there for a one day interview. Steve shook hands with Kerry and asked him whether they were going to work out that day. *'Yeah, yeah sure.'* McCoy said to Steve, but McCoy never came back to workout. I think from there Mocco made a decision. He felt he was snubbed by McCoy, who didn't push for it. The next day he signed with Oklahoma St. He was looking for workout partners and he found them in Cormier and Lawal."

Gable did not have the chance to convince Mocco to stay. He could not sell the Iowa program as the NCAA dominant force. He could not say that he had the nation's best workout partners for the reigning NCAA champion heavyweight. He could not sell it with the same truth that John Smith could because OSU had more to offer the heavyweight and while Mocco is being called a traitor by the Iowa fans, with one look across the OTC room at the gold stock of American wrestling, Mocco looks like he made the right decision.

The powerful heavyweight no longer arrives to the OTC after a long drive from Iowa City as he did months earlier with Hawkeyes Mike and Bill Zadick. At the moment, Mocco was sitting next to Zach Esposito, a former high school teammate and now a sophomore All-American at OSU. He trades stories with former Cowboys Cormier and Lawal, his two new workout partners who have taken to him easily. Success has a way of developing camaraderie among teammates and Mocco was known to train as hard as any heavyweight in the country. As a key to any partnership, Cormier and Lawal would benefit from the transaction as well. But this new sub-plot in the heated Hawkeye-Cowboy rivalry that was the subject to much debate and finger-pointing on wrestling websites, was not the focus of the Olympic training camp. The focus is on the seven individuals who would represent America in the Athens Games.

With an air of confidence in their movements, the Olympians revel in an environment that revolves around them. Old rivals and Olympic Trials finalists, Heskett and Hartung, Henson and Lawrence are at the camp, but the open-level dynamic has been altered as well. Months earlier, every athlete in the OTC room was treated equal.

But things have changed. Rivalries have been put aside. NCAA grudges are on ceasefire. Many of the non-Olympians are careful not to attract much attention as if they were walk-ons to a major college wrestling team just happy to receive two t-shirts, a pair of workouts shorts and a locker with their nameplate.

Nevertheless, there isn't a hell of a lot of male bonding going on. The Oklahoma State wrestlers practice with their same training partners. Iowa guys aren't extending any invitations. Some lines are too clear to be crossed.

And two gold medalists, two symbols of their countries' athletic excellence, two men who had conquered the wrestling world, stand in the center of the room dispensing knowledge in hopes of creating another golden boy to duplicate their accomplishments. The wrestlers sitting on the mats were looking up at the two men whose presence captured the facility but there was an invisible elephant in the room as well. A dark, unseen presence that lingered on the mats, that was transparent in the thick, hot air of the facility. It was something that many did not want to acknowledge and others couldn't deny, something that divided these two symbols of athletic excellence and drove a wedge in their coaching partnership.

There was a rift between the two that had begun long ago. Between Sergei Beloglazov, who was walking across the U.S. practice mats on his toes with hunched shoulders with the energy of an eager youth and Jackson, who was moving about with equal vigor as the leader of the American program.

Watching grainy videos of Beloglazov's competition days, one can see the fleetness of foot, the precision of movement, how he competes aggressively nonchalant while remaining mysterious to the opponent. During his prime, Beloglazov was fearless, peerless, predatory, possessing a sixth sense, a great white shark on the mat, all 125-pounds of him.

When he walked off the mat after winning another world championship in 1983, he was exerted but not exhausted, content but not overzealous and the first one out to greet him was his twin brother Anatoly. The siblings embraced lightly and walked off together and one knew by reading their relaxed body language that victory was expected by both, that whatever didn't get said between the two was already understood and that a brothers' bond was unbreakable, their loyalty to Mother Russia unshakable and Kevin Jackson understood this better than anyone.

Jackson, the gold-medal winning U.S. Olympic coach, had felt his own swellings of pride and victory and worldly accomplishment that few men held. He had felt the blood and adrenaline rush through his body after winning a title like Beloglazov had, dropping down on his knees, sweat oozing from every pore, clenching his fists, ensuring his place as an Olympic Champion. But Jackson had experienced this in a different system, for a different country, wearing the red-white-and blue.

Only now, the two men, the two individual greats, the two symbols of their countries' athletic excellence were supposed to fuse together in an arranged American coaching marriage. When the union began showing signs of failure, suspicions arose, lingered, strengthened and filtered in and subsequently out of the OTC room, into USA Wrestling office hallways and into select wrestling gyms across the country, permeating like the stench of a cigar in a non-smoking facility. People noticed and something had to be done. Mistrust was an issue. Politics were paramount. The very sound of the accusations: *'RUSSIAN COACH SELLING OUT THE AMERICANS!!'* made for front-page newspaper headlines reminiscent of Cold War propaganda and quickly a rivalry that had simmered, boiled up again with rumors and innuendo stirring the pot. Whether it was true or not was another thing, as it was, the U.S. was sleeping with the enemy.

"Forgive your enemies, but never forget their names."

-JOHN F. KENNEDY

Political Games
XXV

Sergei Beloglazov can remember it clearly. So can John Azevedo. The year was 1980 and both had qualified for the Olympics Games; Beloglazov earned the Russian spot months before the Games, Azevedo accomplished the same feat in the U.S. During this era, the rivalry between Russia and the U.S. had intensified due to the Cold War.

"It was very bad feeling," Beloglazov said. "Politics, sport always mixed. We go to World Cup in USA, some people cheer against us, they were very angry. But we were 100 percent sure U.S. was coming to the Olympics. We talk to U.S. wrestlers and although they mentioned the boycott, they were sure they were coming. We lost the World Cup so we want to wrestle these guys."

Before an Olympic training camp, the U.S. athletes heard rumors of a boycott being proposed. Most of the team ignored the claims and continued to focus on the training. "I didn't let it bother me," Azevedo recalled 25 years later. "I figured we'd go." A few top U.S. wrestlers were not as confident, some even used the rumors as an excuse not to cut weight for the Olympic Trials. During the training camp leading up to the Olympics, the speculation intensified and the reality of not attending gained momentum, but it wasn't until U.S. coach Dan Gable addressed the American team that everything was confirmed. The U.S. would boycott the 1980 Moscow Games. Beloglazov found out while watching a Russian news broadcast. President Jimmy Carter's announced that the U.S. Olympians would pull out of the Moscow Olympics in protest Soviet action in Afghanistan, a decision that would have aftershocks for years to come.

American Olympians were later invited to Washington D.C. for three days of activities at President Carter's request. The athletes were given special medals on the steps of Congress, but not all of the Olympian's accepted the gifts and some held protest signs. Later in the weekend, at a dinner in the Olympian's honor, many of the athletes wouldn't shake hands with the President.

Beloglazov, after carrying the Soviet flag into the Moscow Olympic stadium, went on to win gold in 1980, but the void of U.S. competition dampened his experience. "We were very upset," Beloglazov said. "I know the feeling of U.S. athletes. These guys get symbolic medals and most throw them away."

Four years later, Beloglazov made the Soviet team again and prepared for the 1984 Los Angeles Summer Games. At the last training camp before departure to California, Soviet athletes were informed of the decision in much the manner that the Americans had experienced in the previous Olympic cycle, the Soviet sports federation would pay back the U.S. and boycott the Olympics, opening the door for nine U.S. freestyle and Greco-roman gold medalists.

"Totally wrong decision 1984, I talk openly to media about it," Beloglazov said. "They try to convince other countries to boycott, some people like this, but ninety percent of the athletes against it. Terrorists? It wasn't serious. I watch Olympics on TV, Japan and U.S. level very weak. I was 28 at the time, I think maybe I should quit. I was an officer in the police academy and married with children. World Championships become nothing to me, my wrestling career was almost over. What happens if I work hard only to maybe boycott again? Lots of people quit."

Azevedo never made another U.S. team, pulling out with a knee injury weeks before the '84 Olympic Trials. Beloglazov decided to continue training and won three more world titles, but he ached for the Olympic competition. The Seoul Games of 1988 were called the real Olympics by the athletes because there would be no boycott. Tensions were high in Seoul, with a heavy security presence stiffening the atmosphere. "Too much politics involved," Beloglazov said. "Everybody try to provoke. Our coaches never say, *'We wanna beat USA! Oh we wanna beat USA!'* Russia already good. We wanna be ready, wanna wrestle, wanna win."

This would be the last summer Olympic competition featured a unified Soviet Union team. With the breakup of the country in 1991, the power of wrestling in Eastern Europe shifted like faults after an earthquake. When the dust settled, the economic inequality of Russia widened and many sporting organizations were taken over. Russian wrestlers, who had always fought for one spot, could now pick and choose a country to train for. If a talented athlete failed to make the formidable Russian squad, he could attempt to qualify for one of 15 post-Soviet states: Armenia, Azerbaijan, Belarus, Estonia, Georgia, Kazakhstan, Kyrgyzstan, Latvia, Lithuania, Moldova, Tajikistan, Turkmenistan, Ukraine and Uzbekistan. All over Eastern Europe, Russian athletes shifted to different regions, adopted fresh colors and became free agents in a new wrestling world.

"I could have won the Olympics living in the gutter."

-TOM BRANDS, 1996 OLYMPIC GOLD MEDALIST,
SPORTS ILLUSTRATED

Patriot Games
XXVI

Tom Brands is the son that Dan Gable never had, the embodiment of what he preached in his two-fisted approach to the sport. Physically, Brands is not far removed from his peak shape; his forearms are thicker than his biceps and his hands are gnarled and strong as a climber's; his legs built by endless runs of the Iowa's Carver-Hawkeye Arena steps.

In college, competing at 134-pounds, Tom and his twin brother Terry were known to be stronger than the heavyweights on the Iowa team, wearing out one practice partner after another. Their in-your-face wrestling style bore a similarity to a heavyweight boxer who threw punches with such willful intensity that it was only a matter of time before he cracked the opposition's defense. In the final period of matches, the Brands brothers left opponents weary and beaten, hardly resembling the physical shape they carried onto the mat only six minutes earlier.

Brands was the very caricature of Gable. He won a world title and then dominated the Olympic competition, shutting out his adversary in the 1996 gold-medal match. Like Gable, Brands was back at work the day after winning gold, driving all the way home from Atlanta to Iowa and found mowing his lawn the following day by a neighbor.

Brands is more than two cycles removed from Atlanta, but he remains wild-eyed and restless in the practice room; intensity his most pronounced characteristic. *"Up and going!"* Brands says with a twirl of his finger. With that, the best amateur wrestlers in the U.S. begin circling the OTC room. They stop for pushups, then sit ups. Then they pummel back and forth, the sounds getting louder, the action more intense. Brands voice reaches Abas and Guerrero who are blasting through on takedowns. His voice reaches Williams and Cormier who are sprinting up the side mats. His voice reaches everyone in the room who wants to improve. Brands marches up and down the surface, becoming the conductor of the afternoon practice, banging his hands together as if they were musical symbols.

"Sprawl!" And legs shoot back, hips drop and forty wrestlers hit the deck.

"Hit! Hit! Hit!" And the room choreographs into one shooting motion and quickly all the rivals colors on the mats, Iowa and OSU, black and yellow, orange and gold, meshed together like the blood, sweat, rips of athletic tape and bandages that had fallen onto the mat.

"Joe Williams!" Brands yells at the former Hawkeye star.

"Eric Guerrero!" He exhorts to the former Cowboy standout.

"Sprawl!" And fifty men hit the mats in one powerful swoosh. Brands continues to drive the drive the potential of the great U.S. team further, whose keys have been handed to him for a day.

"You can't be a winner if you're afraid to lose."

MARC CUBAN, MAVERICK

Cowboy Up
XXVII

The dream was real now. Days were falling off the calendar. The things that the Olympians had worked for, the things they had chased after were coming true, making them walking success stories, inspirational...

"I CAN GUARENTEE YOU'RE NOT WORKING AS HARD AS THE RUSSIANS OR IRANIANA!!" Bobby Douglas yells to the U.S. team before practice. "We can come home with a lot of medals, but I don't see that intensity, I just don't see it. We're gonna do some things you might not want to do. Some of you would rather be home. There's 12 days left. If you aren't sore, if you aren't tired, you're not working. What you do the next 12 days will have a big impact on the Olympic Games," Douglas says with urgency. "These next 12 are the most important of your career. Since you were young, think of all the work you put in to get to this point. If you still want to be a gold medalist, don't let 12 days stop you. These games will leave you where you stand in your career."

Olympic coach Kevin Jackson takes over the floor. "Do whatever it takes to get that gold medal. Finish this cycle off strong and earn that day off. Once you're at the Olympic Games, it's up to you to get it done."

After a one hour workout, practice is over. But, Jamill Kelly's workout partner, Zach Esposito, a sophomore at Oklahoma State, keeps going. Like the others, wrestling has become so much of what Esposito is. Shaping his psyche, his goals, how he went about his day, imprinted on his body by ears that looked like they were smashed by hammers, the shaping of his back, the scars that were remnants of past battles. This is what the sport has given him. The daily enduring of pain was worth it, to many even enjoyable, because the payoff would come during competition, in the people, the experiences, the NCAA team titles that can never, ever be taken away no matter where the future takes him.

National high school wrestler of the year two years back, NCAA-runner-up the year before, Esposito works to advance further, to move to that next echelon, so he drills a seven minute match by himself: stance drill, shots, sprawls, touching the mat, fake, fake, fake. A dreadful exercise, Esposito goes non-stop as if pushed by something that is not in front of him, intangible, abstract but whose presence lingers in his head just the same, that justifies him pushing his body to exhaustion and beyond. The pain is essential for redeeming the NCAA individual title that eluded him by a single loss. The next two college seasons will be a success only if Esposito rises one step, only if he wins the final NCAA championship match. These are not only the OSU coaches' expectation, but his own. They are trained to think this way, the only way, to win. To not settle on past accomplishments no matter how ripe they may be.

So Esposito presses on, alone in the center of the room. Some watching, others not. No matter, Esposito is lost in the blood-pumping, mind-numbing process of taking that next step, not settling for the last one, even if that next step lies a year away it would justify this moment, tomorrow's and all of the rest. To be a champion, to strive years and years for a singular goal, there is a high price to pay for that moment when the elusive, euphoric, drug-like feeling washes over the body. The one many wrestlers have written down on their walls, in journals, telling themselves over and over again before setting about everyday on achieving it, but few had. For it is a combination of ability, speed, power, guts, toughness, technique, experience, coaching, motivation, all qualities which Esposito possessed, but the present is all he could control for now.

Work.

When the moment arrives, Esposito will have to seize it from an opponent who will want the NCAA Championship just as bad, and this too, he is preparing for. For now, Esposito is doing his part as are the others in the room. Some are going for gold, others are putting themselves in the position to do so down the road; Esposito is chasing an NCAA title. Many of the Olympians and coaches have achieved what he desires, have been where he wants to go and just by being in these surroundings, training with this level of competition, Esposito is getting closer however small the daily gain. And possibly he, like others in the room before him, will arrive at that championship moment and walk out on that NCAA finals mat feeling that the outcome of the bout is a mere finality, his destiny regardless of opponent, circumstance, whatever comes his way.

This is the only way to think. To doubt, would be the questioning of potential, the very questioning of purpose. This would breed slivers of uncertainty that are potentially more powerful than an opponent's attack, more damaging than scorched lungs in the final period. What the opposition is doing is a never-ending race, a nagging question that never vanishes. The opponent will always be there, so Esposito cannot dwell on this. He can only control his destiny.

Esposito would have to put in the work and the moment would be his and amid other finalists, he would get his due at the NCAA's, the grandest stage of American wrestling. Perhaps he would run into the corner to hug John Smith as Cormier and other Cowboys had or point into the stands at the friends, family, teammates who had been there through the ups and downs every competitor faced. Or, perhaps, Esposito would square-off with an opponent who was just as prepared, just as talented and believed just as much as Esposito that the NCAA title was his for his taking. And as they spar back and forth the match would reach its breaking point and the opposing wrestler would seize it for his own glory. Then the pain of defeat would find its roots in moments such as these, the sacrifices and cycle of practices that weren't justified by a title in the end. This is the risk that every gladiator faces.

But, like others in the room, Esposito was a dreamer of the day, one who set about achieving his goals in the agony of the practice room and not in the fleeting shallowness of the night when all feats are believable, when anyone, lying on his back preparing to sleep, could dream any dream possible.

Whatever the competition was doing at the moment couldn't have been much more grueling than this: Sprawl, fake-fake-fake, shot, fake-fake-fake, sprawl. Sweat falls off Esposito's forehead with each rapid movement. Fake-fake-sprawl, shot-shot-shot, down block, Esposito does not look up. Not once does he look up. Tiring halfway through, he gets a second wind with the encouragement of Jackson's voice.

"Four minutes down!" Jackson calls out. "Three left!"

Fake-fake-fake, shot, circle, sprawl-sprawl-sprawl.

"The most dangerous men are the ones who have nothing to lose. Not honor, nor reputation, nor a title that accompanies a name, a man with no conscience is a man to be feared."

-MICKEY STRAIGHT, LOS ANGELES RABBI

Training Days
XXVIII

The best wrestlers in the U.S. wait for the signal. They are lined along the walls. They sit on the metal bench. They wait on top of the mats. The facility smells like a locker that hasn't been aired out. There is friction in the air. The wrestlers are distancing themselves from one another. There are several quiet conversations, but the majority saves their voices. The wrestlers know what is coming. The coaches are going to deliver it. Today's practice is going to be murder.

After a brisk warm-up, no-holds barred action ignites across the room. At a wrestling competition while sitting up in the stands, the battles look fluid with the sounds of the competitors drowned out by the crowd. But watching mat side, it's a violent and ceaseless struggle for leverage that evokes images of two giant rams charging one another in the nearby Colorado mountains. Mo Lawal slams Daniel Cormier who aggressively attacks. Lawal sprawls and instead of trying to spin, opts to hop right over Cormier who is rushing at him. Lawal, falling backwards in the air, hits the mat on his side. Cormier spins, Lawal recovers, each coming within inches of scoring before they mash each other into the padded blue wall.

210   NICHOLAS HOPPING

Doug Schwab, out of Iowa, sweeps Jamill Kelly's leg and drops him hard onto the surface. Abas and Henson are competing as if there is still a score to settle. Tolly Thompson tackles McCoy across ten feet of mat, McCoy rears back and pounds him on the next takedown. Jackson keeps escalating the intensity, heaving instructions across the room as the assistants continually wipe down the surface. The squeak of shoes, the dripping of sweat, the heaves of lungs, have turned the mats into a slip and slide; the room is a massive, swelling *Fight Club.*

The carnage is racking up. One wrestler lies face down, bleeding from the chin, as the trainer tries to apply strips of white tape around his jaw. His shirt offers evidence of an attempted knifing as it is ripped down along the armpit and extends to the bottom of his ribcage. Additional bandage is applied around his forehead but the sweat has loosened its hold and shards of loose material hang off his eyelids, impairing his vision. But the wrestler could care less, he's already negotiating with the reluctant trainer to continue battling.

"We gotta spread out!" Jackson yells. "You've got to control yourself! This is where we get better! Right here, right now!"

Williams rushes under Esposito and explodes his hips while wrenching him around the waist. Esposito rockets six feet off the mat. It's at this peak point that Williams is in complete control of Esposito's medical future. He can slam Esposito and break his bones by blocking his arm and cutting off the devices that will soften the blow. In a split-second Williams can crush Esposito, but at the peak of the lift, the Olympian releases his grip, point proven, allowing the 150-pound NCAA runner-up to plummet to the surface unscathed. As Esposito lay motionless in recovery, Williams nonchalantly walked over his body the way one does of a passed-out homeless man on the street.

Then Williams squares off against Joe Heskett and while they had narrow battles at the Olympic Trials, Williams dominates their practice matches. Heskett has taken time off after the Trials while Williams has been training non-stop at the OTC. In many countries Heskett could be the 163-pound Olympian, many top national coaches felt he was capable of capturing a world medal, but Bobby Douglas, Heskett's coach at Iowa State, didn't think he was getting enough training while working as an assistant coach at Cal Poly-San Luis Obispo. At least not like he could get in Colorado Springs where he face national competition every practice. Heskett was married with a young daughter and held a coaching assistant position where NCAA athletes were his only workout partners. "He's not in the right training environment to be the Olympic champion," Bobby Douglas, his former college coach said. "Everyday he needs to be working on freestyle techniques."

Heskett was like other elite American wrestlers in the room, he had priorities other than wrestling while working as an NCAA assistant coach, which was a job with its own set of commitments. "The NCAA colleges sell our elite level athletes a bad bill of goods," Ron Groves, an OTC resident athlete said. "They tell the assistant that they can train full-time but then they have to be at every practice which is geared toward the college guy. If you're hired as the academic advisor, you might spend an afternoon chasing a kid down for bad grades. That takes away from training, it's a distraction. The Russians aren't working two jobs, they work one job and they train full time. It's hard for an amateur athlete to be a professional athlete."

During a break, Brands calls out across the room, "Troy Letters!" he says, motioning for the Lehigh NCAA champ to match up with Joe Williams. In 2008, Joe Heskett will be 29, the same age of Williams and he figures to be the Olympian if Williams retires after this cycle, but there will be someone else ready to challenge him and that someone could be Troy Letters.

Like a gunshot at a track race, the whistle blows and the wrestlers are off, jostling for position. Letters, with one leg forward, shoots in on a high crotch leg attack. Letters is too strong and in too good of a position to be denied and finishes for the score. Then another score near the center and another on the edge. In several minutes Letters has been able to accomplish what the rest of the U.S. couldn't, scoring repeatedly on Joe Williams. No one in his weight has taken him down as many times as Letters has and as they continue to spar, the best coaches and wrestlers in America have noticed. The whistle blows, the room exhales, the last round is over.

"Hey-hey-hey!" Jackson says, crouching, arms extended. The room turns to face him for a quiet, tension filled two seconds. "Overtime!"

Williams is sapped, depleted, staggering at the knees, the strain of the sport robbing another supremely conditioned athlete of his balance, technique and motor skills.

"Put it in the bank," Jackson exhorts. "Put it in the bank." The wrestlers stagger around the room in a slow jog.

***

The Lehigh University wrestlers who were at the OTC are especially close. Back in Bethlehem, Pennsylvania they were the show. Their matches drew thousands of fans and were broadcast over local radio and cable stations. But at the training camp, they are just another group aiding the process of the Olympic movement.

At night, after showering at the facility and eating a meal in the cafeteria, the Lehigh group catches a shuttle to a nearby hotel. They cram into two double-bed rooms, already littered with towels and workout gear after a day's use. Nearly every wrestler has a scar or fresh scrape to signify his reason for being in Colorado Springs. The television and radios are blasting as teammates shift in and out of the two interconnected rooms. After scrapping together whatever their budget will allow, several of them make a local liquor store run for cheap beer and pretzels while others trade stories and play cards to pass the time.

Jon Trenge, an NCAA athlete who took a redshirt season to train for the Olympics, is energized by the arrival of his teammates after spending a season living at the OTC. Trenge missed the camaraderie of his college mates and seemed to have lost spirit for the Olympic pursuit. During a qualifying tournament in Athens, Trenge had a match overturned by an official, was pickpocketed and lost his passport and had to spend an extra day at the American embassy. And throughout the season away from college Trenge traveled to far reaching tournaments that did not match the excitement of the NCAA level. But with the return of his peers, Trenge is yelling and hollering and acting like an undergraduate again.

Trenge is seated next to his Lehigh teammate Troy Letters, who he describes as a sort of wrestling genius. Letters, who makes no plans when heading into the match-improvising off the whistle instead, made no boasts of his taking down the Olympian Joe Williams in the day's practice. Instead, Trenge, Letters and his teammates have fun at each other's expense. They spit chew into empty beer cans and while watching the Simpsons on TV, they swap clothes and playfully slap each other on the back. There is no practice the following day so later on that night the Lehigh outfit heads to the nightclubs downtown. Some couldn't get in because they were too young, and their IDs too fake but they continued to party because they are like other NCAA teams and programs across the country. The season, the sport is a grind and in the process of exhaustive training, there has to be down time.

Years from now, it will be impossible to share this. There will be families and careers to worry about, jobs and futures to secure. In NCAA wrestling, athletes from high schools and junior colleges come together to places like Ann Arbor and Norman, Stillwater and Lincoln; roughnecks, squares, honor roll students, model citizens and rowdy types, unite for better or worse to make a college wrestling team; a fraternity built based of each member's athletic prowess and not by funny handshakes, intiation rituals or monthly dues.

And as a team there are certain rules that went unmentioned in the NCAA handbook that go along with that. They, like others, would fight for one another. Borrow clothes if needed. Introduce girls when the opportunity arose. If one couldn't get into a club, the others would produce an ID to try and make it happen. If one was having a bad week in practice, the other would pick him up, point out his flaws and guide him through. If a dangerous situation arose, one wouldn't bail on a teammate. College teams bond over four years. They train together, live together, study together, struggle, fight and party together, so they arrive at tournaments as an organized, disciplined band of brothers and because of the physicality of the sport, because they fight out their battles separatly but together, college wrestling programs seem closer than most.

The Olympic team is different; they have seperate priorities. Guerrero and Williams are married with children. At the end of practice Kelly, Cormier, McCoy and Jackson swapped stories and joked like old friends, but their unity is temporary. While they dine together and play video game tournaments in their downtime, while they watch DVDs in between workouts and purchase matching dog-tags at the local mall, there unity is short-lived and life will soon force their separate ways. The innocence is lost on the open level.

***

The parking lot of the OTC is nearly empty. There are no tours scheduled for the day. Inside the sports complex, the weight room doors are locked and the lights are off. But for the U.S. wrestlers, the Olympics begin today. Referees wait in the center of each mat. Time and scoring are recorded appropriately. Thirty second breaks are taken and wrestlers are called by name to compete.

"Stephen Abas on mat one!" Jackson says with urgency.

Abas walks through the doors tonguing his mouthpiece, sweat glazed on his face, eyes failing to meet anyone. And he is quickly tossed to his back. Tilting and twisting, Abas desperately tries to get away, but his opponent's hold is firm and keeps him exposed for several seconds. This is the last thing Abas and the coaches want. They want domination. They want sharpness. They want injury-free action. They don't want some college kid sticking one of their gold medal hopes. They don't want McCoy to be passive against Mocco. They don't want Williams to shut down. They don't want Guerrero to have trouble scoring. Specifically, they don't want their athletes losing confidence, the edge they need to win medals, so the referees decisions tilt in the Olympians favor and the reassuring of the Olympic ego never ends.

Williams rushes through the door to the music of *Rocky*. Williams attacks Doug Schwab relentlessly, taking him down in the first ten seconds. After a break, Williams isn't nearly as aggressive. It was in the first flurry of action, the first moments on the mat that he was a world-beater and the lighter Schwab didn't stand a chance. The opponent was helpless because Williams was bigger, longer, more athletically gifted than anyone near his weight. It was moments such as these that coaches know that Williams was a gold medalist contender.

But getting Joe Williams to attack non-stop was another story simply because Williams didn't have to wrestle this way to be the best 163-pound wrestler in the U.S. All Williams had to do was sit back in his matches, put his long arm out to defend against his opponent and when he felt like it, blast him across the circle with one of his double-leg shots that was unstoppable. Williams didn't have to fulfill his total potential to be the best wrestler in his U.S. He knew it, his opponents felt it and it is why Schwab, an elite U.S. 145-pounder can look over-matched in one period against Williams and hang with him the next. In the U.S. Williams didn't have a thing to prove, he had been the top American wrestler three years in a row, but for he and the rest of America's Olympians, the stakes have risen.

It was now U.S. versus the world.

"When the president of the Russian sporting federation can threaten the life of everyone on the FILA staff there is a problem. At the Olympics in Australia he threatened to kill everybody on the FILA board because of the officiating, an American referee was one of them. When things like that are allowed then you have a corruption problem."

-BOBBY DOUGLAS, U.S. OLYMPIC COACH

Russia
XXIX

You don't fuck with Russian wrestlers. Sometimes they couldn't get Visas. Sometimes they had problems entering other countries. But they always got respect. Maybe not from the codes of Amnesty International, but the type of consideration that pulled them to the front of lines in nightclubs and got them the best tables in restaurants; the type of deference that made others step aside.

"In the Soviet Union, the wrestlers are part of a racket, syndicate, mafia, they serve as bodyguards, whatever you want to call it," Bobby Douglas said. "They are the most feared athletes, they have the reputation as the heavy lifters. It's the same thing in the former Soviet-Bloc's, Turkey and Iran. People you don't want to mess with. Nobody bothers them. They don't look at themselves as gangsters. They were the soldiers, the kings, the generals, the ones on the front lines during the war. People in their country respect them because of there discipline, wrestlers are the people they look to in order to solve their problems; they were the leaders. Look at Ghenghis Khan, he is history's greatest conqueror and he was a wrestler."

The legendary Mongolian emperor considered wrestling an

important way to keep his army in good physical and combat shape. Wrestling was also used occasionally as a way of eliminating political rivals; Mongol history records incidents of Khan arranging to have political enemies killed via a wrestling match. During the Manchu dynasty from 1646-1911, the Imperial Court held regular wrestling events, mainly between Manchu and Mongol wrestlers.

Many of the conflicts that Khan's army engaged in took place in the mountain regions of southern Russia, areas like North and South Ossetia and Chechnya, and many Russian gold medal winners have come from these areas. "We have good wrestlers because we are survivors," Makhavlock Khadartsev said. "It is in the blood. We are descendants of the Alani, who were massacred by Genghis Khan according to local legend. Our ancestors were the ones who filed into the mountains, who survived. The weak could not survive, only the strong. We Ossetian's have always fought for our lives."

Eastern-European wrestlers have a presence in their cities that appease local strifes. "I've been in some countries where we had dangerous situations," Douglas said. "Places like Turkey and Iran, but I was unfazed because once people found out we were wrestlers, they went away. Problems started, but the presence of other wrestlers quickly took care of it. They treat you like royalty if you're a wrestler in Russia, Iran or Turkey, they put a bounty on the gold medal. Buvaysa Saytiev is a millionaire, Ivan Fatsiev is a millionaire; they're worth millions because the federation takes care of them."

The head of the Russian Sporting Federation, Mikhail Mamiashvili, was a three-time world Greco-Roman champion and 1988 Olympic gold medalist. Anyone who encounters Mamiashvili sticks to words like fierce, intimidating or intense, and it is general parlance that it would be best to leave his name out of your mouth, one USA wrestling employee going as far as to say that the failure to do so might leave one, 'Swimming with the fishies.'"

At the 2002 European Championships in Finland, Mamiashvili's VISA was denied to enter the country, much to the chagrin of the Russian Olympic Committee of whom Mamiashvili is an executive member. The Russian sporting leader, former director of the Russian Army's central sports organization CSKA, is not without friends in high places. Mamiashvili is a personal friend Russian president

Vladamir Putin as well as several foreign ministers. When his VISA was rejected, calls flooded the Finnish Foreign Ministry from Russian officials. The Finnish police denied his entrance based on their suspicions that he was one of the most influential godfather figures in Russian organized crime.

Some of Russia's most notorious figures are former wrestling or boxing stars. Boris Fyodorov, former head of the National Sports Fund, was nearly murdered in 1996. Oleg Karatayev, Vice-President of the International Amateur Boxing Association and former heavyweight champion was murdered in Brooklyn, New York in 1993. Otari Kvantrishvili was killed in a public sauna in 1994 and Valentin Sytch, President of the Russian Ice Hockey Federation, was murdered in 1997.

But Mamiashvili could not be accused of being a sporting leader who fails to take care of his athletes. Russian Olympic champions are paid $500,000 for a gold medal and $4,000 a month for a world title and $3,000 a month for a European title. Mamiashvili also brokered an agreement with the Armenian Olympic Committee for Russian wrestlers who compete for Armenia; they will receive $500,000 from the Armenian National Olympic Committee in the event of winning an Olympic gold medal.

The wrestlers are funded in part by Suleyman Kerimov, a Russian billionaire industrialist known as 'Russia's Richest Civil Servant,' and is listed No. 35 on *Forbes'* World's Richest People List. Kerimov is believed to control a majority of Nafta-Moskva Oil Company and Russian wrestlers have the company's logo etched across its uniforms and singlets.

The U.S. wrestlers are largely supported by Jim Ravannack, a Southern business man who co-founded Superior Energy, a company valued at $1.5 billion. With USA Wrestling, Ravanack takes care of travel expenses and logistics of athletes and their families, but Ravanack cannot dictate the way the sport is received by its own country. While most American wrestlers remain obscure and struggle to make finances meet, Russian athletes are treated like national heroes and metal arch gates are built in their hometowns if they win Olympic gold.

"In Russia the oldest sport is a way of life, they live with honor and respect," Valentin Kalika, a former Russian national coach now living in the U.S., said. "The Russian system allows no volunteer coaches. Russian wrestling coach is a wrestling coach, that's their profession. It's a full-time job, that's what you do all your life. You have to have degree that's higher than physical education teacher. Sport clubs have professional system with a government sponsored budget, professional coaches with 42 days vacation, training facilities and camps where kids do not pay money to compete. In America you have non-profit clubs run by volunteers."

Unlike the U.S., Russia practices freestyle wrestling year-round in a system where the influx of talent breeds champions. "Russians practice all their life one style," Kalika said. "For seven, eight months I work with four, five world champs, ten guys practicing together. It's like cooking a soup. Throw the best wrestlers in the world with the best training partners and you get the best wrestlers ever. In Russia, if you get gold, you are like God. Nobody remembers who wins bronze. Every sportsman wants to be Olympic Champ."

In September, several U.S. wrestlers made the trip to Krasnoyarsk, Siberia to compete in the Ivan Yarygin Tournament, which was named after the brilliant Russian wrestler who died in a car accident. The Yarygin, considered one of the toughest tournaments on the planet, took place in the heart of Siberia and the U.S. group that attended got a glimpse of what the sport means to the Russian people.

"In Krasnoyarsk wrestling is a professional sport," Jamill Kelly said. "People who couldn't afford the price of a ticket sat outside in the cold watching matches on the big screen on the side of the arena. There's an excitement and energy that you rarely feel in American tournaments. You go over there and you see how you wish you were treated."

The Russian national team is selected by the coaching staff instead of an Olympic Trials format. While there is a national tournament that is a base for selecting the Olympic team, the Russian national champion is not always selected to go. In 1972, only two of the Russian national champions were named to the team, but the 2004 Russian Olympic team is the first to name each winner of the national tournament as the Olympian. Russian head coaches face immense pressure from the media, fans and the state department and there are vast differences in philosophy, styles, and budget between the Russian and U.S. wrestling programs. "In the U.S. is a committee," Beloglazov said. "In Russia head coach decides what to do, he chooses the coaching staff and the entire team. As a coach, if we lose, we all out, it's very simple."

For men this competitive, a defeat was like death. So the trained, bled and pushed their bodies beyond the brink so when they stepped into the circle, losing was not an option. Russian wrestler's pride is revealed in the talent of 163-pound Buvaysa Saytiev; the country's premier wrestler in its premier sport. At the 2003 World Championships, Saytiev was scored upon by Senegal's Jean Diatta early in the first round. Saytiev proceeded to run up a score of 33-2, choosing to continue the match after the ten-point slaughter rule, going about his business with the cool detachment of a professional hit man. There was nothing quite like watching a superior wrestler pick apart an inferior one, something that could get lost in the numerous bodies of a team sport, but was visible and open as a surgical wound on the wrestling mat. Like a black widow catching a defenseless insect in its web or watching a snake corner a helpless mouse, the exchange between Saytiev and his counterpart at the World Championships was a Discovery Channel dissection where the viewer watched knowing who was in control.

And if character is revealed under pressure, what does stepping into a ring alone reveal about a man? His physical strength? His inherent weakness? His genetic code? At what point does he mentally break? When will he quit? Or will he fight, take pain and dish it out? The mat yielded answers six minutes at a time. It was the reason why all the posturing that went on before a street encounter, was scarcely witnessed within the wrestling arena because each true gladiator knew that what could be said with words was best revealed with action and Russia's Saytiev accentuated this point at the World Championships with every definitive score until the ref raised his hand in a 33-2 victory, battling as if being scored upon was an insult to his skill, his county, the very trace of his family bloodlines.

**

"Don't get the idea that I'm knocking the American system."
-AL CAPONE, AMERICAN GANGSTER, 1899-1947

The way Russia and the U.S. tried to embrace one another politically, attempting to diffuse tension with public relations language and forced smiles, was a mirror image of the deteriorating coaching partnership between Beloglazov and the U.S. program, and the struggle the Russian coach had with several American athletes.

"Huge difference in U.S. between number one and number two wrestler," Beloglazov said. "There is huge talent in U.S., but wrong selection process. NCAA is the biggest problem here. NCAA doesn't care about Olympic Games. So the athlete thinks NCAA is everything."

While coaching at Lehigh, Beloglazov became frustrated with the NCAA system and its athletes goals. "America has talent, but very wrong selection. NCAA is all business. But this sport is all about Olympics, you have to set goal all the way high. Here they think about NCAA glory, get out of here," he said dismissively. "I want to be All-American, NCAA Champ. I think, I don't want to work with these kids it's a waste of time. They reach top three NCAA and think what could be better. I don't waste time with those kids. I don't care about NCAAs, I don't care. Coordination, speed, strength, I care, but again, so different situation economically between these two countries. A great example is the U.S. resident program is very good, but unfortunately, USA Wrestling has nothing to offer these guys. You want to give something to the wrestlers family, apartment, rent, something. In Russia, I follow my coach everywhere. It's no discussion. Coach says something, I do it. It's respect. Whatever he said we follow. I tell Lee Fullhart what to do. I say Lee do this to train. He says, 'I go lift.' He coaches his own self. I ask Lee if you here please follow schedule, but he not trust me. I think fine, go wrestle somewhere else. There are too many stars in the U.S. wrestling room. Discipline first in Russia. It's hard to change right away in the U.S. They had five, six coaches before me. Russian practice is total control, you have to follow."

"I don't trust any Russian. I don't trust Beloglazov."

-BOBBY DOUGLAS, U.S. OLYMPIC COACH

Cold War Residue
XXX

At the Ivan Yarygin in Russia, American wrestlers saw the other side of the sport. A Cuban wrestler approached an American heavyweight about throwing a match for money. "I have four children, I lose to you for $4,000."

The practice of buying medals was nothing new to the international scene. Many athletes from impoverished countries are responsible for taking care of large extended families and the sale of a medal could feed them for half a year. For some wrestlers, the trade-off is no trade at all, it's a responsibility.

In the 1960's and 70's, Russian coaches and athletes began to work and train in Cuba. They developed a good relationship with a small country that consistently turned out amazing athletes. In Cuba, money is scarce. In Russia, it flows freely within elite circles, where politicians, oligarchies and organized crime have the biggest stakes of influence. According to data from the Russian Finance Ministry, the income of 10 percent of the richest Russians citizens exceeds the income of the same amount of poor people 15-2. The inequality has been growing for several years and the lines between legitimate businessman, politicians and mafia are blurred.

"Personally, I try to avoid the mafia crowd," Beloglazov said. "But in a way it's unavoidable, all mafia show up at my police officers friend child's birthday. I come to say happy birthday and there's an obvious criminal on other side of table. What can I do? That situation is typical. I ask my friend what is this guy doing here? People get guilt by association. I wrestle, I coach. I have old friend I used to wrestle with and ask me to come to dinner. You can't say no to get dinner. Wrestlers who are now mafia they have kids, family too. I know people, doesn't mean I want to be friends with them. If you're a good athlete in the Soviet Union, mafia gives you money if you win. Criminals make easy money, but my life is different. I'm not connected. Same thing in Russia is in Chicago, New York. People who own restaurants want security to protect them. Russians call these people 'Roof,' for protection. That's called mafia. People pay for protection every month, unofficially, as a problem solver. It wasn't law. Russia very different, sometimes athletes are involved but they're not really killing anybody. Mafia tries to be around well-known wrestlers because it looks good on them to support us. All people sit at the same table in Russia."

One former U.S. world team member, now a Division I coach, recalls Beloglazov during his competition years as a political guy. He heard rumors that factions in the Russian and international wrestling community viewed Beloglazov as a sell-out for coaching U.S. athletes.

This awkward coaching partnership was exemplified when Beloglazov was sent to the Yarygin Tournament as a U.S. coach. Put in the position of aiding a rival against his blood country, Beloglazov chose to sit in the stands and failed to make it down to the mats. "He wasn't really coaching me, I didn't like that about him," Stephen Abas said. "He's not in my corner and it didn't make sense to me. I don't know how to explain that. I didn't think it was right. He's not sure what kind of a role he has."

Beloglazov was not on the floor for the American matches widening the wound in their trust and the feelings spread to other U.S. athletes and coaches. There were suspicions that Beloglazov was calling his brother Anatoly in Russia and breaking down how to defeat the American wrestlers he coached. The questions of Beloglazov selling out the Americans came and went but could not be answered. For every person who believed Beloglazov, there were several others who didn't and slowly the Russian coach was fazed out of an arrangement that seemed destined for failure at the start.

When Iowa State coach Bobby Douglas first began competing internationally in the early 1960s, there was hostility between Russian and U.S. wrestlers even then. Wrestling was an Eastern European dominated sport. When matches got tight, Americans always felt that the judges from communist countries would rule against them.

"We hated the Russians, we hated them," Douglas said. "I wrestled a Russian at the Olympics and he felt like Superman, superhuman strong. I competed against him months later and he felt normal. I know that they were using drugs. A lot of their athletes showed it. There was no drug testing back then." To counteract their physical and technical strength, U.S. coaches and wrestlers developed a style that relied on conditioning and hard attacks. "At the end of the day we wore them out," Douglas said.

In the eyes of Douglas, the 1992 Olympics epitomize the corruption within factions of the sport. The USA wrestlers won the tournament point-wise, but the title was officially given to the United Team. "I have yet to find that country," Douglas says with sarcastic disgust. "There was a way that the powers that be were able to manipulate the system. Greatest farce ever produced at the Olympics. *People ask me if I'm prejudiced?* Yes, yes I am. I'm prejudiced against that system. I don't trust any Russian. I'm very frank, I don't trust Beloglazov. It was a psychological mistake on our part to hire him. It was not the smartest thing to do. I think we could have gotten everything he did on video."

Beloglazov's advanced wrestling technique usually involves three to four transitions to complete a move. It takes time to grasp and apply in competition. "I wish there was a magic bullet to shoot into athletes to let them learn technique," Douglas said. "But that doesn't happen. I respect Beloglazov as an athlete, as a coach, but it was uncomfortable for him to be in the practice room. Talking to the athletes, I never got that impression they were comfortable with it either."

But there are those who come to Beloglazov's defense. "I love Sergei," Ron Groves said. "He knows how to deal with professional athletes. He's always asking me about things away from the mat, about my family, he enjoys life and doesn't take this sport too seriously."

Douglas, however, cannot be convinced of these virtues. "Beloglazov said he was interested in working with younger guys, not interested with older guys," Douglas said. "Alarms went off in my head. At Lehigh, what kind of impact did he have on guys with 50 percent growth left in them? Minimal. If a guy is there two years, can he have an impact? Now you want to evaluate him while coaching the cream of the crop? With Olympic guys who have maybe ten percent growth left in them? Ask any former Olympic coach if they would have done that. Do you think Beloglazov's brother asked him what the Americans were doing to prepare? He's a twin! They probably don't even have to say anything; they could read each other's mind. He knows everything we do. Would I love to be in Russia's training camp? Of course I would, but the Russians would never hire an American coach even if they needed us. *They would never do it! They would never trust us!* I asked a Russian athlete what he thought about the Americans hiring Beloglazov. The Russian laughed and replied with a question, 'If you were going to fight a war would you hire the opposing general to lead your troops?'"

***

"I have my faults, but being wrong ain't one of them."
-JIMMY HOFFA, 1913-1975

As a result of the rivalry between the two countries and the clashing coaching philosophies, Beloglazov became the odd man out in a partnership that seemed destined for failure. No matter what Beloglazov said, his allegiance was viewed as skeptical. The more widespread the rumors became, the less input Beloglazov had in the OTC practice room. He became defensive and began to question the U.S. training program.

"Kevin make mistake, push too hard," says Beloglazov. "Nobody teaches training process. Problem is nobody knows training process. Here they do long train then lift. Kevin's supposed to have short, quick practice. In Russia, we have three times a week blood tests to help recovery process. They lift too much last camp. Your body doesn't work properly. 'I say Kevin, hey, be careful.' But they don't listen to Russian. My experience is like this, fine. I think I could be useful. I don't want complete control. I would focus more technically. I mean

Zeke Jones? Who Zeke Jones? Who he?"

Only in a room of this caliber, only from a mouth of such accomplishments, could this statement have even half a credit. Beloglazov is widely viewed as one of the top three wrestlers ever while Jones is a former world champion and Olympic silver medalist who was once recognized as the most technical wrestlers in the world. But Beloglazov's dismissive statement of Jones seems to have less to do with a personal beef with the energetic Olympic assistant coach than the fact that Jones has been appointed to take over the mat that is essentially Beloglazov's office. Jones is a running today's practice while Beloglazov is assisting on the side. While he blows off the situation, there's pain in his voice and it was apparent that the situation bothered him.

"I work one year here and Zeke Jones come for one camp and is now Olympic coach," Beloglazov said. "I'm here for one year and I don't run one Olympic camp. Head coach decides nothing in America, Russia head coach decides everything. I went to Russian Nationals, made a video and gave it to Kevin to scout. Whatever I do, I do professional. I wanna win, I don't wanna lose. I think why work with you? What do you expect? I told Kevin that the Cold War was over a long time ago."

The differences between the two men had less to do with personality and more to do with upbringing. Jackson was an American, as proud to wear the colors as any. Beloglazov was a symbol of Soviet technical dominance, a rival from the other side. Jackson never felt it was necessary to bring in Beloglazov a year and a half before the Olympics, he felt he was pressured to show too much.

"Sergei and I never got on the same page," Jackson said. "Because the people who influenced him led him to believe that I wasn't his boss. He shouldn't have been here. We definitely could use him. We wanted to use him for tactical preparation. That's what I was looking for, but those things didn't happen. As Americans, we honor loyalty, friendship. Abas was here a year and a half and Sergei never came down to his mat at the tournament in Russia, to slap him on the back, wish him good luck. I invited him over to my house a couple times and for whatever reason he never came. When it came down to it, Sergei's not like Bobby Douglas, he's not like Tom Brands, Zeke Jones or John

Smith, *he's Russian.* He believes in their structure, their system. He believes he's better than us and that our system will never be able to catch his...*and he might be right.*"

*"I don't have many people I want to get revenge on, but I am
sure that there are many who want revenge with me."*

BUYVASA SAYTIEV, RUSSIAN CHAMPION

Chechen Fighter
XXXI

Buvaysa Saytiev was born on March 11, 1975 in Khasavyurt,
Dagestan, a land rich with old, gas, coal, minerals and located in the
North Caucasus Mountains in the southernmost part of Russia. The
most common language is Russian, but there are over 30 local dialects
spoken among the population of more than two and a half million
people. The climate is dry and hot in the summer, but the winters bring
brutal cold. Because navigation is rugged through the mountains, the
region impedes travel and communication and is largely tribal. There
is a variety of ethic groups, but 90 percent of the populace is Muslim.

In Russian, Grozny is interpreted as fearsome or menacing, which
is a proper way of describing their wrestlers as well. In Chechnya's
capitol of Grozny, there are several facilities that cater to combat
sports and in every city of the Chechen republic there is a school of
freestyle wrestling. In these clubs there is a mix of youth wrestlers,
professional competitors and post-war soldiers needing a place to
release their anger. In the Russian military, fighters from Daghestan,
nicknamed *Dags*, along with other Chechens all had some form of
martial arts training and were known as the toughest and most fearless
soldiers in the Russian service.

Grozny was the site of the First Chechen war in mid-1990's, a fierce battle that lasted three months and resulted in the seizure of the city by the Russian military. Much of the area was destroyed and thousands of Russian and Chechen soldiers and civilians died; unclaimed bodies were later buried in mass graves on the city's outskirts. However, Chechen guerilla units did not surrender. They pestered and demoralized the Russian military with raids and surprise assaults, ultimately recapturing the city with a few thousand militants in a sneak attack that led to a ceasefire in 1996.

The Second Chechen War produced the same atrocities, leaving Grozny in a condition that the United Nations described as the, 'The most destroyed city on Earth.' Even though the war officially ended in 2000, murders, bombings and clashes between Russian forces and separatists continued after; estimates of civilian deaths range from 35,000 to 100,000 and more than 500,000 people were displaced. Local uprisings, guerrilla warfare and rebel fighting remain common in a region that has also produced some of the world's best wrestlers.

Saytiev grew up in a family of three brothers and two sisters, which is not considered large in a region where women commonly rear eight to ten children per clan. His father, a bricklayer, built his own house and other homes around Dagestan after finishing contracting school. In Russia most housing construction is funded by the government, but Saytiev's father was skilled enough to be courted for private projects. "He had golden hands," Saytiev said. "He was a master of what he did. There was always a long line of people waiting for him to build their house. My brother Hakim followed in his footsteps and became a major contractor as well."

One day, Saytiev's father was driving a car with two other passengers when a bus traveling from Rostov to Baku, Azerbaijan t-boned him from the side. Saytiev's father wasn't wearing a seatbelt and he slammed his head on the steering wheel upon impact. Initially the accident didn't appear serious; none of the passengers were bleeding. "It was a Soviet car that kind of looked like a coffin," Saytiev said. "My father had his liver severely damaged and he experienced internal bleeding. The accident beat his liver out of place. In that state, he came out of the car, sat on the curb and had a cigarette. A couple people walked by and asked him how he was: 'I'm fine,' he said. They asked him if he was going to go to the hospital and he said, 'No, I don't really need the hospital.' At that moment he died. It was 1988."

Blizha, Saytiev's mother, was working at a building factory when her husband died. Quickly realizing that she wouldn't be able to raise all the kids by herself, and relatives from both sides of the family began pitching in. "Not only were we the only kids, but there was my uncle's kids whose mother had died and father was in jail, so we were taking on an extra four children," Saytiev said. "But we made it because everyone helped out," Saytiev said. "Everyone went to school, nobody was a really good student but we all tried. If we missed school one day we would get in a lot of trouble. It never crossed my mind to miss school. I had 15 A's in one-quarter, I had a very good memory and I was a sponge, I sucked up all the literature and the geometry I could."

Saytiev's favorite poem is called, *"Being famous is not attractive,"* by Nobel Prize winning Russian writer Boris Pasternak. In 1988, Saytiev's trainer brought it to him and instructed him to memorize it before a match. "It came into my heart right away," Saytiev said. "I repeat it before every match."

"I don't think being famous is very attractive. That is not what lifts you up. You don't have to build an archive. You don't have to panic over your number of volumes. The object of a masterpiece is giving yourself away."

"These words are going to stay with me for the rest of my life," Saytiev said. "It will be very hard to forget them. These words have defined my life both inside and outside of sport."

"It's not about the noise, it's not about the success. It's embarrassing that just because you've created something that you're on the lips of other people. Just because you've achieved something doesn't mean that everyone should be talking about you. Just because you've won. It is only a piece of you defined." -BORIS PASTERNAK

"When I truly understood this poem," Saytiev said. "It was in the moment when somebody was lifting up my hand up as a champion wrestler and I realized that this is all bullshit. I am the only one who understands how much I put into this victory and whether or not I deserve it. Already from my youth I had an abstract view of victory,

I had different goals than my opponents. Even when I was a child I thought that if I become the champion of my city it is not going to be important. All I really wanted to know was my limit. Because of the attitude I carried, I once had astronomical score in the finals of the USSR championship, winning 17-0. Everyone said it was unreal."

Saytiev walked heavy and at times looked like an angry tsar and in others his eyes were serene as a monk who had reached peace with his life. He had straight hair and wore it long, sloping down to the peak of his eyes. With a conservative haircut Saytiev could pass for a doctor or lawyer and he struck many people as having the level of intelligence and capabilities to succeed in any field.

Saytiev was tall and trim, appearing to tower over his opponents, because most middle-weight wrestlers competed in a low-square stance. Saytiev kept his legs straight and bent over at the waist and would pursue his opponents with his arms close together like a diver about to hit the water. When he got a hold of an opposing wrestler Saytiev would lock around their waist with arms that stretched like a slinky, rolling them repeatedly on the mat like a crocodile drowning his victim.

"I got my strength from my ancestors," Saytiev said. "From the streets and my trainers who brought me up, but I give the most credit to my mother." As a youth Saytiev enjoyed billiards, soccer and chess, but his desire to wrestle overrode other hobbies and would reach a point where he was too good for him hometown competition. "They locked me out of the gym," Saytiev said. "I reached a certain level and they locked me out. We didn't blend with the local grey masses, and God grant me that I never blend in anywhere."

A trainer in Krasnoyarsk promised better facilities, and his older brother Abdul-Hakim took him to the Siberian city at the age of 17. Abdul-Hakim was a master of sport and was successful in wrestling, but he was the only child who was old enough to care for their widowed mother. It was difficult for Buvaysa to adapt to Krasnoyarsk but his Chechen friends helped him with the transition. "Chechens stick together," Saytiev said. "But I quickly understood that I needed to abandon some of my old traditions in order to make a new life in Siberia."

Saytiev grew up in the old U.S.S.R. where a radio was built into the wall of all Soviet apartments and was ceaselessly broadcasting news and political material. He awoke every morning at six a.m. to the Soviet Union national song:

> *Unbreakable union of free republics,*
> *Great Russia has joined forever!*
> *Long live the created by the will of peoples*
> *United and mighty Soviet Union*
> *To Glory, our free Fatherland*
> *The stronghold of the friendship of peoples*
> *Party of Lenin is the power of the people*
> *It leads us to the triumph of Communism*
> *Through storms the sun of freedom shone to us*
> *And the great Lenin lighted us the way*
> *He raised peoples to the right cause*
> *He inspired us for labor and for acts of heroism*
> *In the victory of the immortal ideas of Communism*
> *We see the future of our country,*
> *And to the Red banner of our glorious Fatherland*
> *We shall always be selflessly loyal*

Saytiev would go on to win six world titles and two Olympic championships, and did not lose from 1994-2000, but all he ever wanted to do in the sport was to win a clean match. "I didn't have the desire to just win," Saytiev said. "I only had one situation where I wanted revenge and that person just disappeared and I never saw them again."

In the 2000 Olympics, Saytiev was upset 4-3 by Brandon Slay from the United States; Slay went on to earn the gold medal. "I let this person take me down in the second round. I didn't even know who he was. I had to look him up in the Internet. I think he shouldn't have been in the Olympics at all, he was like a plane fly-by, he flew in, flew out, and he didn't have much to offer. Maybe they fed him something. He appeared, caused havoc and disappeared. Kind of like that Rulon Gardner, but Rulon at least fights there somewhere. That Slay guy disappeared for good. He's not even worth my thoughts. If somebody asks me a question about him only then do I remember, otherwise he doesn't exist for me."

Saytiev has achieved a good deal of fame in Russia. He is recognized everywhere he goes in Krasnoyarsk and is known as a trailblazer for

Chechen wrestlers who train in the Siberian city. "Everyone receives me like a son," Saytiev said. "All the policemen know me in Siberia, all the people recognize me, all the dogs respect me." Despite the conflicts between Russia and Chechnya, Chechen wrestlers continue to migrate to the Russian city to train. One American wrestler summed it up: "The political calamities that exist between the two countries have to be put aside by the Russian coaches and Chechen athletes because as a Russian coach, in order to win, you better bring in athletes from Chechnya. Everyone who trains in Krasnoyarsk is from Chechnya. Saytiev's success put Chechnya on the map."

At 20 years old, Saytiev was champion of the world, but as he got older winning became more of a challenge. "Technique and having the fighting character are necessities required to win the first time, but I've found that the hardest thing to do was to keep my identity and focus, to respect myself all the time. Everything depends on your life philosophy and how you react to things that happen to you. You need to realize who you are, because victory can destroy you or make you better. In a deciding moment, win or lose, life or death situation, you need that instinct to prevail. Your instinct will know what time it is to apply it. I have this instinct; it is not something I take for granted."

Saytiev's ability has put him in the public spotlight in Russia, a place he does not wish to be. One month after the Atlanta Olympics, Russian swimmer Alexander Popov was stabbed in the stomach during a dispute with three Moscow street vendors. "I know this guy, he is very intelligent," Saytiev said. "I don't think he started this conflict. If I was in that situation I would have done something also, not because I am a wrestler, but because of principle. Unfortunately, we are all mortals and periodically things like this happen. At times I also get very angry and violent as well, but I have never been in a situation where I have been cut with a knife. I regret when I do get mad and throw out an angry word or throw out a punch; afterwards I am surprised that I even got that mad. It usually happens at night when I am hanging out with friends and some smart-ass kids decide that they are physically able to take me. I give them a good push and they're even stupid enough to try and give one back. It is better not to be recognized, it is a very big problem for me, it really stresses me out. I can't learn to live with this. The reason I don't like it that people know me is because you are not really all that white and fluffy in reality and people have a different opinion of you when they see you on the street versus the TV. For example, one time when I was parking my car and an old lady said to me, "Where the hell are you blocking the street!"

I got out of the car and told her: "You should direct your questions to the administration of the city. Don't you see what is happening on the street? Where the hell am I supposed to put it? There is no parking lot, there is not shit anywhere. I need to get into the store and everyone else put there car where they felt like it so what am I supposed to do? Go see the Governor!" I told the lady. "Then the old lady recognized me and her face lit up and she said in a sweet little voice: 'Buyvasa why are you so thin? Are you hungry?' And I look at her and think where the hell does she know me from? Go figure."

***

Saytiev's athletic talent has also placed him into influential Russian business and political circles. He is friends with many wealthy metal company owners in Moscow, including the likes of Iskander Makmudov, who, according to *Forbes*, has assets totaling eight billion and is listed as the world's 86th richest man. Saytiev has also met with Alu Alhanov, former President of the Chechen Republic about building a sports facility in Chechnya, but the Russian wrestler does not see himself as a political man.

"Personally, I don't really give a shit. I really don't want to do that because it is painful for me to see stupid, incompetent people who are trying to get into power in our country. Same with our great committee in Krasnoyarsk, there are a two or three professionals plus a couple of half-ass motherf**kers. In Russia, politicians are not very smart. It seems as though they choose a location and base the whole politics of the country on that location as if these people don't even know the geography of our country. These people close the doors to their offices, think of some great ides, and they don't really take anyone else into consideration and then they pump this into the veins of the people. Why the hell are you guys closing your office doors to the people? Our strength is in unity and integration, but no, you close up and you threw the dust into people's eyes. Krasnoyarsk is such a potential geographically rich area in terms of its resources. Why can't we use these resources in a more productive way? There aren't enough people who are going to get the oil out of the ground. They are going to bring outside workers and they can't afford it. Even though I am a citizen and I understand and respect the politics of the Government, very often I want to beat up all these people in power. I don't need to get into politics right now because I can't pretend. I don't know how to lie. Sometimes I think about it, because I am a popular person. I have very many friends who you can easily call the strength of the world. I met with President Vladimir Putin and the Governor. It turns out I am very bright person in this area."

"The only person who cares is the Governor, but he doesn't do anything about it. The people are out for themselves and most sit on their butt. The problem of a person from Krasnoyarsk is he sees this famous person only through the TV and he judge's life based on what the pictures tell him. It is not his fault, but at the same time it is his fault that he is incompetent. He doesn't have the time to keep up with the current events because he has to go to work and feed his family. They don't know how they can help their own city. I would never consider being a diplomat for Chechnya, it's a very unstable place, if it quieted down I might consider. I am afraid to live in this world because of the situations in Saudi Arabia and Israel where people justify the fact that they are bombing each other based on trivial things. It shows that a lot of people in this world aren't built to be honest and strong. That is probably why I don't want to go into politics."

***

"When I feel low, I go fishing," Saytiev said. "In 1998, I felt like other people were living my life for me, I drank a lot and just lay in bed all day. Finally the people who care about me got me to wrestle again. As soon as I got back on the mat, I felt alive. Sometimes when I lose, I burn and suffer inside, the higher a person rises, the more painful the fall. I really want to live a normal life, but I need to learn to be happy with what I already achieved. I don't want all the gold in the world. I don't want to think about the day I put my hands down and my legs are going to be hanging out of a hammock. I have a problem with time, I don't know if other people suffer from this, but I always have a feeling that I can never get anything done. I feel like everything is moving a little too fast. Even though I am always flying to different places, I'm always doing something, I still feel like I am standing still and everything is rushing by me. I feel that my youth was very short and the sport that I choose was very difficult. It is hard for me to find the golden middle. I want to leave the chaos, but I do not want to destroy what I started."

There are times when Saytiev longs to be like others when he is out at restaurants, drinking and smoking cigarettes and relaxing. But when he does smoke he doesn't inhale and he doesn't enjoy listening to loud music in dining places. He can't hear who he is talking to and it only makes him feel like he is wasting time.

As a part of their tradition, Chechens receive expensive presents for their birthday and because of Saytiev's success as an athlete he often receives gifts he would otherwise never purchase. Such as the time he was given a $30,000 watch by somebody he doesn't even remember or the expensive cell phone he received that he didn't have use for. After Saytiev won another championship, the Russian government purchased a Mercedes in Moscow and delivered it to Saytiev's apartment in Krasnoyarsk. "They put it under my window in my village and I kept looking out the window at it for two days," Saytiev said. "Then on the third day I went outside to see if it was actually real. I don't know what the hell is wrong with me. Why am I so ungrateful just because I don't like the car? I try to give people presents but I really don't understand these things. I think spending money on presents is a waste."

Saytiev owns two pieces of land outside of Krasnoyarsk but he has yet to find the time to build a house. He and his wife Indira, have two children and they rent an apartment in Krasnoyarsk, but adjusting to domestic life has been trying. "I really don't know how to deal with kids. They are so much smarter than me. They do all the talking and I just listen to them. I believe that you should get married in your mind, any sort of emotional or life event shouldn't be the reason. Marriage is a very responsible step and you have to approach it in a very cold and smart way. You have to live the rest of your life with this person. You risk making a mistake to break up your life, her life and the lives of your children. You have to weigh it out. You have to understand what type of family they are from, their genetic build and moral foundation. Of course, you can't know everything, you have to at least know that both of you are deciding the most important thing in your lives. I don't think it is good when people say I can't live without you, lets get married, that's very stupid. Wrestlers don't get married until they really understand it. A lot of them put it on the backburner, because they have experienced defeat on the mat and they don't want to be defeated by a woman. But a lot of my friends who are wrestlers got married young."

"I have been close to God my whole life. Religion gave me everything. Battle between good and evil, God and Satan is present in every single one of us and that is why we as humans find it difficult. Technically a Muslim will pray five times a day. But there are days when I don't pray at all. It gets very difficult for me. I experience depression and I lose my focus sometimes. If one really feels his prayers, everything seems to come back together again. But I do not want to be a fanatic; religion is a science that I am willing to learn for the rest of my life. I feel like everyone should be afraid of death, because then you will live more responsibly. I feel very close to God and Islam. It is a very tender feeling to know God, however I cannot really put the word God into context. It really depends on how you live. The way you live determines how close God is to you. If you spend a month fooling around in crazy orgies, then you won't really know who God is. If a person is focused and lives a clean life he will know him better."

"I order, you follow, if you're not good enough-goodbye."

MIKHAIL MAMIASHVILI, RUSSIAN WRESTLING PRESIDENT

Mamiashvili
XXXII

"Our wrestling team is not a private affair," Mikhail Mamiashvili, head of the Russian Wrestling Federation said. "We answer to the President Vladamir Putin and our sponsors if we fail, but first and foremost, we answer to ourselves. The government gives us colossal financial help, but it is not enough. We cannot organize a completely self-sufficient training process. We need the government's money. I put a colossal amount of money into the Russian Wrestling Federation, which is provided for me by Russian businessman."

Leonid Tyagachev is one of those businessmen. A former sportsman who was once voted the best ski instructor in the world, Tyagachev built skiing facilities throughout Russia. In 1991, Soviet Union sports programs deteriorated after the fall of the communist regime and Tyagachev was voted unanimously as the Vice President of the Olympic Committee, carrying the burden of making sports relevant again.

Tyagachev has large holdings in several Russian industry titans that have pumped millions of dollars into Russian sports: Gazprom, which is the biggest extractor of natural gas in the world; Lukoil, which is the country's largest producer of oil; and Sberbank which is the largest bank in Russia.

"Sport is a big part of the political framework of a country," Tyagachev said. "The Olympic movement is the top of this gigantic pyramid in which the prestige of a nation is synthesized with the biggest companies of the world. Sport has become a world industry, one of the most effective spheres of business and the state puts in a lot of energy to build up athletes. Only certain people can be put out on this pedestal: rich managers, masters of sport, or people who have the authority in the world of sport. I want to provide the athletes with bodyguards and give them better training centers, but they need to cooperate with me so that I can provide more for them. But only the best athletes are going to have me standing behind them."

Many Russian wrestlers wear uniforms with Nafta-Moskva stamped across the front. Headquartered in Moscow, Nafta-Moskva advertises itself as a leading Russian Investment Group with ties to gold and silver production and oil exportation with subsidiary companies throughout Europe and the United Kingdom. Suleyman Kerimov, who is believed to control Nafta-Moskva, is the Deputy Chairman of the Russian State Duma Committee of Sports and another wealthy financer of Russian athletes.

The Russian wrestling federation has the financial backing and with it came the pressure to perform on its coaches, administrators and athletes; sporting president Mamiashvili shares the bottom-line philosophy of his Russian sponsors. "We don't have the opportunity to put in money to athletes that do not produce," Mamiashvili said. "If I see an athlete excel, I will provide him with an extra income for his to success. I order and you fulfill my order. The government pays for you to excel and that is normal in our country."

Ron Groves, an American wrestler who has spent time competing in Russia, believes that Russians are under more pressure to perform and are willing to do whatever it takes to win, even if that meant taking morality out of the equation. "The accountability is much bigger in Russia," Ron Groves said. "Terry Brands and Jackson embrace the accountability but overall the culture of American wrestling is the coaches are not on the hot seat, you would never see that in an American football program. It changes the type of coach you could get. Many American wrestling coaches couldn't take criticism from the media. Our sport is a cult, it's closed off, our coaches are not under the gun. The Russians are willing to do whatever it takes to win, they want to ensure victory. It's not an issue of the draw I get a good draw. The Russians turn over every rock. Their attitude is that they're going to guarantee victory. If one of their athletes can't get in great shape, they will find a supplement that will help. People accuse the Russians of using steroids, but it's their mentality that they have to guarantee victory and their not willing to lose. That gives them the edge."

A controversy arose in Russian wrestling circles when Mamiashvili cut off the salaries of trainers he felt weren't good enough; Mimiashvili dismissing the criticism with evolutionary connotations. "If you're a bad trainer or a weak athlete, I refuse to put money into you because you don't bring me the expected result. If the athlete isn't able to meet expectations...*goodbye*. All the main government trainers answer to me, they respect the federation and they respect me. I am the only one who can accredit these athletes. If people around me are failing they will fall off. The world will put everything in its place. Just because I was born in a lower caste doesn't mean I will die in one."

Mamiashvilli was raised in Knotop, Russia and moved to Moscow to train as a youth. He rose to prominence after a successful career as a Greco-Roman wrestler, winning three world championships and a gold medal at the 1992 Olympics. American officials describe him in hushed tones, comparing his intensity with that of super heavyweight Alexander Karelin, but there was a soft side to Mamiashvili as well. He likes to play with his dog and while he isn't fond of giving toasts at banquets or dinner parties, Mamiashvili is a sucker for Ukranian folk songs. "My father was Ukrainian, that's why I love the folk songs. I grew up in a small town and my parents were very hospitable, so they would always have the neighbors sitting at our dinner table. The women would sing Ukrainian folk songs, they were really melodic and beautiful and they stayed in my memory. To this day when I hear them, my soul sings along." Mamiashvili, also a fan of the *Sex Pistols* punk rock group, has been rumored to sing to his wrestlers when they win and there are numerous Russian articles that joke about his love for the music, but meeting Mamiashvili is nothing to laugh about; he is undeniably a man in charge.

He still looks as physically ruthless as when he was winning World and Olympic titles and he enhanced his reputation with a shaved head and expensive tailored suits. He entered rooms with a stride that was smooth and powerful as a Bengal tiger on the prowl and he greeted others with hands that were thick as a leather baseball mitt.

"I have unprecedented influence because for the first time in history, two representatives of Russia, Nancy Yarygin and I, are on the bureau of FILA. For complete support for our nation we need to realize that we are all after the same exact thing-victory. The only people who have the strength to rival Russian wrestlers are the U.S."

"Joe, you know me, I don't do things halfway."

-LAWRENCE TAYLOR ON A PHONE CALL TO JOE THEISMAN AFTER SHATTERING HIS LEG IN A NFL FOOTBALL GAME.

Unbound Rule
XXXIII

American wrestling was a close group. The coaches used to compete against each other, they knew each other's strengths and weaknesses, their vices and virtues, and it was much of the same familiarity with their athletes in the OTC training camp. They knew who hung with what clique, who were religious men and who were tail chasers, and who were legitimate Olympic hopefuls and who were just bodies in the room. The coaches and the athletes didn't have to wait till the end of a season to watch it play out, because every training camp practice was like an audition of American Idol, there was no hiding the talent or lack of it.

Mo Lawal and Cael Sanderson meet on the center mat. It was quite apparent that Lawal taking this present encounter with Sanderson as seriously as their duel as U.S. Nationals. Lawal wanted what the Olympians had and specifically, Lawal wanted a piece of Cael Sanderson. Lawal wanted to kick Sanderson's ass in front of the entire practice room. In front of John Smith who had done his share of domination of elite wrestlers and Kevin Jackson who was no stranger to taking out big-shots himself. And Lawal knew that it wouldn't hurt his reputation to perform in front Olympic assistants Tom Brands and

Zeke Jones, Sergei Beloglazov and Bobby Douglas, in front of the six current Olympic wrestlers or all the NCAA Champions who were watching on the mats. Lawal wanted to make a statement about how quickly he was progressing, about how good he could be. These type of ambitions can't exactly be hidden in this sport and Lawal wasn't going to try and hide them. Unlike most others in the 184-pound class, Lawal believes he can beat Sanderson and he would probably go into an alley to prove it.

Sanderson knows this but he doesn't engage. He waits to wrestle but doesn't get caught up in his opponents' pre-match routine. He doesn't watch the youthful, crowd-pleasing Lawal vertical jump high in the air. He doesn't watch Lawal's feet peak at his own shoulders. He doesn't allow Lawal to get inside his head. There is an absence of malice on Sanderson's face as he calmly leans down in a half stance and keeps staring at the floor as if ready to sketch a design in the padded surface.

The two wrestlers smack and paw each other on the head like Golden Glove boxers, and while Sanderson tries to hide his annoyance it slowly creeps through. Sanderson attacks in and a scramble ensues with Lawal. Down in par-terre, Lawal tri-pods and Sanderson latches on. Lawal locks Sanderson's arm and rises, before violently whipping backwards like a deep sea diver out of a boat, catching the big fish on his back and is nearly pinning him. But Sanderson enjoys Lawal's company so much he immediately returns the favor, squirming out and rolling Lawal into a tilt to score three points.

The athletes and coaches begin to watch other action around the room, but the West Texas product knows how to reclaim their interest. Lawal was an aggressive wrestler whose ambition bordered on reckless intent, figuring that was the point of the sport. On his feet Lawal looked for one move and his opponents knew what was coming but few could stop it. Lawal wanted to double-leg everyone he faced. He wanted to plant his head into his opponent's sternum and drive his legs until he smashed them to the mat or hit em' where it hurt and he didn't seem to have much of a preference for the two; as Lawal said after an Olympic Trials match, "This is wres-tlin, you tryin to hurt sum-badey." It was this type of maneuver that Lawal was looking for on Sanderson as they started the second period of their practice match.

Lawal shoots a double leg, clutching Sanderson's knees. Driving towards the boundaries, he pumps his legs furiously toward the padded wall because this is his chance to take out USA Wrestlings golden hope, to finish what Fullhart couldn't, to put Sanderson down, so Lawal kept driving, but Sanderson swiftly answers this challenge as well. Falling back, he uses Lawal's aggression and whips him to the side, twirling him for three points. With one swift rejection, Sanderson proves his undeniable command over Lawal and wouldn't allow him to get the best of him in a simple practice match nor the edge he desperately craved.

Sanderson's from Utah. Sanderson's a church boy. Sanderson grew up in a nice place, with nice people, in a loving, nurtured environment. Heber City isn't exactly East L.A. or Chicago hellhole Cabrini Green and Sanderson went to Wasatch High, which certainly didn't cultivate the environment of Plano East, where Lawal stole money just to eat lunch off-campus, or where is was natural for kids to break into cars in order to buy some new sneakers or get gang-jumped by guys on their own high school football team, and all these facts might lead one to say that Sanderson was soft compared to Lawal, but there would be no truth to those who told it because when speaking of Sanderson there just isn't much soft in em.'

Sanderson had the same edge of an inner-city Chicago boxer, or an East L.A. street fighter, because if you strip away the tattoos and bleep out the cusswords, the competitive levels aren't much different. Sanderson hated to lose. Sanderson was rough enough to win. Sanderson was not going to be denied. Sport crosses languages, cultures, races, and barrios; those who rise to the top all have it just the same.

Sanderson doesn't enjoy these bouts as much as Lawal, questioning why Jackson had him wrestling against one of his rivals. Jackson's philosophy was simple. Sanderson needed the daily challenge in the practice room, needed it much like Jackson needed when he trained at the now infamous Foxcatcher training facility in Pennsylvania where wrestlers would pass each other in the middle of the night on long distance runs. Needed it just like all the Olympians did, and that's why Steve Mocco is waiting to challenge Kerry McCoy, one wrestling mat away.

Mocco and McCoy's hyped match up at U.S. Nationals fizzled and they never met at the Olympic Trials, but this practice match essentially meant nothing and everything at the same time. However, neither wrestler does much of anything during the contest. McCoy wins on criteria, but a victory cannot be taken from this. McCoy was passive and held on, adding to the frustrations of the American coaching staff.

At some point in his career, Jackson felt McCoy lost an edge. "Somewhere along the line Kerry got soft on me," Jackson said. "Even when playing Playstation football he lost a little of his competitiveness. He wasn't like that in 2000, definitely not in 1998." At the world championships in 1998, McCoy faced a Russian in the first round who was favored to win the tournament. He defeated the Russian, then his following opponent from Turkey and then the Cuban in the semis. After the match the decision was reviewed in the back room and eventually overturned, costing McCoy a world championship that would have ripples of effect for years to come.

"Stephen Neal was the best heavyweight in the world in 1999," Jackson said. "International wrestlers were happy when Kerry showed up. In the heavyweight division, the best athletes usually win. Neal was the biggest, most athletic, most explosive heavyweight and he was hungry, Stephen was a bad dude," Jackson said with admiration. "Once Neal found out he could get paid for wrestling he would go into a match thinking, *'I'm killin 'em. This guy's trying to take my money. This guy's trying to take food out my mouth, I'm smashing him!'* That was Neal's mentality. I wasn't sure I saw that in McCoy. After Neal won in 1999 and lost in 2000, he was getting heavy. Kerry should have won the world championship in 2000 because he was the best guy. Stephen gained weight while Kerry trained at the OTC with a freestyle focus every day, that's why Kerry got better, those skills carried over. McCoy beat Neal because Neal stayed in Bakersfield to train."

In 2001, Stephen Neal retired from international wrestling to pursue a football career with the New England Patriots, going on to win three Super Bowls while playing as an offensive lineman. "Losing Neal hurt McCoy."

Jackson suggested indirectly that McCoy wasn't a killer. It wasn't physical. It wasn't experience. It wasn't something that could be changed in the practice room. McCoy was too nice, too polite, too unlike the beasts that had conquered his weight class in the past. The truth was that once Neal left to play in the NFL, Kerry McCoy lost his truest companion towards achieving gold. McCoy had nobody left to be challenged by and to McCoy the U.S. heavyweight title didn't mean a thing; he backhanded all challengers. Tolly Thompson was beaten like clockwork. Mocco was just a new face. No one pushed him.

International waters were different. There was Artur Taymazov of Uzbekistan, the world champion who had flat-backed McCoy at the World Championships in New York. That possessed considerable height and formidable strength. That was not dismissible like the American challengers and projected all the desire of a perfect nightmare.

The image of an Olympic heavyweight wrestler is that of a horror movie beast. Men who looked as if they were locked in dungeons with only steel weights and thrown slabs of red meat to eat. Who had hairy overgrown shoulders and giant gnarled hands. Who tore apart practice partners and frightened everyone in their path. But this was not Kerry McCoy who spoke eloquently, nodded at doormen and had acquired a higher education; was stately, diplomatic and humble. McCoy helped up his practice partners, laughed easily and said all the right things and it might be easier to find a certain member of Al-Qaeda than someone who had evil words to say about the gregarious American heavyweight. McCoy was not a monster, was not a beast, was not what many Olympic heavyweights appeared to be and certainly not Alexander Karelin, the Russian wrestling great, the fearsome, awe-inspiring Greco-Roman wrestler who went undefeated for much of his career and whose lone Olympic loss was the story of the 2000 Olympic Games.

Karelin was a man so physically unique, so athletically gifted, that if the great evolutionary explorer Charles Darwin had crossed the globe in search of unique athletic specimens and not animal species in the Galapagos Islands, had bushwacked through jungles, taken to the high seas and scanned the seven continents, Darwin might have taken an account once he reached Eastern Europe and written about men who were fearsome, athletic, flexible, imposing and who trained to no end, who came in various shapes and sizes but held similarities in their cauliflower ear, thick-necks and V-shaped backs.

After observing this group for several days, Darwin might have noted that wrestlers were an athletic species perpetually in strain, could survive harsh conditions while pushing their bodies to severe limits, were mentally tough enough to take the desert without food or water, were physically capable of climbing large mountains, were able to adapt into whatever environment they were in as surely as a chameleon. With these notes and observations, with these sketches and varied thoughts, Darwin might have returned to his place of origin, his room of study, and drafted out a long article in his journal like I just have, linking wrestlers as the fittest of species, one that if given no external benefits, would prevail in a survival of the fittest.

And Darwin surely would have retrieved his notebook and referred back to his drawings and notes of other wrestlers across the globe, drawing parallels of strength, power, physical ability but upon retracing his visit to the Eastern Bloc, he saw something distinct in these wrestlers, the difference as subtle as the color white and off-white, and after several days of observations and research, after much wandering and searching, perhaps Darwin would have heard eyewitness accounts of the vaunted Russian heavyweight who was a species all together his own. Based off this premise, it was not conceivable that Darwin would have tracked the footpath of Karelin barreling through the forest full of snow on two-hour runs or heard proclamations of him bear-hugging a refrigerator up eight flights of stairs or taken note of the Russian heavyweight's astounding flexibility that allowed him to do a split of the legs while standing.

But Kerry McCoy was not Karelin. McCoy didn't run through the Siberian forest. McCoy didn't carry refrigerators up eight flights of stairs. McCoy was an athlete who looked physically capable of playing pro-football in the practice room and then, after showering, dressing into street clothes and fitting on his reading glasses, appeared polished enough to have a lengthy discussion about the current state of world affairs.

McCoy was not a beast. McCoy was not Karelin, Neal or Taymazov of Uzbekistan. McCoy was the best heavyweight the U.S. had, motivation or killer instinct be damned.

"The only cure for grief is action."

-GEORGE HENRY LEWIS

Cormier
XXXIV

Daniel Cormier comes through the wrestling room door slapping his head, his arms, making a straight line to the wrestling mat where he is the man, the Olympian, the most important wrestler in the America at 211-pounds. Cormier toes the line and greets the hand of practice opponent Tim Hartung with a slap. At the Olympic Trials, Cormier abused the former Minnesota star, beating him soundly. But on the mats of the OTC, Hartung tosses him immediately. On his feet, Cormier is recharged for a few moments, attacking with intent, but ends up on his back again, shoulders rolling across the mats as he put up a half-hearted fight. Hartung, with Cormier's head and arms imprisoned inside his grip, looks up at the ref and waits for the whistle to signify the pin. Cormier is flat, defeated, having already given up but the referees don't call a pin because the Olympic coach yells for the match to continue.

It was eating away at Jackson that Hartung was beating Cormier at the moment. It bothered him that Faust had held off Cormier a week earlier in practice too and perhaps even more so when Cormier responded by hurling a wild punch at Faust that missed by enough to know that half of it was directed to the target and half was directed at himself in frustration.

One can see traces of the anger that got Cormier involved in the sport in the first place. One could envision the story of the high school wrestling coach who broke up a fist fight between Cormier and another youth, channeling his aggression into the wrestling room where he eventually won three Louisiana state titles. And since then the sport had taken him on quite a ride. From Metairie, La. to one of those crossroads junior colleges in Kansas that was a last ditch effort for talented but troubled athletes who didn't have grades, might have had a checkered past and was staking its tenuous future into two years of school, two years of wrestling and hopefully not two years of delinquency.

But Cormier succeeded in Kansas because he was not a failure, was not some punk jock. Cormier was raw, powerful and gifted and that's why John Smith signed him out of Colby College, turning, molding and whipping Cormier into a multiple All-American at OSU, the U.S. National Champion two years running and that's why he pounded Hartung at the Olympic Trials, ate him up really, ate him up like a lion in the jungle, leading Cormier to be given the key to his hometown city, become America's Olympian, wear the red-white-and blue warm-ups, feeling the prestige associated with such an accomplishment all of which meant jack shit at the moment, that was not of any significance in the current case anymore, Cormier's accomplishments might as well be thrown out as inadmissible evidence, because they were useless to the jury of the mat where wrestling was nature, primal, the great equalizer where titles, rankings and politics didn't mean a thing, because if one knew nothing beforehand and had just walked into the OTC practice room, it was clear to see that Hartung was the superior wrestler, Hartung was the lion in the jungle, Hartung was whipping Cormier and Jackson was letting him take it, allowing the match to proceed like a dad watching his son take a beating from a peer no matter how much his pride wanted to stop it.

"Hey!" Jackson says, sternly waving his finger at the ref. "Don't call it!"

The action continues until Cormier scrambles off his back by his own will. Coaches don't like to see athletes quit, especially Olympians. Afterwards, Cormier storms off the mat and for the rest of practice

McCoy attempts to tranquilize the frustrations of Cormier, who has slumped against the wall. Jackson comes over to offer encouragement as well. Hartung gives Cormier a pat on the back, as the disgruntled Olympian looks down at the floor and cannot hide his displeasure for not dominating his own practice room. To be the best in the world, Cormier feels practice domination is a given, but he must move on. He must leave the defeat behind. He must pretend it didn't happen.

The morning comes and goes, but during the afternoon practice the coaches are still concerned about Cormier. "Where's Daniel?" Jackson asks. "Jamill you seen Danny?" Moments later, Cormier emerges, slaloming through a group of visitors, dropping his backpack to join the others. Cormier is different from his two other Oklahoma St. Olympians, Guerrero and Kelly, in that he didn't watch his diet as fervently. Guerrero and Kelly lived wrestling year-round and both have been described as being compulsive about their eating habits, cautious of whatever they put into their bodies. Cormier trains in cycles, pushing hard for several weeks at a time before competition and generally eating whatever he wants, even the popular fast food chain Popeye's Chicken. Cormier will get far overweight between tournaments, in the 230-pound range, before having to cut extensively to make the 211-pound classification.

There was something about Cormier that was still un-harnessed. He was raw and big-boned with muscles in all the right places for the sport; thick thighs, hips, arms and chest. "Daniel's got so much rawboned athletic ability," Jim Ravanack said. "He doesn't have to lift as much in the weight room to stay strong, he can cycle-train."

While Cormier moves around the practice room in cracking jokes with teammates, calling Lawal his personal assistant and trash-talking with Jackson about his basketball skills, it wasn't so long ago that he had quit wrestling and his prospects of Olympic glory were as dark and closed off as the curtains to his bedroom window.

Following the end of practice many wrestlers stay behind for extra work. As multiple conversations take place throughout the room, as bodies continue to train, John Smith's son Joseph is play wrestling with his younger sister, folding and twisting her like a doll, perhaps unaware of the infant's fragility and his own strength. And despite the multiple eyes around the situation, it is Cormier who is the first to catch the potential danger. *"Hey!"* Cormier yells across the room at Joseph, the oldest of Smith's four children. *"You gotta stop that!"*

Perhaps it is luck, or circumstance, but it is Cormier who keeps the closest eye on the young children as several other wrestlers engage around him. Coach Smith's son, Joseph stops and puts his sister down. Moments later, Cormier's face is still sober and severe, one of the few times when he appeared serious when not competing.

It was a little more than a year ago, in June 2003, that Cormier's three month old daughter Kaedyn, who bore a striking resemblance to her father, was killed in a car accident in Killeen, Texas. Kaedyn's mother, Carolyn Flowers was a passenger in a different vehicle from her daughter's when it collided with a semi-truck. Flowers called Cormier who heard her scream on the phone when a Texas state trooper informed her of the crash. Cormier hung up, called the state highway patrol headquarters and was given a confirmation of the fatality.

***

Daniel Cormier is no stranger to ill-fated events. He grew up in Louisiana, a part of America where hurricanes would wipe out towns and setback generations of development. His hometown of Metairie sits at an elevation of three feet. New Orleans is its eastern neighbor and Lake Pontchartrain sits just to the north; storm surges often cause the lake to overflow and flood the surrounding areas. Metairie caught the wrath of the Fort Lauderdale Hurricane in 1947, putting it under six feet of water, Hurricane Betsy did a number on the city in 1965 and the Flood of 1995 wasn't exactly cause for a Mardi Gras celebration.

Cormier was a Southerner. He liked to eat and laugh and didn't appear to take life too seriously. He did not have the steely demeanor of his teammate Eric Guerrero and he did not watch his diet with the same calorie-crunching discipline. There were times when Cormier got on Jackson and Douglas' nerves because he wasn't as focused and they knew he had all the worldly potential that couldn't be taught.

Cormier had a lot in common with his fellow African-American workout partner Mo Lawal. Both enjoyed rap music and they talked and clowned each other like the best of brothers, but maybe not as much as they enjoyed pulling out the landing mats in the OTC wrestling room to hone their WWF moves. Lawal and Cormier were mock tag-team partners for half an hour at a time, usually after a short practice where coaches allowed the wrestlers to work on their own. Cormier and Lawal would slam and pummel, toss and dip and clip each other into padding the size of a queen mattress. Cormier taunting Lawal and Lawal clothes-lining the Olympian who pretended to not be watching, while Guerrero was locked into extra drilling or Kelly was slashing down the sideline in sprint. While the re-enactment of staged violence could be considered a workout, it wasn't exactly a Dan Gable instructional video on Olympic mental preparation, and might lead a critical mind to think that Cormier wasn't serious enough.

Cormier seemed like the type of guy who was always fooling around in the back of class but would inevitably get caught because his voice would carry to the teacher in the front of the room. While some adolescent class clowns eventually graduate to criminality, Cormier could not be confused with this lot. He was a big, sweet kid who liked to have fun and possessed the type of talent that would lead him to the highest echelon of athletics.

Cormier was a five-foot-eleven inch package of power and could be the most explosive athlete on the Olympic team. He had a baby face with eyes that were friendly and disarming despite an upper body so bulked with muscle that he appeared to be wearing football shoulder pads under his warm-up jacket. Cormier's physique wasn't sculpted to the degree McCoy, who could get side work posing for fitness magazines, but he wasn't at a loss for power. He had whipped McCoy to his back in a recent workout with the same dynamic force that he did to an opponent at the World Championships and he once was an all-state linebacker in a region of America where football sat next to God or at least had a reservation as the same table.

Like most residents of the storm-ravaged community of Jefferson Parish, Cormier grew up with the knowledge that life would face dramatic events, but nothing could have prepared Cormier for the number of tragedies that he would go through.

When he was young, his father Joseph was killed by a relative during a Thanksgiving Day argument. In college, Cormier was a roommate of Daniel Lawson, one of the ten members of the Oklahoma St. basketball and media staff that died in a plane crash in a Colorado snow storm. Just as he had dealt with the other climatic situations in his life, after his daughter's death, Cormier withdrew.

He holed up in his apartment in Stillwater and despite the calls from the OSU coaches, Cormier would not return to the wrestling facility. He didn't talk much to his friends either. Many days went by where he was secluded in the darkness of his room. He gained weight. He lost desire. He cried himself to sleep on some nights. The national tournament came and went and Cormier still hadn't competed. Those closest to him, his wife Robin and OSU coaches and training partners, knew all that he had worked for was falling apart.

"I could have sat around saying, 'Why did this happen to me again?'" Cormier said. "But what would that have done? It wouldn't bring her back." Cormier applied for a deferral from USA Wrestling and in a special wrestle-off he defeated national champion Dean Morrison in three matches to make the world team.

While Cormier dedicated the Olympics to his daughter and talked about the sport being an escape from the pain he feels for the loss of Kaedyn, there are moments in the wrestling room where he cannot forget.

"We've been sold on mediocrity. So few people find out what they're capable of because they rarely push to the limits. They're too busy thinking about the odds."

-CURT SCHILLING, CHAMPION

Olympic Training Camp #3
XXXV

Jamill Kelly didn't slide into the room or yell across the mats with the amplified voice of Daniel Cormier. He walked in slowly, focused, taking everything in, setting his gear down and finding a wall to put his back against before practice began. He would scan the mats as he tied the laces of his wrestling shoes, usually next to the affable Cormier, his closest friend on the team, who was calling people out as they entered the Olympic facility. One couldn't tell that Kelly had been here before, and people didn't think he would be here again.

The U.S. media had forecasted a strong showing for the American wrestlers in Athens and assistant coach Bobby Douglas called the 2004 team the most talented the U.S. has ever had, but when they reached the last and least-known member of the team, prognosticators and sports writers just wrote Kelly off. They'd never heard of him, he didn't have much of an international resume, so who would predict him to do anything at the Olympics? Kelly had his lapses of doubt as well.

When he traveled to Russia in February, Kelly lost in the first match of the tournament. "I lost to a nobody after leading 5-0," Kelly said, shaking his shaved head. On the bus ride following the competition Kelly, for the first time ever, cried over wrestling; completely broken, he questioned his place in the sport. "I didn't know if I had what it takes."

Upon returning home, Kelly put all his focus into U.S. competitions and making the Olympic team. The experience in Russia spurred him to work harder and to clean up his technical skills. Kelly believed the Americans had become too predictable, while foreign opponents were difficult to gauge, remaining passive at times and aggressive at others.

It was only six months ago that he sat down with sponsor Jim Ravanack and had a serious discussion about moving on from the sport. "Jamill wasn't getting anywhere," Ravanack said. "And the reality is if you're not improving to achieve your goal, you got to try something else. It wasn't working. He saw that he had to change."

Ravanack, who lives in Louisiana and had a close enough relationship with Kelly that he would eventually entrust him to look after his two young sons while they attended high school in Stillwater, explored options for the former OSU wrestler. They discussed the proposition of Kelly moving into coaching youth wrestlers full-time, a position Kelly had a natural affinity for. But Kelly wanted to continue competing and once Kelly reached that decision, Ravanack and John Smith brought in Rob Herman, a Greco-Roman Olympic coach, to help Kelly work on different locks and maneuvers from the clinch position. Kelly, always a student of the sport, soaked up Herman's teaching and what was once a weak position became an area of strength.

Still, nobody was picking Kelly to win an Olympic medal. His bio in the media guide was several paragraphs less than any of his teammates and as one American wrestler referred to Kelly, "He's the stepchild of the Olympic wrestling team."

In college, even when ranked No. 1 in his weight, even while starting for the powerful OSU Cowboys, Kelly assumed that some of his opponents were better than him. After graduation, things slowly changed. During the 2000 Olympics, Cary Kolat brought Kelly to Sydney as a workout partner where he first got to hang around Jackson, who gave Kelly pointers and encouraged him to continue training. He began to feel calm in big stages and the doubts he had in college showed up less. "In freestyle, nine times out of ten, the more technical wrestler will win," Kelly said. This brought reassurance to

Kelly because he was a technical wrestler.

Although Jackson felt Kelly was the most skilled man in the 145-pound weight, up until a year ago the Olympic coach wouldn't have told anyone that Kelly was a lock for the team. Like others, Jackson thought Chris Bono or another American in the stacked weight class had a better chance at making the team.

It's many of these same coaches who are now focusing their efforts on Kelly who is working near Bono on the mats. During the OTC workout, Bono steals a glance at Kelly and while he is upbeat and training as hard as if he were the Olympian, this defeat is a hard to swallow. Bono is now a training partner, not much different from the NCAA wrestlers on the mat.

Months earlier, in the practices leading up to the Olympic Trials, Bono, like other hopefuls, entered the practice facility with potential. But the coaches no longer viewed the group the same way.

Bono was like a decorated college athlete returning to his old wrestling room after his senior season, a room where he was once king, a room in which he once drew the most attention and praise from trainers, a room where he dominated, was revered and followed by peers, a room that was all too familiar. He knew the hard spots on the mats and he might even remember his old locker combination, but now it was a room that no longer felt like his and was much like returning to a college facility after leaving school for good.

For Bono to be significant in the OTC wrestling facility it would take some time, another run at a world championship, another chasing of a monumental goal, to feel the hope and purpose he once had in Colorado Springs, it will take another four years.

***

"Let you guys know what's going on today and the rest of this week," Jackson says. "Smoking crack is not allowed in the dorms, that goes with anything, OK? Guys, don't be stupid. Last camp some guys got a case of beer and took it to their dorm on the last night. They left a half-empty can in the room, now they're banned from the OTC for a year. Women after 11 p.m. are also illegal. Don't leave trash on the floor, respect the room. This training camp cycle will be two days on, one day off. You also should have time to get an extra run and lift in. Start off strong."

"Abas, Guerrero, Kelly," Jackson points to a section of the mat. "Those are your spots. We want you to be comfortable here. You won't be comfortable in Athens. If you're not a ranked guy, you college guys stay-wrestle off to the side, we gotta have our Olympians ready. You might not have a chance to wrestle but be ready!"

Wary of injuries, the coaches give the seven Olympians ample room to work with while the rest cram the perimeter and fend for themselves. Jackson was speaking to elite NCAA athletes; many of them are the best at their schools, tops in their conference, champions of their nation. There was national high school wrestler of the year C.P. Schlatter and All-American Nick Simmons from Michigan State. There were athletes from Arizona State, West Virginia, Delaware Valley, and just as they had once been the focus in rooms filled with lesser talent they were now just another component in the four-year cycle, no more irreplaceable as a water cooler or a training table full of food.

With one look around, blue-chip recruits could be found in every direction, but now, in a way, they were just food for the sharks: tossed into the center of the mat, chewed up by the Olympian and spit out with each 30 second whistle.

The Olympians stand stoically in the center as another feeding awaits: Abas does not budge from his spot, neither does Williams; Sanderson lingers restlessly for the next offering. To take a break would cede leadership. The seven had worked to be in the center of the mat and to leave, to walk off just because their legs were tired, their lungs hurt, would be stepping off the pedestal they worked so hard to get on. So the Olympians don't budge from the center, while prized recruits, All-Americans, present and future NCAA champions are funneled in. *NCAA champion? Who gives a damn?* The whistle blows. *It's your turn kid. Whatta ya got? What have you done lately?* This wrestling room is of the highest pecking order.

A song begins blasting through the stereo, a number by Local H, and the wrestlers hear the beat and it gets their blood pumping, their testosterone flowing, the rhythm picks up and the thoughts in the mind clear, instinct takes over and the men start attacking each other, coaches start coaching and the room temperature ratchets to a feverous stage. Despite the curses and grunts and occasional screams the wrestlers seem numb to the struggle, almost pacified by it, because they keep getting up for more.

One athlete hits the deck hard. He pushes off the slippery surface on his stomach while clutching his left knee with both hands like a wounded soldier trying to find cover from an enemy sniper. Others keep their distance as if a small disease has hit the air, spreading apart as he throbs in pain. But the wrestler does not besiege help or beg for pity. The wrestler wants to keep going, but the Olympic trainer must clear him for injuries. One visitor observing the action turns to another and says, *"Wow, these guys work hard."*

And the visitor is right, the wrestlers go hard. Real hard. Hard enough that the walls sweat and spectators perspire. The music is cranked. Bodies are catapulting. Slamdowns. Takedowns. Beatdowns taking place everywhere. Turns. Counters. Snaps. Twists. Pulls. Tugs. Switches. Flips. Attacks. Escapes. Double-legs. Single-legs. Minds breaking. Lungs searing. Feet stampeding. *"Workhard?"* "This is the United States Olympic Wrestling Team dammit! *What the hell did you expect!?!"*

High Price
XXXVI

The mood is lethargic after practice; Sanderson and Jackson are the last ones on the mat. With a whistle and stopwatch dangling from his neck, Jackson discusses technique with Sanderson. Earlier in the year when Sanderson wanted to quit the sport altogether, Jackson was able to reel him back in and keep him training.

Jackson knew Sanderson didn't enjoy coming to Colorado Springs. He knew he didn't like wrestling Lawal. Jackson understood why Sanderson questioned it, but Jackson had a quick response for that as well. "You have to be challenged on a daily basis at a higher level than what you would find in competition," Jackson said. "Dave Schultz, Chris Campbell, Melvin Douglas they prepared us to be world champions. My practice partners were better than the guys I faced in competition. I remember John Smith trying to score 100 points in a practice match. As a result, Smith wrestled the same way in competition."

"It doesn't matter when a coach is watching," Jackson said. "It matters more when no one's watching. I paid too high a price to lose. I could go train with the best guys in the world. The Russians have that.

All the other republics have that. We don't have that. But we still have success. I attribute that to the American will. When a person makes his mind up that he is going to be a world champion, then those things can be overcome. That's what Brandon Slay did, he stayed within parameters, using his tactics. You can't tell me he was a better wrestler than Saytiev. The reason why he won was he was working on the exact skills that a world champion needs. We haven't had that in all these other weight classes. Joe Williams has never been challenged since Slay left, neither has McCoy once Neal went to play football. How do they expect to beat the Russians? Iran is in a system where they have competition every other week. You got guys who train from January to September. Their athletes are in a structured environment."

Jackson spoke of those willing to pay this high price in the way a general does of a few good men. The ones who go beyond what was required. The ones who could separate from the group, from the rest of the world. Jackson spoke of this high price as the only way to approach a goal in life, because for him, for all the champions he'd known, it was. The opportunity to win a gold medal is so small, the moment so brief, that every day of hard training is crucial. So when the moment finally comes, there is no second-guessing of ability, no doubts of what will happen, the athlete has paid too high a price to lose.

The receipt, the proof of this, is in taut muscles which were built, shaped and cut to precision. In the pride written on determined faces. Jackson's goal is to have his athletes rely on muscle memory, to allow their training to take over, to not think, but react in the competition.

But sometimes that didn't happen. Sometimes Jackson had to push Williams into running the COG Trail up Pikes Peak Mountain. Sometimes he had to ask McCoy to come back in the wrestling room for extra work after a bad practice. "At times I have to guilt a couple of our guys into training," Jackson said. "I don't have to guilt Sanderson to do that." Jackson understood that each athlete is unique. "Sanderson for his own mental health knew what had to be done, he knew what his body needed. He ran the mountain five times in the summer. He came to the OTC 22 times in two years. He wanted to move his feet the entire match, so from a confidence standpoint, Cael had to get in more training than others. 'I gotta get some more,' Cael would tell me. The same training Sanderson did in college carried over to the open level."

"Bring a certain energy, motivation, a certain hardness that will help you," Jackson said of his wrestling philosophy. "I hated my opponent when I wrestled. If Joe Williams felt that, he would never lose to those guys. If you hate your opponent it's a lot harder to lose to him. Somewhere along the way some guys on the team missed that." Jackson felt it was a carryover off the mat, as well. "It could be anything, everything. You have be a good dude, a good man, a good person. Even with Saytiev from Russia, as much as I want our guys to beat him, I know he's a good person. Everything's a carryover. On the mat training's got to take over. In the heat of the moment, you don't think, you react. From life to training to everything, morally right, physically right. If you know those things are incorrect then it carries over to competition."

"I don't believe some guys on our team are doing everything to be the best in the world. You have to be self-motivated. For some reason," Jackson says with detachment as he leans back in his office chair. "They're not self-motivated enough. It could be anything personal that holds one back. You gotta deserve to be the champion."

***

Jackson, like other national and world-caliber U.S. wrestlers, had fought in the UFC after his wrestling career. Dan Henderson, Matt Linland, Randy Couture, Chuck Liddell and Tito Ortiz who had dominated the UFC's hierarchy over the years and were just a few of a slew of former wrestlers to find success in the octagon.

Yet, there seemed to be little acknowledgement to the long-held truth that wrestlers made the best organized sport fighters. With the majority of all conflicts, street or organized, ending up on the ground, turf, concrete, what have you, wrestlers were adept at rising to the top of the rumble. Therefore, if Cael Sanderson and Muhammad Ali were to meet in such a setting in the prime of their careers, with both athletes nearly equal in height and weight, both long-limbed and swift of foot, each personifying all the qualities of a consummate champion, both highly intelligent and capable of adjusting to an opponent's greatest strengths, Ali specifically with the rope-a-dope technique that overcame the powerful George Foreman and Sanderson, with his unique style that defeated the relentless pressure of Lee Fullhart, it would be a clash of sports and styles.

But, unless Ali the boxer caught Sanderson with a punch and stunned the grappler from the onset, Ali would likely be forced into an unnatural position of fighting from the ground, throwing punches off his back with little of his usual speed or force and would be defeated by Sanderson the wrestler, more times than not. However, the mere mention of this argument to the mainstream would be preposterous for those who knew of Ali, once the most famous man on the planet. Millions grew up with Ali's image adorning bedroom walls as a sporting and cultural icon. They were likely to know little, if anything of Sanderson except as the guy from Iowa St. who went undefeated.

Wrestling's lack of mainstream popularity is the chip it can never knock off its broad shoulder. There have been several attempts to raise its profile with professional leagues on cable television. But perhaps wrestling was not meant to be a glamour sport in the U.S. Maybe it was better off without publicity. Would the extra attention make it more pure? Truer to its primal roots? Or, possibly, it would wander down the wrong path and turn out worse than its brother sport of professional boxing, with its numerous shady organizations and dysfunctional committees. But the attempts to gain entry into the national sporting consciousness by wrestling leaders will never stop, because many are afraid the sport will otherwise die off.

Wrestling has survived because of the fundamental physical struggle between two athletes that is imbedded in human's animalistic nature. Wrestling was never a fad, a novelty. The sport is primal. And it remains humbling to those who pursue it.

Out of all the Olympic sports, wrestling and boxing have the most in common: training, discipline and mentality. The mutual respect between the U.S. Olympic wrestling and boxing teams could be seen in their brief daily exchanges in the cafeteria, the direct eye contact and silent nods of respect, the easy conversation that follows between the representatives of the two fighting disciplines in the hallways and lounges of the U.S. Olympic training facility.

To step into a ring, a circle of battle alone, one has to be his own psychologist in order to deal with inhibition, fear, hesitancy, strategy, the opposition because there can be no more humiliating sporting feeling than being broken, beaten and worked over by an opponent. The wrestler walks out alone. He competes alone. He wins, loses and has the chance to be humiliated alone. And for precisely these reasons, high-stakes, high-level wrestling contests are fought with the bloodthirsty intent of a back-alley scrap.

"Only the mediocre are always at their best."

-JEAN GIRAUDOUX (1882-1944)

Master of One
XXXVII

Eric Guerrero is a terrible athlete. On the basketball court he looks unsure of himself nor is he the fastest runner; in a local pickup game he would be one of the last participants picked. But none of this matters, because Eric Guerrero is a brilliant wrestler.

On the mat he is fast, slick, relentless and had an uncanny sense of how to win. Guerrero was not a three-sport letterman at San Jose's Independence High School. He didn't trade activities season to season. Guerrero excelled at one sport and one sport only and he was the best 125-pound high school wrestler in the country. In college he was an NCAA champion from his sophomore year on. So when teammates and coaches go participate in another sport to get a light workout on a day off, Guerrero is an easy guy to track down. And while growing up on the West Coast, he took to surfing, reading and playing the guitar to relax, he is not exactly a laidback California local. He had a pride and dignity in his appearance, his dark hair always seemed perfectly combed in place and even in the wrestling room he tucked in his shirt carried himself like a professional.

As rain falls from the dark Colorado sky, as other Olympic team members play basketball or run the COG trail, Guerrero uses his hour on the mats. Shadows of a beard are beginning to form across his face. His grey workout clothes are damp with sweat. His red-white-and blue wrestling shoes match the color of the wrestling mat in the facility. John Smith sits just outside the red circle on the first mat. In a t-shirt and shorts. Smith silently watches, chewing on the end of a pen. Instinctively, he checks on his son Joseph who is roaming around the room. There is a weightlifting tournament next door and the clangs of falling weights carry through the walls. After being given instructions by Smith, Guerrero begins sparring in one minute increments. There is little of the usual clamor in the wrestling facility, there is no dialogue between Smith and Guerrero or his workout partner, at least not until Guerrero is taken down.

"DAMMIT!!"

Guerrero slams his hand and furiously rises to his feet to redeem himself. He pounds his workout partner twice in the head, demanding under-hooks with forearm uppercuts to each shoulder. Throwing it by, Guerrero manages a faint grip of the leg but is too competitive to be denied, driving his partner to the mat. Now, Smith's son is seated right beside him, a football cradled in his arm, watching as intently as his father gets up to demonstrate. "You're hitting that flat-foot-ed," Smith says with a slight Oklahoma cadence. "You need to be here."

Guerrero's next shot is flawless. Moving in, hovering low, faking a few times, he creates a slight opening before slicing through and closing without much physical debate from Kyle. Then a quick pitter-patter of the feet, like a boxer showing off, to snatch a single-leg, stalling a moment on the liftoff of his opponent then, within a blink, reversing directions and whipping Kyle violently to his back.

Guerrero's next two shots are stopped and he begins to puff in and out with anger. Then he is taken down for the first time in this session. But Guerrero gets the next score within 15 seconds. Then the next one a single-leg. And the next, as Smith nods with approval. And the following one on a double-leg. For the rest of the workout, Guerrero will own Klye, but this can benefit both of them in different ways. Guerrero's confidence and fluidity will only grow sharper. As a result, his partner will undoubtedly get tougher; in the U.S., Kyle's competition can only go down.

***

"We should not be more than 13 to 14 pounds overweight," Jackson says. "Let's prepare like we're gonna wrestle the Olympic Games. We'll go over to Athens and tone it down a bit. About ten more training days. No more surprises from here on out." Bobby Douglas, veteran of the last two Olympics, cuts in. "It's United States against the world, including the referee." Douglas says. "If the girls get four golds and Greco team does well, you think we're gonna get calls? You gotta make the calls. Wrestle the way you been training." After the coaches address the team, wrestlers work on their own. Some are finished in 30 minutes; others are still on the mat at the end of the hour.

"That's him!" a boy says to his mother. "That's Cael Sanderson!" Sanderson is oblivious to the attention as he works with John Smith. The young fan runs to the edge of the mat with a disposable camera and waits 15 minutes with a sharpie in one hand and a t-shirt in the other as Sanderson confers with his coaches.

Soon thereafter, he signs the kid's t-shirt who hustles back to his mother to show off the fresh autograph. Sanderson is the last Olympian to leave the room. On the way out, he receives an Olympic packet. Each member of the United States Olympic Freestyle Wrestling Team is given a team bag with his name stitched in, 50 Olympic collector pins, a t-shirt, an envelope full of cash and plane tickets to Greece.

*"There is no greater glory for a man in all his life than what
he wins with his own feet and hands."*

-HOMER, THE ODYSSEY

Athens
XXXVIII

I arrived to Athens in the middle of the night. $1,300 in my pocket,
one pair of jeans, shorts, couple of t-shirts, a camera, Olympic tickets
jammed into a small backpack and a name of a hotel. It was midnight
and the city was buzzing. Warm Mediterranean weather. Energy in the
air. Youths riding motorcycles. Young Greek women moving about.
But I couldn't party, couldn't get distracted, had to get a roof over my
head, had to find Mohammed Lawal. The rest could wait.

"Park Hotel," I said leaning into the window of a cab. The cabbie
nodded with confidence. I sat back as we rode into the city.

The previous two days I had been stuck on standby in the Frankfurt,
sleeping on benches that were as comfortable as a coffin, being
awoken every 15 minutes by German airport loudspeaker warning
travelers of security alerts, and as I waited sleep deprived and hungry,
I thought about all the things I had to do just to get to Greece, just to
follow this story. I had driven across Colorado through Utah and into
Nevada doing 95 plus to arrive at the National Championships in Las
Vegas with no hotel room, no press pass, no one awaiting my arrival.
But I found a room, got the story, then headed back across the Western

badlands, where, after talking my way out of the wrath of the Utah highway patrol, I reached a Colorado blizzard with a bad tires and no windshield wipers; spinning out three times on the mountain highway as diesel trucks barreled down the road in second gear, but somehow arrived back home safely.

A month later I rode across the Midwest on a train, arrived at the Olympic Trials in Indianapolis, got the story, and went home after witnessing more wrestling drama than I ever thought possible. I had been to Arizona, Wyoming, Kansas, Oklahoma, Iowa, Nebraska and throughout California to follow the story. And at times the journey was boring, daring, inspiring, pathetic, but I had made it.

Then I thought about the athletes' quest. Abas had to wait four years for another shot at defeating Sammie Henson to make the Olympic team. I had witnessed Eric Guerrero crying, doubled over in pain underneath a staircase in Madison Square Garden after losing at the World Championships. I had seen Jamill Kelly get defeated not at Worlds, not at U.S. Nationals, not at the state tournament, but ten years earlier at the San Joaquin high school sectional championship, so what were his odds of making it? Joe Williams was in a McDonald's commercial for the 2000 Sydney Games, but was upset by Brandon Slay, failing to qualify for the team. Cormier had to emotionally recover from his daughter's fatal car accident to continue training. McCoy once again had to survive the qualifying process. Cael Sanderson lost his passion to compete and wanted to quit the sport; dealing with expectations and pressure that no U.S. wrestler ever had.

The seven had made it. I had made it. The cabbie and I rode into Athens in silence. 20 minutes later we pulled up at the entrance of a swank hotel. This must be it. Moments later the hotel clerk told me it wasn't the Park Hotel I was looking for. He stubbed out his cigarette, pulled out a phonebook, dialed a number and handed me the phone.

"Mo…I'm at the Park Hotel."

"It's a different one," Lawal said over a scratchy telephone connection. "Up by the airport, I'm not sure if I can get you in."

"What do you mean?"

"Heavy security," Lawal said. "A couple of armed guards patrolling and checking ID's out front."

The Park Hotel is located on a narrow one-way street just off a main drag. The parking lot is small and shaded with low, overhanging trees that covered a narrow path that leads to the front door manned by security guards who checked credentials for anyone attempting to enter. Once I fooled the protection unit into believing I was an American athlete, I was allowed through the front doors. I climbed two flights of stairs and found the room where I could crash on the floor for free.

When I arrived at the gym the next morning, I took my usual spot in the practice room, off to the side of the mats, and began taking notes. A couple of the Olympic wrestlers nodded in my direction, but they quickly went back to their routines. I always kept my distance. These were intensely focused athletes. They didn't have to tell me what they were going through.

I already knew.

In college, I had awakened at six a.m. and been on the stadium track running sprints at 6:30. I had spent many afternoons in boiling wrestling rooms. I had thrown up while working out. I had pushed my body to hellish limits. I had locked myself into the solitary confinement of the weight room to improve strength. I had fought with teammates. I had fought for them. I had pulled on plastic sweat suits, thrown pieces of gum in my mouth, left my college pad when my roommates were eating dinner and ran until my legs burned, my clothes were soaked and I weighed what I needed to weigh.

During my time in the sport I had experienced all the things a wrestler could feel: victory, defeat, arrogance, humiliation, revenge, exhaustion, rage and satisfaction. I had been broken, exposed, vindicated, impassioned, obsessed and focused. I had stared across gyms at opponents, warmed up beneath shadowy bleachers, crushed my hands into lockers, thrown my headgear in frustration and been tossed out of tournaments. I had been academically ineligible and a student-athlete All-American. I'd been a leader and a follower, passive and aggressive, head case and headstrong. I had stood ashamed at second place and silently proud above medal stands. I had gone 0-2 and 5-0. I had experienced success and failure on three levels (high school, junior college, NCAA Division I) but never consistently had a grip on the sport, always one more challenge ahead.

I had ridden in cars, vans and planes as a member of a Division I team, to reach tournaments in Boise, Reno, Dallas, and Chicago; it didn't matter where the competition site was, the routine of a wrestler was much of the same. Run, lift, spar in the off-season and pre-season, and when arriving to the competition day, doing whatever needed to be done to make weight. Converting hotel bathrooms into makeshift saunas: close the door, blast the hot water, spit into the cup while the mirror fogged up, make small talk with teammates who also needed to wither away the last several wretched pounds in agonizing heat.

I had risen on the mornings of tournaments, dehydrated, sucked-up, thinking only of the moment I would step on the scale. After that, drinking water, that in moments of extreme dehydration, tasted holy. I had stood on the perimeter of the mat anxious to compete, slapping my muscles awake, shaking out my nerves, building my competitive edge with any source of anger I could find. For nine years it was like this. But after my last collegiate match, after being defeated in the Pac-10 Conference tournament, after getting a tooth knocked out and losing all my meal money in a hotel room poker game to a teammate, after nearly a decade committed to the sport, I no longer had the stomach for it.

I was tired. My time was up. I was done.

A year had passed and I no longer lived the athlete's journey. I had it easy now. I only had to get a story and survive in an expensive city on a thin wallet. I didn't have to feel as if every movement leading up to competition needed to be limited, every ounce of food thought for, every drink of water calculated. So the Olympians didn't have to tell me how they felt because I had once too been immersed like them and solely focused my practice movements, on victory-success-winning, to care about anything else. I had once bled the sport, loved the sport, wanted to tell its story and that's why I was now standing on a street corner halfway across the world, with no reservations, no one awaiting my arrival, carrying only a backpack and tickets to the Olympic wrestling event.

***

The Park Hotel is situated in a quiet Athens neighborhood where modest apartment buildings mix with simple one-story houses that have small, well-kept gardens and trees that shade narrow streets where cars are economically parked halfway on the curb.

It had six floors and slender hallways in which short, petite maids worked diligently to keep clean. The entire hotel staff couldn't exceed ten people, and the U.S. contingent had bought out the building for the month of August, which limited the diversity of the crowd mixing in the lobby. In fact, anyone who wasn't the cauliflower ear type was treated with a rude arrival. Their bags were checked, they had to show forms of I.D. and were generally interrogated by men with guns about their reason for visiting. But the staff had their orders, and those orders certainly had their reasons.

For the year leading up to Athens Olympics, the media had focused exclusively on things that were going to go wrong. Stadium construction wasn't going to be finished in time. Security was going to be lax. A terrorist incident was imminent.

The Park Hotel felt like the American wrestlers were in the witness protection program for Olympic athletes. It was miles away from the Olympic Village and it hardly contained the environment of the world's largest sporting event. There is a stong anti-American sentiment during the Games, USOC officials warned the athletes to avoid displaying their American athlete credentials in public and every time they opened a newspaper they were given the latest updates on terrorism threats much in the manner of their own country after 9/11. The security guards standing outside the entrance were certainly not the flashlight and walkie-talkie types. They carried high-powered weapons and patrolled the grounds day and night with the requisite paranoia of any F.B.I. agent.

A few of the athletes and training partners took to one of the guards, an attractive femme fatale archetype with long brown hair that nearly reached the gun on her waist belt, spending the hours after dinner and talking her up while her partner smoked cigarette after cigarette and pretended not to pay attention to her colleague's conversations.

A five-minute walk from the hotel is the American College of Greece, which is nestled at the foot of a mountain filled with pine trees and red rocks. Perched above the city at the breach of a small shopping center and a neighborhood terrace, is the adopted headquarters of the U.S. Olympic Committee.

On the outside of the ten-foot green metal gates, positioned every hundred yards, blue-shirted security personnel sit underneath umbrellas that shade them from the blistering sun.

The A.C.G. is similar to a small liberal arts college with an enrollment of 1,500 students. Like most campuses on a summer vacation, students are nowhere to be seen and despite the assortment of grocery markets nearby, the foot traffic is confined mostly to local elderly population walking their dogs. The trees and quad area are compact and the facilities are well-managed. It's a controllable atmosphere, precisely what the USOC was looking for to avoid the myriad distractions that exist at the Olympic village, which has gained a reputation as a free-for-all love fest between international competitors who, during the three weeks of competition and subsequent release, exercised all the restraint of a college freshman dorm. The USOC is here to produce medals and anything that deters from that objective is brought to question; the selection of the Park Hotel for the wrestlers went along the same line of thought.

At the ACG, bomb-sniffing German Shepherds are collared by U.S. secret service agents. Like the incessant chirping of birds in the trees, one can't see the totality of the state department security force, but they're everywhere. Snipers are on alert day and night. Each person wishing to access the grounds is given a thorough shakedown. Visitors are required to empty their pockets and turn over any personal belongings for inspection. Each vehicle that enters the facility has its exterior swiped by a chemical detecting device resembling an acne medicine pad. The entire procedure takes roughly three minutes per automobile. Hoods are popped, inner contents checked, as the team of guards conduct the modus operandi with professional suspicion, but they seem to understand that mostly they will be getting paid for a suntan.

Inside the A.C.G. there is a pool, a track stadium, basketball and volleyball facilities, workout gyms for judo, tae-kwon-do and Olympic fencing teams along with a weight-room, cafeteria and meeting rooms for USOC employees. At the top of the steps and to the right of the track is a blacktop basketball court and an unassuming green gym where U.S. wrestlers are concluding a practice that leaves them less than two weeks away from Olympic competition.

It's a Spartan training facility. The windows are cracked for minimal ventilation and there is not a trace of air conditioning. Three rows of concrete seating curl down a stairway that connects to the hardwood gym floor. Greek lettering is etched in between the eight basketball backboards. Two mats are separated from a wall by a few feet. Waist-high water coolers filled with ice and bottled sports drinks sit next to the bathroom. Sponsor banners hang from the ceiling. On the two mats that cover half of the floor is USA Wrestling's version of Noah's Ark. The two fittest athletes in each weight class, coaches, trainers and essential support staff.

The U.S. team arrived early in order for the athletes to assimilate into Greece and adjust to the time change. Essentially, everything is the same as the OTC in Colorado Springs. The mats, the trainer, the coaches, even the dining facility where the USOC brought personal chefs and flew in American meat products to protect from food-poisoning. Energy bars are laid out on tables. Sports drinks sit inside glass door refrigerators. A projector is aimed up at a screen to update the day's Olympic results. An assortment of athletes: boxers wearing unlaced high-top Adidas shoes, swimmers in lightweight warm-up suits with damp hair pulled back into ponytails, sprinters with legs like thoroughbreds wearing short-shorts and loose jersey tops and wrestlers with beaten ears mixing with USOC workers in polo shirts and khaki pants.

In the late afternoon the weather becomes overcast and the wind temporarily blows away the pollution that hovers over Athens. Above the cafeteria on a road that winds up a mountain, there is a clear view of the Olympic stadium in the center of the city where the opening ceremonies were held several days earlier. But the U.S. wrestlers are not reminiscing on the ceremonies or snapping photos like the tourists who have bombarded the area, they don't see the Mediterranean Sea beyond the cityscape nor the blue skies that have suddenly cleared; the wrestlers are under the cover of a gym, on the mats, back at work.

Sanderson smoothly takes down Tim Hartung while Zeke Jones refs and coaches simultaneously; Hartung changed his wrestling style to accommodate Sanderson. After training together in Minneapolis, Sanderson chose the former Minnesota star as his workout partner because he can rely on him to be punctual for morning workouts and not go out drinking every night. Their partnership seemed to be an easy fit. Like Sanderson, Hartung is a natural athlete who excelled at multiple sports in high school. He is well-respected in the tight-knit wrestling community for leading Minnesota to back-to-back NCAA titles, the last of which came in dramatic win against Fullhart of Iowa.

Cody Sanderson watches his brother from the opposite corner, taking note of his difference in attitude. "He seems to have regained that passion for the sport," Cody said. "That little kid smile that disappeared in college that I didn't see again until now. Cael's relaxing and enjoying himself and it has to do with him regaining his faith, church, spirituality."

Jim Ravanack, the USA Wrestling Team Leader, had a different take. "Cael ain't going to like me saying this, but if there's anybody who inspired him to win a gold medal, it was Lee Fullhart."

Coaches observe the action from the weathered wood bench below the bleachers, while others follow from atop exercise bikes, the squeak of their wheels resounding throughout the gym as Sanderson continues to work on the single-leg finish. Attacking the leg comes naturally for Sanderson and the reasoning among the coaching staff is that if he can finish his takedowns, there's not much that can stop him.

Sajid Sajidov of Russia and Yoel Romero of Cuba are going to be his toughest competition. He has not beaten either wrestler and in his previous bout with Sajidov at the World Championships, Sanderson was unable to finish on the leg attack with time running out. If he converted the move, he would have been the world champion. Some American wrestlers thought officials were trying to give the match to Sanderson, the home crowd wrestler in New York, but the Russian Sajidov won by a point anyway. But the referee would not be a homer in this Olympics, not that Jackson, Douglas or any of the American coaches instilled this into their athletes. Sanderson is a wrestler; it is up to him to win the gold.

On the other side of the gym, the American fencing team jousts up and down white strips of surface, prodding one another with flimsy metal foils. Strapped by cords connected to electrical equipment a few feet away, each athlete badgers back and forth, every score punctuated by a two-second fire-alarm beeping sound. On the opposite half, the U.S. wrestlers' practice moves at a quick pace. Each minute broken down to what the coaches can squeeze out of it: thirty-second sprints, ten-second goes, one-minute overtime periods; the training as systematic and organized as a Microsoft Excel spreadsheet.

During the late afternoon practice, Abas and Guerrero start drilling slowly. Once their bodies get warm and sweat begins to pour, they turn the corner on their shots with razor precision. A decade earlier, this scene was visible at California Junior National Team practices, where teammates would sit after practice and watch as Abas and Guerrero. This gym is like the others they have inhabited over the years. Hardwood floors, bare walls, heat trapped by closed doors and windows. The two Olympians could have been preparing for competitions in Fresno, San Jose, Atwater or Tulare. It could have been at Five Counties, Reno Tournament of Champions or the CIF State Meet, with Abas and Guerrero no matter what the bounty, the focus never changes and that is why they are in this bland gym, in this remote part of Athens, preparing for the biggest sporting event in the world, and not back home wondering, agonizing, *what if?*

"Wrestling has taught me this: Even if you fall very low, the most important thing is not to be afraid, because everything can be done with your own hands."

-ALEXANDER KARELIN, 3X OLYMPIC CHAMP, N.Y. TIMES

Perfect Frustration
XXXIX

Kevin Jackson surveys the practice scene between the two mats. Then he moves to the corner, rolling the whistle on the tip of his mouth like a cigar. "Guys, come in here real quick," he announces, while reading off a small sheet of notes in his hand. "I'm sure they explained at the hotel that we have ten minute interviews with NBC. Remember we're still a little ways out. Rest, recovery and massaging, those types of things are very important. After this cycle, no more walking back and forth to the hotel, catch a ride instead. Questions? Concerns? Everybody alright? Get a good, strong warm-up drill."

Cormier looks sloppy as he is turned by Lawal, Smith walks away shaking his head. "Daniel come on," a coach calls from the mat. Despite several coaches urging him to continue Cormier quits on the rest of the match. Weigh-ins are a week out and with each pound of body weight that Cormier loses his patience seems to be getting thinner as well. He keeps saying to himself that he should be in tip-top shape, that its far too close to competition to not be wrestling perfect. He should be able to grasp that perfection. He should be able to attain what he felt on other days when his shots were fluid and his body felt powerful. When he scored at will and felt unbeatable, where his technique felt precise, where he was on his way to capturing the gold.

But this was not one of those days. On this day Lawal was beating him. Lawal knows Cormier's moves and essentially has nothing to lose from the experience. The Olympians can get injured and lose momentum, or even worse, they can lose confidence. How could Cormier win gold if he couldn't win a takedown on his practice partner? He tries to ignore this question, telling himself to shake it off, that the only reason why he wasn't dominating was because Lawal knew his strategy so well. He tries to blow this thought away like he did with the coaches' calls with the wave of his hand, but they seem to hang in the air like the humidity. As he sits despondent on the bench, the feeling is inescapable and must be dealt with in a swift manner. "That's alright," Jackson says, with voice optimism. "That's okay."

While success on the mat relies on motor skills and muscle memory, on technique and a desire to win, the coaching staff is in the business of brainwashing as well. They will not let the Olympians take the short walk back to the hotel, they pump up psyches so on the day of competition the Americans will believe that no one trained harder, rested more, had access to better coaching and proper nutrition, and when they step onto the mat they expect total domination.

Cormier moves further down the gym, distancing himself from the team. Earlier Smith watched with restraint as Cormier boiled with frustration, but now there is a release. With a stern face, Smith gestures with his hands to the mat, pointing animatedly while Cormier, staring at the ground with perspiration rolling off his nose, listens with the ear of a dutiful son. Minutes later, Kelly walks over in a white towel and sits next to Smith and quickly the coaching is extended to him.

This had not been an Olympic champion performance from Cormier. Smith wants more. Smith expects more. And he is letting Cormier know. His hands come up from the shadows, lit up by the sun that shoots through the windows, palms open to reiterate a point, snapping his fingers to accentuate repetition, "Boom, boom, bam!" Smith goes on for another ten minutes as Kelly and Cormier nod silently.

The wrestlers return to the hotel after practice, clutching Olympic weightlifting and boxing tickets they would use later in the evening. Twenty minutes after his teammates leave, Cormier sits in the stands listening to a USOC sports psychologist, taking in her words and her coaxing.

***

On Sunday morning the complex is deserted. The fencers have already competed and moved their gear out of the gym and except for a slight hum of a generator, the room is still and quiet. The heat is sweltering, even small movements lead to sweaty pores. A whistle blows and Eric Guerrero begins a bout against his partner. Smith watches, arms folded, wrestling shoes untied and while the Oklahoma St. coach is known to offer praise sparingly, he jumps off his knees and slaps his hands together as Guerrero takes down Kyle again. Then he returns to his seat on the bench next to Sergei Beloglazov, four Olympic gold medals between them, and sits side-by-side with the Russian.

When Beloglazov talks about wrestlers he rejects NCAA Champions sweep of the hand and Olympians don't faze his standards either, but when speaking of Smith there is a hitch in the Russian's voice, a sportsman's appreciation that he seems to hold for few others.

They met once in competition, at an All-Star meet in Pittsburgh, it was Beloglazov in red, Smith in blue. During the six minutes of action, the two wrestlers folded and twisted each other like a rolling rubrics cube, each wrestler always making the right shape, each shot and counter a clinical exhibition, but Smith prevailed against the smaller Beloglazov 4-2, scoring repeatedly on shots. But with Gable, Beloglazov's tone changes and there was less admiration for the Iowa style. Beloglazov came from a background that placed value on technique over brute force and relentless attack. Beloglazov didn't feel the sport could be dominated by the Hawkeye will alone, and others must have felt the same way because USA Wrestling brought Beloglazov over from Russia for his technical skill.

But now, in the American practice facility in Athens, Beloglazov is reduced to a glorified janitor of sorts. He came into the room quietly, almost unnoticed, to clean up sloppy technique and training methods. He sweeps across the mats in search of things others might have missed, picking up clues with his keen sporting eye, but his impact is hardly known. It is Kevin Jackson who is in control of the team, who comes through a side door and begins coaching Sanderson even before he has put on his shoes.

All over Athens the Olympics are in full swing. Meanwhile, the wrestling facility seems far removed from the pressure of the world's oldest sporting event, but there were signs that they were about to be swallowed whole.

Eric Guerrero's every movement is gauged. He watches other athletes train but follows the action with his eyes, not with his head. When he walks over to the water cooler his steps are slow, relaxed, economical, cutting straight across the surface instead of walking the long way around the side. When he sheds weight, he wears a full jump suit and climbs on the bike. Then he gets up, removes his shirt and wrings a puddle of sweat out of it. As he does this, his eight-pack of abdominal muscles appears and disappears with each breath. Guerrero grabs a piece of ice out of the cooler, closes the lid and pops it into his mouth.

Zeke Jones calls over to Guerrero and instructs him to call when he needs a ride back to the hotel, the coaching staff refusing to let the wrestlers squander even the smallest amount of energy on the five-minute walk any more than they would allow them to dwell on a bad practice.

"I know there are those who have done these things usually keep quiet, and those who haven't done them talk."

-THE PICKPOCKET

Lone Star Hope
XL

Plano, Texas is a long way from Athens. It is a wealthy suburb north of Dallas, a staple of American corporate headquarters: Frito-Lay, Cinemark Theatres, Perot Systems, and JC Penny are just a few that call the city home. Located in Collin County, Plano's affluence helps it rank as the wealthiest county in Texas and part of 1% of the wealthiest counties in the U.S.

Residents of West Plano are stereotyped for driving a Mercedes-Benz, Audi, Range Rover and other high-end cars. Troy Aikman, Lance Armstrong and former Presidential candidate H. Ross Perot have at one time or another lived in the city and maybe if Lawal were to make something happen on the wrestling mat they would be willing to include him in the notable residents list.

Lawal knew of a different side of the city while attending Plano East High, which had a program they called the Ivy League where they would bring in students who had scored well on standardized tests. "They brought in the smart kids and built homes through a Blue-Ribbon program, but we still had problems," Lawal said. "Cars in the parking lot were broken into, checkbooks were stolen. I stole sometimes too, I was tired of eating the free lunch, nasty cheeseburgers and milk, I wanted to go off campus where the rich people lived. All my boys sold drugs. I got jumped by guys on my own football team. Older guys from the neighborhood would come and try to fight the high school kids. But hey, shit happens."

Lawal, perhaps sensing that he could not become a serious wrestler in Plano left the city right after his senior finals or maybe Lawal, like most teenagers, just wanted to get the hell out of his hometown. One can picture a youthful Lawal riding across the Texas plains, leaving the state where football was king and arriving to Oklahoma, a place that had the caliber of wrestling programs that could shape his raw talent.

Plano's population, well over 250,000, cared far more about football than anything that involved a mat and two athletes fighting within it. And in the beginning, they must have laughed at Mohammed Lawal because wrestling was a joke sport where he came from. It was the sport that received the crappy facilities and runoff funds of powerful football programs. It was a sport where athletes had to move mats into cafeterias and makeshift practice rooms, serving as part-time maintenance workers who washed germs off the surface. Wrestling was simply not something they celebrated in Texas, especially not a six-foot, 195-pound African-American with slabs of raw muscle and natural ability, who could jump out of the gym, who could explode with power, and had that anger-induced reckless abandon that seemed destined for release on the gridiron.

Guys like Lawal were Division I hit men, major college football safeties who flew around 100-yard fields, monsters of the secondary who dominated their territory like dope dealers on a private gang playground, head-hunting opponents and delivering punishment any shot they could get. So to have Lawal recede from this Texas schoolboy destiny must have been met with skepticism from his ball coaches, especially for a sport that was eclipsed in the towering shadow cast by Texas prep football. But it seems that Lawal could have the last laugh now, he could smile that big childish grin of his that even the most loyal KKK member couldn't help but feel guilty for not smiling along with him, because Lawal was far from that place of Plano, Texas and much closer to the elite of the world wrestling scene.

As the Olympians prepped for defining moments, their training partners worked in anonymity. The training partner would not get his picture in the paper. The training partner would not compete. Their duties required them to practice at three-quarter speed and conceded scramble situations to the Olympians. It was a role that was tailored for an athlete to coast given the fact that any meaningful competition of his own was several months away and that there were plenty of distractions around. Athens was full of pretty girls, nightclubs and bars that didn't close until you stopped putting money on the counter. Lawal and other training partners were in an Olympic atmosphere that was much a business trip for them as it was a party for Olympics fans and tourists, and many people visiting the city were going to do things like they did in Cancun, Belize and other places that didn't deserve regrets. But no matter where the night took Lawal, he showed up on time for the morning practice as hungry for a workout as if he were eating off the Olympians plate because if he was going to be the American representative in 2008, then the process started in 2004.

After watching him compete at practice, one could tell the sport was a drug to Mo Lawal. The explosion and drop of an opponent was like an injection of a needle into the arm, everything becoming heightened, the sense of feel strongly acute, the sounds becoming muffled, and in moments like these, Lawal kept going, kept attacking, kept hitting the most basic wrestling move with the most eruptive burst of power… *BOOM!*…and Lawal would do it again because to him the drug was not something cheap, not something found on a street corner, but something he had worked for in the practice room. As a natural entertainer Lawal was also there to entertain, to invoke cheers and incite rival boos, to keep people on the edge of their seats and jolt them off with direct explosions of the opponents body. To Lawal, competition was the drug of choice, everything else was paraphernalia.

***

He was the type of individual that drew a crowd wherever he went and was able to have a good time in every country in the world. At a Mediterranean nightspot he had a large crowd of foreigners mimicking his dance moves as if the DJ had handed him the microphone and let him take over the party for himself.

He appeared so undeniably American, so confidently at ease as he walked the streets of Athens listening to headphones with a white towel wrapped around his head like he was the Sultan of Egypt, evoking an easy charisma with Greek street peddlers that prompted them to take with photos and shout out his name after just two minutes of interaction. *"MO-HAM-MED!"* the vendors said with reverence. *"MO-HAM-MED!"* Taking in the surroundings with a slow gangster gait that said time was his bitch and he didn't mind keeping it that way.

But around his coaches, around men that could help him, Lawal was constantly on the pursuit. Always asking Jackson, Brands and Smith questions because he wanted more, more of the experience he had not gotten enough of in college and really hadn't tasted in high school.

With Lawal, wrestling was relatively fresh, new, seen through the wild-eyed wonder of youth. He wasn't burnt out like so many wrestlers his age, men who had competed since they could walk, had cut weight since they stepped on a scale, who had known the grind of the sport for too many years, no Lawal was a bit Huck Finnish, he had no prejudices, no fears of the unknown and was ready to take the journey of the sport to the top of the world.

He was deferential in the presence of his mentor John Smith, the hard-minded, hard fought, champion athlete and coach. One afternoon between practice in Athens, at a cafe in between the airport and the center of the city, Lawal, Smith and other OSU training partners unburdened by the preparations of competition, had lunch at a sidewalk café. The topic of conversation went numerous directions but eventually the subject turned to Lawal, and Smith, a man not loose with praise, remarked that, "Lawal was the only man in America who could beat Cael Sanderson."

Smith threw these words in Lawal's direction, and because the coach's words didn't come cheap, because they came from the source, because Lawal had to earn the flattery through years of work in the Stillwater wrestling room, through the meat grinder of the NCAA tournament, through sparring battles with Cormier, Mocco and Sanderson, it was significant. So Lawal nodded in silent acceptance but didn't say a word, didn't boldly raise his hands like he did to urge a foreign crowd after taking down his Russian opponent or yell into the air like he had after drilling an NCAA coach off the platform at the Olympic Trials, Lawal just nodded and didn't say a word as Smith continued on as the voice of assurance to the other dining mates, "This is the only guy in the country that can take Sanderson."

It went to show that Lawal was not some punk black athlete that some whites tended to write him off as. Lawal was not some attention-seeking prima donna. No, Lawal was a Schultz, a Jackson, a Smith, a silent gladiator who always wanted more.

Time Shaving
XLI

The U.S. Olympic wrestling team is killing time and the very thought of it doesn't make any sense. Every day, every practice, every match over the last four years is now down to killing time.

Kelly pedals aimlessly on the bike. Williams is getting stretched by the trainer. Cormier listens to rap music on his headphones. Abas is napping on the mat, preserving energy like the rest of the team. The athletes are battling to find the right balance of working out hard but smart, loading up but not overdoing, enjoying themselves, but not losing focus. They have spread out in much of the manner that any team or large family would at an airport, or a bus station, people who have been broken in and bonded to one another but now in the dead times went to find their own space. They sit on bags. They watch from seats. Nobody says or does much.

They had spent the prior evening sitting around the lobby of the Park Hotel playing Texas Hold Em' and watching Olympic highlights on a 22-inch T.V., but mostly anxiously waiting to compete. Some would read a book or hook up their video game consoles and burn a couple hours with Madden football but there was no way of escaping the thoughts of what the coming days would bring.

Their dreams are no longer those of a child. They were due to check into the Olympic Village in the afternoon and for the seven American wrestlers the Olympics were now very realistic. And in this practice room the Olympians are trying to 'seize the moment' before 'the moment' occurs. And right now that means killing time. The chirping and jabbering between wrestlers is gone. The cafeteria is nearly empty and most of the athletes who once filled its space have already competed. How they performed, how the Americans ran, sprinted, boxed, swam, synchronized, dived, balled, jousted, gyrated-flipped-twisted-turned, how each Olympian fared is tallied up by computer printouts that measure accomplishments the way they do in the Olympic Games: gold, silver, bronze.

The athletes' families arrive to the gym in the afternoon; Abas embraced his brothers Norman and Gerry while Guerrero greets his father and uncle by the entrance. The athletes are given total freedom to work on the mats or play basketball, but Joe Williams sticks with his sport. He fights with one hand held out high and the other down low, extending his arms out like a hawk displaying his wing span to its prey. Watching Williams, there are glimpses when the whole world seems attainable. This has been the lure of those trying to coach the former Iowa star, those trying to squeeze out his golden potential.

His exterior is pretty much unmovable. His hair is never long enough to get out of place, the length of the sides makes it seem like he has a barber fade it every three days. His expression is never rattled, when teammates attempt to trash talk with him, Williams just gives a half-smile and nods before going on with his business. He could snap, explode and pummel those with antagonizing words, but he seemed to have a principle that wouldn't allow a reaction to such things.

Williams heads to a side bench to keep his sweat going. Wearing dark blue jogging pants, a light gray sweater, and a plain black baseball cap pulled low on his head, he looks like an undercover cop passing off as a transient in a sting operation, rocking back and forth on the bench like a hobo huddled up against a shivering wind. Eight years removed from beginning the cycle to train for Sydney, Williams is now less than 48 hours away.

As he rocks back and forth at the apex of an eight-year buildup, it is hard to imagine how it will all turn out, which direction his Olympic dream will go. *Would Joe Williams finally attack with fearless abandon? Would he go after his opponents like never before? Would all his talent and ambition finally come through?* There is only one way Williams could leave this competition with his career justified and that's by having the gold medal placed around his neck.

The way he looked in the past week, how he went about his training in a machine-like manner, offered evidence of why he could soon have the gold. Twisting and ducking under his training partner with such a precise explosiveness that it was hard to imagine a better athlete, it was hard to envision a more prepared wrestler, watching Williams it was hard to conceive that any country in the world had created a better built specimen at 163-pounds.

***

As the early-round pool match-ups are finalized in Olympic meetings, the wrestlers are no longer distinguished by name, but instead by country; the Russian, the Cuban, the American. They are now representing their nation's colors and with that comes a sense of loyalty, obligation and duty. An emotional outburst could be viewed as a projection of a country's arrogance, good sportsmanship a symbol of its grace, a gold medal proof of its dominance; under the microscope of the world's eye the Olympians carry responsibilities bigger than themselves.

Money was spent, strength testing conducted daily, sport psychologists utilized, organizations built. Every angle has been covered, every precaution was taken. With the technical skill of John Smith and Zeke Jones, the motivation of Bobby Douglas, the intensity of Tom Brands, all under the watchful eye of Kevin Jackson, the coaching staff attempted to concoct the peak performance out of seven unique athletes, each having different psyches, backgrounds, physiques, abilities and needs. But now the staff would have to let their prized prospects go out on their own, they have done all they could.

Along the way, there had been trainers advising them, parents supporting them, opponents challenging them, training partners sharpening them, and at the end a four-year cycle, numerous USOC employees assisting the final, grand act. Athletic trainers at the ACG watch the big-screen televisions throughout the day with the same hopes that friends or family would have. Fans, confidants, lovers and others who knew their stories and the process that led them here. Others, International Olympic Committee big-wigs and the powers that be, tuned in with other motives, watching the way an agent eyes his ballplayer, knowing a gold medal could lead to a windfall of financial sponsorship.

While Olympic bids can be bought underneath the table and event judges can be swayed by power, there are certain things that don't have a price. Whatever their reason for watching, whatever ties and investments they have, however strong an influence they sway, it is not their moment. This moment belonged to the athlete.

"For what you do in life echoes in eternity."

-MAXIMUS ARELIUS, GLADIATOR

Olympia
XLII

The lobby of the Park Hotel slowly comes to life. Early morning sun creeps through an opening in the curtains and lights up the front doorway. Coffee and orange juice is set on dining tables. Slowly, as the morning carries on, members of Olympians' families come down the tile stairs while others emerge from the lone elevator by the front desk. Outside in the parking lot and throughout Athens, it is gray and quiet.

Inside, Guerrero and Kelly's families wear red, white and blue hats and T-shirts bearing their namesake. Abas' siblings move between the groups forging an easy camaraderie. McCoy's mother, radiant and outgoing, works her way between several tables, beaming with pride. As they pass the time eating pound cake and boiled eggs, as they sit on leather couches and converse, four families become one. Their hopes have become the group's hope, for the parents of the athletes, the roles had been reversed; with a child-like anticipation of Christmas morning, the adults can hardly wait to see what will unfold.

Meanwhile, on the outskirts of Athens, in the locker room at Ano Lorissa Olympic Hall, the Olympians arrive hours before the morning competition. The arena, built upon a vacant sandlot, stands out amid a barren Mediterranean landscape. A hot wind sweeps across the dry brush and sandy hillsides; small signs of plant life patch in the surroundings.

Wrestling appeared in a series of Egyptian wall paintings as many as 5000 years ago and when the Olympics began in 776 B.C., they included wrestling. When the Olympics returned to Greece after a 1500 year absence in 1896, organizers chose wrestling as one of the main sports. What was once a medival setting is now a pristine, state-of-the art facility equipped with all the modern amenities where flags of the world gently sway from the rafters in two neat rows, audio receptors hang from the ceiling, falling down halfway to the mats, two giant TVs record the athletes movements. While the venue of Olympic wrestling has changed over time, the sport has not. Back in the old world, in the most ancient of Olympic sports, the crowd is roaring.

"Hel-las! Hel-las! Hel-las!" The Greeks cheer for effort, for valiancy, the Greeks cheer for pure sport; a three-point move scored by their countrymen makes it too loud to think.

"LET'S GO KERRYYYY!" After debating, then waiting for this moment since Sydney, McCoy steps on mat, 9:48 a.m. Athens time. Wearing the light blue singlet with blue kneepad on his left leg, white on the right, he inhales and exhales while waiting for the opposition. Jackson takes his spot in the coaches' corner and leans against the blue waist-high platform.

Days before, the American wrestlers looked ordinary in college T-shirts and practice gear, but their uniforms as well as their presence have changed. McCoy moves onto the mats with a statesman's duty and quickly takes control. At the break, a stone-faced Jackson walks up the stage, clapping and wiping sweat from McCoy's upper body with a white towel. The U.S. coach cuts a figure of complete, utter confidence, displaying not a hint of worry and his muscular heavyweight conveys much of the same. This early-round domination was expected from the American heavyweight and international coaches assumed as much.

At the top of the stands, along the walkways, their video cameras are lined across the arena like railbirds in a pool hall staking out a future opponent. The foreigners watch, just as USA Wrestling officials watch; the Americans have three cameras recording, every move is scouted, everyone is spying eachother. McCoy's toughest test would come later, when he is expected to run into Artur Taymazov, the Uzbekistan heavyweight who had all the attraction of boxer Gorgeous George from *Snatch*: tall, bald, hairy and imposing, Taymazov looking like he had resided in a Soviet dungeon for the last several years, been thrown small animals to feast on and trained by pushing a tank up a mountain. But McCoy had not gotten to the world champion Taymazov yet, the American heavyweight still had business to take care of with his current opponent.

McCoy fights off a takedown while stilted on one leg. After several fruitless attempts to finish, his winded opponent releases his grip as time evaporates off the score clock. With his free hand the American clenches and points to his country's flag-waving section. He jogs past the media area and disappears at the end of the winding route to the locker room, Jackson shadowing every step of the way.

Up in the cheap seats, just below the rafters, Sergei Beloglazov is sitting among the fans. He wears a dark gray jumpsuit, but not a U.S. coaching warm-up that would signify his current coaching position. When Beloglazov runs into old friends he is quick with a smile and sure with his easy charm, but he looks out of place clutching a ticket to the sporting event he made his name at. He is easily distinguishable among the wrestling crowd, many eyes follow his path through the walkway and during his time in Athens, he will be honored at a dinner where he will be inducted into the FILA Wrestling Hall of Fame, but Beloglazov is not allowed down in the warm-up room like Jackson who is waiting next to Cael Sanderson who is shifting and kicking his legs out in anticipation.

He displays his blood rag to the ref, slips it back into his red singlet, shakes hands and drops to his stance as heads turn in the crowd. Sanderson's Belarusian opponent is long, lanky and thick-muscled, but stands flat-footed and moves with a crab-like defense: side-to-side, grip-ready, paranoid of any sudden movements.

Sanderson hunts the ankles, the Belarusian is neither quick nor nimble at moving his, and this is where the mismatch lies. He continues clubbing Sanderson in the head, but this is all he can do. He tries to counter, but he is too slow. He attacks and Sanderson bobs, weaves then re-attacks. Sanderson's opponent is left to stand, wait, then guess and this too is tardy; three takedowns leave it at 9-1. Despite his lead, there is not a look of pleasure on Sanderson's face, like an artist who isn't fully engaged, he does not enjoy the easy ones. Before leaving the mat, Sanderson glances at the American section where his three brothers, Cody, Cole and Cyler rise and cheer but Cael continues off the surface unemotionally. After arriving on one side, he exits through the other, past photographer's row, through the opening in a metal barrier decorated with Athenian decals, before being stopped for TV interviews; the glare of cameras following every match.

While Kelly, McCoy and Sanderson have relatively good draws for their pools, Abas is thrown to the sharks. He is paired with former Cuban world champ Rene Montero and Moldova's Ghenadie Tulbea who defeated him a year earlier. With no choice but to hunt or be hunted, Abas attacks immediately, hitting a quick low single, yanking up the right leg and rolling his opponent across his back for a 5-0 lead. *"Yeah! Yeah! Yeah!"*

Gerry Abas stands and yells, banging his hand against the metal railing at the foot of the stands. Abas is loose, prime, and ready; he is flowing. As Tulbea lowers to shoot, Abas' head is there to meet him; when he charges, Abas rides his force out of bounds; down in parterre, his opponent lifts Abas up in the wheelbarrow position, Abas kicks out-then in, teetering and shifting his balance on the brink of allowing points before falling safely to the mat. Abas' eyes, narrow and focused, don't make their way up to the stands as he walks off in victory, hardly breathing.

None of the U.S. wrestlers has time to enjoy the other's victories as the afternoon moves quickly; one American after another comes out of the tunnel. The building is clearing out by the moment, but several American supporters make their way to mat three where Jamill Kelly competes amid an emptying arena. In a poker sense, Kelly has been dealt a good hand with his tournament draw, now it comes down to how he plays it. He attacks in, but is reluctant to commit and backs out. Scoreless at the break, they go to the clinch. John Smith leans over to the edge of the mat as they lock hands.

If the lock breaks, Kelly loses. If the lock breaks, he will drown in his pool competition. If the lock breaks, the Olympics are over for Kelly. So the lock cannot break. That would make everything leading up to it a waste. Kelly leans in, grips his fingers together and swears they will not come apart. His opponent cannot keep the grip and Kelly's hand is raised. The American's Olympics are not over yet; he nods silently as he leaves the mat.

During the second session of the day, the gaps in the seats that existed in the first round begin to fill up. Abas' coach, Dennis Dellido, is on the top of the first row, howling down at the mat with his hoarse voice. Neither wrestler is ready to strike, each circling patiently in the center. The Cuban puts Abas down in par-terre and turns him for two points. Abas' chest is pressed against the mat as he army crawls to the perimeter with the Cuban latched on top.

Dellido tugs on the metal barriers, cringing and gyrating, touching down on his seat before shooting upright again as if the chair was a hot stove. Abas is in serious trouble. Down 3-0 with a minute left, Montero, with a hand ready, is already on the defensive, poaching for a mistake. Family members chant in the stands but if fades as fast as it begins and Montero is not budging from his dominant position. Stalling is called, the Cuban is put down on the mat, but the American cannot turn him. 31 seconds remain. Abas charges after Montero, faking, shooting, adjusting, finishing and cutting the lead to one and with 15 seconds left, Abas hijacks the match. Wrapping his arms around Montero's midsection, Abas gut wrenches him slowly and with one last push, flips him over the mat for two points.

Dellido jumps out of his seat and bangs on the barrier. Gerry leans over the railing and screams at his younger brother; the American flag, once lifeless, whips violently in his hands. Riding an adrenaline cocktail of triumph Abas gets up bug-eyed and points both fists to the stands as the Cuban sits stunned on his knees.

As he walks off, a familiar voice breaks through. *"Stephen!"* Dellido yells. *"Stephen!"* Abas looks up as he goes down the steps, smiles slyly through a red mouthpiece, and winks at his college coach before heading to the media section. Montero exits slowly, unsure of existence, with the look of someone who was pick-pocketed in broad daylight.

***

Kerry McCoy shakes Greg Strobel's hand and heads out for his last pool match. Kevin Jackson is on another mat and this, in addition to the fact that McCoy was bumped out of scheduled order to compete, seems to have distracted the American heavyweight.

Strobel tried to ignore this because if McCoy were to advance from here only two more wins were needed to wrestle for the gold. Two more wins and McCoy can quiet his detractors. Two more wins and his Sydney defeat will be a distant memory. But first he has to get by Marid Mutalimov, a wrestler McCoy pounded 5-0 at the 2003 World Championships. McCoy, looks bigger, better, stronger and faster than his Kazakhstan opponent. Mutalimov is pale-faced and bushy-haired, owning a stomach that sticks out further than his chest. If anybody looks the part of Olympic champ, it is McCoy. But Strobel does not see a good omen as McCoy settled into his wrestling stance. "He was nervous." Strobel would say later. "He was all nerves."

Therein lies a principle of wrestling. Coaches cannot substitute or trade one Olympian for another on a bad day. McCoy is America's Olympian and he earned his spot by proving he was good enough. But being good enough to win is not always sufficient, while being good enough in the moment always is. Strobel has no control over how McCoy wrestles. Only McCoy does. And McCoy is all nerves.

Up 1-0, it seems to be only a matter of time before McCoy's ability takes over the match, but this rush never comes. He is tentative, the opening never opens and while Murtalimov is not the athlete McCoy is, what he gives up to the American in power is replaced by grit, what he lacks in skill is made up for in tactics, what he looks like isn't what he is. McCoy's attacks are met with fingers in his eyes and his movements are slowed by the pulling of his singlet. With McCoy's slightest hesitation, Mutalimov is able to remain evasive of his more athletic counterpart, but no additional stalling points are called and when McCoy finally gets a hold of him, Mutalimov has a grip as well.

As they lock in the clinch, Murtalimov, the post-Soviet stock of 250-pounds and McCoy, America's best big man for the last eight years, each was on the cusp of Olympic glory, each man spoke different languages, loved different women, ate different foods but was now locking, clinching, and connecting their selfish desires together. Because this was a selfish sport, each man wanted to win by himself, lose by himself, wanted glory for himself and had to be selfish to train when others were boozing, selfish to run when others were relaxing, each were now locking their ambitions that had encapsulated most of their lives, locking their purpose of achieving glory, realizing ambition, boosting ego, gaining sponsorship, greed, power, might, fueled by redemption or rage or whatever drove their genes to spend eight years, ten years, half their life on a padded mat, run along lonely roads in bags of sweats, crisscross their separate countries in search of men who could test them, push them, beat them, yes, both Murtalimov and McCoy had hunted these things out from New York to Pennsylvania to across the United States, from Kazakhstan to Russian to across the Post-Soviet states, because McCoy and Murtalimov's both wanted the struggle, the fight, the battle like any ambitious young soldier wants war and because of that choice, because the whistle had blown and the ill-fated tango had begun, each wrestler was now subject to chance, susceptible to defeat, all these things were going on within the circle and the people who knew them, loved them and hated them from the stands knew this, felt this and were cheering for and against this, but this couldn't be going through McCoy's nor Murtalimov's mind because on the mat, one can't daydream, one can't philosiphize, one... *"OOAAHHHHHH!!"*

The two heavyweights crash to the surface as the crowd rockets from its seats. McCoy attempts to swing his momentum over, but there is no escaping. Desperately trying to reach his stomach, a look of disgust fills the American's face as half his body is pressed onto the mat. It's too late. McCoy is on his back. He has lost three points. His Olympics are over.

Mutalimov rises on one knee and pounds his fist to the crowd, kneeling over McCoy like a hunter over a conquered beast. There will be no Sydney redemption, even the bronze is out of reach. Second best in the world the previous September, McCoy is only second best in his pool in Athens. He runs off with head tilted downward, barreling through the media section, brushing off reporters with a sweep of the hand and disappearing into the locker room.

Back in Bethlehem, Pennsylvania many of the Lehigh athletes McCoy coached would learn of his defeat through the detached view of a computer screen. The official scoring will read 5-4 in favor of Kazakhstan but it will not show the work McCoy put in to get to this match. It will not show Stobel following McCoy's wake into the locker

room, walking slowly pained with his defeat. It will only show that McCoy wasn't good enough on this day for the gold medal.

***

The chants have begun. The drum beats are ceaseless. Gypsy music blares from speakers. At random junctures, fans from France, Germany and Hungary spring from their seats before meshing into the mass of bodies again. While others cheer in spurts for their countrymen's matches, the Iranian's whistle and chant non-stop.

"Toot-toot-toot-IRAN!"

Majod Khodaei, walks out as his countrymen sing. Cael Sanderson is facing the Iranian, but it sounds as if he is battling their entire country.

"Toot-toot-toot-IRAN!"

Khodaei plays the edge of the circle and takes a 5-3 lead with little time left. Khodeai slows his pace, making the clock seemingly move faster, the seconds more precious. The Iranian's game plan, to camp at the perimeter of the mat and sit on his lead, is working perfectly.

The American coaches yell frantically from the corner, but only Sanderson can change this. There is no time to think, no time to dwell on the refs, the crowd, or the score which all seem to be working against him. Down two points with time evaporating, Sanderson has to go. The American shoots in and clutches the leg, reins it in near the edge and cuts the score to 5-4. Turning the corner, he attacks again, but is rebuffed by Khodeai, who lingers near the out of bounds line. Calls for stalling against the Iranian ring out but they are not aknowledged by the officials.

On the mat sprawled flat, Sanderson hooks in his arm under Khodaei, who is clutching onto Sanderson's limbs as if they were a life preserver. But it is the American who has reason to fear for his sporting life at a point in the match where his lungs were screaming like the insides of an insane asylum, but he digs, pulls, tugs at the bracing of the lock with the urgency of a man tied to the tracks of an oncoming train, the press of time bearing down on him, barreling towards him, ready to kill his gold medal hopes. With defeat closing in by the seconds, Sanderson muscles the grip free and spins behind for the score.

Sanderson forces overtime, then he ends it. When Sanderson shoots again at his opponent's ankle, the Iranian is too exhausted to fully react, falling backwards at the edge, ending the match. Sanderson breaks, the jaw cracks, the blank expression changes, Sanderson flexes and points to American crowd. He pumps his fist and smacks his hands together. Sanderson is showing emotion. Sanderson is engaged. He walks off elated by his 6-5 quarterfinal victory.

In the semis, Sanderson is set to meet Cuba's Yoel Montero who is on the mats shortly after Sanderson has disappeared into the locker room. Built like an NFL safety, Montero is muscular, quick, experienced and every bit the athlete Sanderson is. Some coaches in the arena feel that the Cuban is on the downside of his career, but at the moment it is hard to tell. He remains a deft scrambler, making up for careless mistakes and sloppy technique with god-given athletic ability.

The fans attempts to will a Greek wrestler to victory, but when he raises his level, Romero takes it to a new one. Like a pool hustler plotting the eight ball, Romero trades shot for shot, never fully committing, at one point holding off on a finish only for the sake of keeping the action going. As the Greek battles he leaves himself open and it's only a matter of time before Romero chooses any number of finishes. The Cuban sticks his shot, hitting the Greek's exhausted body across the smooth surface until balance is no longer on his companion, finally sinking down in the corner. Romero ends the drama, silences the noise and reveals what he knew all along. While the Greek was immersed in the game, the Cuban was running it.

Romero helps the Greek to his feet, pats him on the head and kisses him on the cheek. On his way to the center, Romero allows himself a sly smile. Then the Cuban raises the Greek's hand as the ref raises his own in victory; keep friends close, but enemies closer.

The U.S. wrestlers are done. It has been a good day, a great one even. Three are in the semi-finals and Guerrero, Williams and Cormier have yet to begin. Other than the defeat at heavyweight, the U.S. record is perfect. But McCoy's loss hung in the air and when he emerged from the locker room after his loss, he was solemn and definitive about the end of his career. "I know I'm done wrestling. So I can enjoy life a little bit and not have to put up with stuff anymore. I guess it's not in God's plan for me to be an Olympic champion."

Shortly after 8 p.m., in a crowded hallway between a staircase and snack stand at the top of the arena steps, the Sanderson family congregates. Ten have made the trip to Athens with the aide of money raised in Utah. Their faces light up as Cael, tallest of the group, arrives and casually embraces his wife Kelly. For this is what they have come to know. Cael, rising to the occasion against pressure, opponents and history, whatever is thrown his way. In the end, despite how much he played the edge, how loud his county's chants became, how much the calls, the clock went his way, the Iranian was defenseless against the American will.

But tomorrow is a new day, bringing new opponents, two of whom Sanderson has never beaten, but his family continues to enjoy the moment for what it is, smiling as they depart together.

With the last match completed, the wrestling crowd climbs the steps and spills out into the warm summer evening. The sun is all but gone, the moon rising for its shift. Transporation awaits the competitors and fans just outside the arena gates. Twelve hours from now, three Americans will return with their golden aspirations still intact.

"Gold is tried by fire, brave men by adversity."

-SENECA, ROMAN PHILOSOPHER

August 28
XLIII

By car, metro and bus they arrive, packing into Ano Lorissa Olympic Hall. Across the arena, media settle into work stations; flipping open laptops. Conversations in various languages are drowned out by rock music. The VIP seating is beginning to fill with Armani suits and flashy sport coats.

The first Olympian ever from Harvey, Illinois takes to the mats. Clean-shaven and with his fingers-tapped around the bridges, Joe Williams, slow and steady, baits his opponent in before rushing forward in a blur, slamming the Georgian to the mat. The American is too quick for Gela Saghirashvili, he is making it look easy; another two points puts him up by four. The second period hardly matters, Williams is too good for this. He wins like he should and advances like predicted; Williams is one step closer to the unknown.

Shortly thereafter, Daniel Cormier wastes little time with an Austrian. He spins behind to score as Abas and Sanderson square off with opponents on the other two mats.

Three mats.

Three countries.

Three battles being waged.

The Americans will win.

The Americans will dominate.

The Americans can't be stopped.

At this point, many fans assume Sanderson's journey to end in a fairy tale, even the Governor of Utah has expectations of such, but stories get twisted on a wrestling mat, it's not like writing, wrestlers don't get a second chance to rewrite the script, which is quite clear watching Romero takedown Utah's favorite son for a 1-0 lead. Romero moves with the graceful assurance of those who were physically superior to all they crossed. He has prevailed over Sanderson both times they have met, each win by a point and in their third match he has the quick advantage.

Sanderson scores at the end of the period to tie it at the break. Knowing Romero is likely to tire, Sanderson begins to move nonstop in the final period. Faking, shifting, dropping and shooting another takedown. Lost in a state of heightened intensity, in the dimension where ambition and talent merge, Sanderson keeps going, keeps attacking, mindless of the previous encounters with Romero as if they never occurred, his legs are tremendous pistons, the product of lung blistering runs up 14,000-foot Pikes Peak Mountain in Colorado Springs, evident in the slices of muscle tissue that trace his thigh and calf, Sanderson is constantly moving, inevitably exposing himself in a free-flowing state of attack; the catch is to see if Romero can keep up.

Sanderson finishes a takedown, the one he had finished on Hartung after every practice as if it was his sworn duty, to make it 3-1. After breaking Romero with a third score, Sanderson withstands the Cuban's desperation assaults. As the clock cements his victory, Sanderson rolls backwards to the mat and points his fingers upward as his training partner Tim Hartung also raises his arms in triumph.

***

Throughout the proceedings, as he walks out for his matches, Jamill Kelly tries to block out the Olympic atmosphere. Kelly wants to treat it like any other tournament because the more he thinks, the worse he wrestles. He centers his focus. He stares straight ahead, thinking only of the match at hand. He doesn't look at the Olympic rings that tattoo every wall. He ignores the hordes of cameramen and shuts out the crowd. But now, as the Russian gold medal favorite waits for him to arrive on the third mat of the Olympic arena floor, there can be no diffusing the situation.

Makhach Murtazaliev's face is pale and bloodless, his eyes dark and deep. He had a sneer that suggested that he knew he was better than Kelly, and he certainly had the evidence to prove it. He has already handled Kelly once, taking him out 3-0 in Russia. He won the European championships by defeating a three-time world champion and he has just taken out Iran's Ali-Reza Dabir, the 2000 Olympic champ, with the potency of a young talent who knows few limits. It was time for the young Russian to get his due, and the American with no name was his only hurdle.

At the Yarygin in Siberia, Kelly learned the young Russian star's tactics. He knew Murtazaliev's offense was to score on top and Kelly knew he had to stay out of bad positions. Kelly also knew if he wrestled nearly perfect, he had a chance. As passionate Russian wrestling fans settle into their seats, their comrade Murtazaliev patiently waits to strike. He makes slow, deliberate movements on the hunt for an opening, but Kelly matches him forehead-to-forehead, hand-to-hand and calmly holds position as the first period ends.

When they lock in the clinch, Murtazaliev quickly whips around for a headlock but Kelly slips out to score the first point. *"Stay calm!"* Smith shouts from the American corner. *"Stay in good position!"* And that's exactly what Kelly does. Put down for passivity, halfway through Murtazaliev's attempt to turn him, Kelly steps over and stops the move. In the front headlock, Murtazaliev grips Kelly around the chin, cutting his air supply short, but fails to score. Kelly is just as strong as the favored Russian, his movements just as quick. Smith digs his elbows into the platform while the anxious Russian coaches continue checking the clock, each passing second playing into the American's hand. *"Right where we want it!"* Jackson calls out to Kelly before overtime. *"Right where we want it!"*

Murtazaliev forces Kelly out of the circle to tie the score. In the next exchange, he looks to finish the match, but in a frantic scramble for position, Kelly relies upon a technique he has not used since his freshman year in high school and exposes the Russian as they flip. In the American corner, Smith and Jackson are jumping and yelling to Kelly. *"Act like you won! Act like you won!"*

But something's not right. The ref grabs Murtazaliev's hand and motions for Kelly to join. Kelly backs away from the hasty sentencing that awaits him in the center and unable to accept the verdict, gestures toward the head table to petition in defiance of the mat referee.

The arena is a chorus of cheers and jeers, whistles and insults and appears one controversial call away from an old-fashioned sporting riot. Russian fans are clutching and shaking the metal railing, appearing ready to rush the officials table. American fans are just as unsteady. After a tense review, in which the divided arena voices its decisions; the Greeks siding with the American, the Russians with Murtazaliev, "KELLY WINNER" flashes across the corner scoreboard.

Murtazaliev wilts to the knees as the ref holds his wrist. Kelly charges to the corner, jumps into Jackson's arms and pounds his fist in the air. Venomous boos mix with cheers. A Russian official continues to argue with the head ref as Murtazaliev desperately turns in every direction for help that will never come. His face quickly turns to anger. He rips off his blue shoulder strap, curses at the ref and refuses to shake hands with Kelly. The Russian coaches storm the mat in protest. Kelly bounds away, vanishing from the scene clutching the back of his head incredulously, victory in hand, medal assured, doubters silenced.

***

Eric Guerrero was smug in the face of defeat, he simply refused to accept it and that's how he carried himself on the mat. And it worked. Guerrero rarely lost and he has had as much success throughout his career as any other member of the U.S. team.

Over the years he had walked into arenas, competitions like the NCAA championships where legends are made in this sport, and dominated. Guerrero had thrashed opponents whose careers had made them heroes in their hometowns, known throughout several cities, had put their names on their college gymnasium wall but, Guerrero had dismissed these challengers like a beating from an older brother, had made them feel like fools on the mat, had given their athletic self-esteem a harsh reality check in six minutes of action or less.

Guerrero had done this in San Jose, throughout California and the whole United States, from high school to college, wearing the patriotic colors of Independence High to the black and orange of OSU, and now full-circle with the red-white and blue for America. But Guerrero had not been able to blitz international competition, and something was off about this, something was amiss and needed to be fixed because the best in the U.S. usually put one on par with the best in the world and Guerrero had certainly tapped out the States, but overseas his dominance didn't carry over.

The U.S. coaches came up with their separate correctable reasons and while Guerrero spoke with reassurance leading up to Athens that it was his time to shine, repeating these positive thoughts in his head, in the arena, competing on the Olympic surface for which Guerrero always seemed destined, things were starting to unravel, the dreams, the goals, all of it was coming apart like a teenager that took years to nurture, and grow but now lay paralyzed by a stray bullet fired in the night.

The dream was dying out there, out before his proud family. After preparing in America and crossing the Atlantic by flight, Guerrero's actually here, trying to pull it out like so many other times before but he's down by a point, can't get a damn thing going, time's leaving him and his Mongolian opponent is not offering favors.

Guerrero had walked on confidently, bobbing his head in anticipation but at the sound of the whistle, the Mongolian Olympian ran him off the mat for the quick lead. The Guerrero family, spread across two rows of seats, watched from across the arena, taking pictures and recording the action with their video cameras; one cousin puts down his binoculars and yells across the arena, *"Stay with him Eric!"*

But at the break they are silent. His father and uncle have their hands on their heads while others cross their arms in frustration. Throughout the years they had answered countless questions to those who had caught a glimpse of Eric's career: 'How is Eric doing? How's his training going? When's he going to bring home gold? And because of this his family has a stake in his success as well. They have been there for all of it. The van rides to local freestyle tournaments, the CIF championships, the NCAAs that he dominated as an OSU Cowboy.

As the match wears on, momentum swings to the Mongolian's favor and the pressure to score saddles Guerrero. His opponent, a two-time

Olympic silver medalist, knows what cards the American is holding and anticipates his play. Guerrero needs to gamble for the big score but the Mongolian's defense grows tighter. *"Get him!"* the American section calls out. *"Get him!"*

One uncle removes his hat, leans back and scratches his head. Guerrero is not bouncing like he was in practice. He is not attacking like he did against his training partner leading up to the Games.

Then the American revives hope with a takedown. Now all he needs is a point to tie it. The Guerrero's believe again, because Eric has always been able to pull these out. In high school and college, he was king of the close ones, always finding a way to win. At NCAAs, at U.S. Nationals, this is how any great wrestler makes his mark, and Guerrero has always been a great wrestler.

While Guerrero's athletic talent didn't grant him a million dollar contract, it did create an opportunity for family members to witness the Olympics, something that they never could have foreseen the day Eric started competing. Such things involved many factors beyond the natural ability and fire which Guerrero possessed. It required going against stellar high school competition while still in middle school. It demanded the type of work ethic that had him skipping rope right after a draining NCAA match, not because his coach told him to, because he wanted to. But now the Guerrero family was in Athens twisting and turning with such intertwined desires, their chants part hope and desperation, nerves and anticipation, their cheers riding on the fragile precipice of glory and failure, that Eric's every move on the mat was a puppet master to their emotions.

In overtime, in the clinch, Guerrero makes six attempts to score: a foot-sweep, a throw-by, leg-attacks that didn't connect, desperately trying to will his way through, looking for something, anything to prevent defeat. With one big move Guerrero can win the match so his uncles clap and lurch forward with renewed hope as the wrestlers embrace, but the lock slips, a move must be scored, something must happen...*and...and...*the Guerreros slide down in their seats as if witnessing a car wreck, not wanting to see, but unable to look away.

No one looked sharper in the last week of training camp, no one seemed more prepared for success throughout their career, but in this cruel and unforgiving sport, it didn't matter. Not to the press who was already on the hunt for its next story, nor the opponent who is having his hand raised in victory. Blood coats Guerrero's lip as he exits the mat, but the lip isn't what is hurting him, the pain of defeat is the only thing thats real.

Six Minutes For Eternity
XLIV

Olympic event workers carry out the medal stands and place them on mat three; first the gold platform, then the silver and bronze. Everything is set; all that is left to be determined is who would stand where.

In the bowels of the arena, beyond view of the crowd, the wrestlers wait in divided packs of six. Two coaches and an athlete line each side, standing on the top of a thin-grey mat surrounded by blank white walls. The competitors walk out first, the two coaches follow. Then the groups split. The coaches sit below the edge of the mat, the grapplers part and climb up the steps, onto the platform and into the eyes of the world.

Abas meets his adversary Mavlet Batirov, a fresh-faced Russian with hair hanging over his ears, on the center mat. Abas is six years older than Batirov and looks just that. He is a fist taller and has a beard forming while his counterpart looks like he never owned a razor. The announcers formally introduce the wrestlers to the crowd, but there would be no introductions necessary on the mat.

Abas defeated Batirov 3-2 in New York at the 2003 World

Championships and he looked just as confident as each lined up in formation for the gold-medal match in Athens. But it is apparent that the Russian feels just as good about his chances, because for an instant, both athletes and the American coach, Abas, Batirov and Jones, look up in unison at their countries flag on the north end of the arena and in their faces, in their eyes, it is clear, that despite the language barrier, the clashing cultures, the continental divide, the Russian and the American are thinking the exact same thing. The American is sure of his place as Olympic champion. The Russian believes only six minutes stand between him and the gold.

Abas attacks in, clutching and twisting Batirov's leg before discarding it and backing out in a flash. When he strikes again, Batirov goes with it, scrambling-holding-waiting-baiting for position and when the Russian finds the hold he wants, the American goes flying head over heels. Two minutes into it, Abas is already down three and the chants from his countrymen are drowned out by those for the Russian.

"BA-TI-ROV! BA-TI-ROV!"

Batirov counters two consecutive shots so smoothly it appears choreographed. His flow is disrupted, but Abas keeps attacking. He bursts in deep on the leg, Batirov counters, Abas backs out. They badger back and forth, neither preserving energy nor tactics, trading violent exchanges for several seconds. The slabs and jabs and half-fisted punches that are thrown do not count on the scorecard, but they are taking a toll on their own. Abas strikes at Batirov who crouches low in a position he seems to be looking for and he heaves Abas up and over for two more points.

"BA-TI-ROV! BA-TI-ROV!"

Abas makes a living slithering out of holds, but is caught and trapped by Batirov as Jackson begins to pace anxiously behind Jones; the deficit grows to 7-1. As the points pile on and the crowd grows stronger, louder, unable to return to its seats, the Russian, seizing his moment, appears to transform before the crowd. Boyish-looking during introductions with a haircut made fashionable by *The Beatles*, Batirov is now confidently gathering in the surroundings, hands on hips, his powerful chest heaving in and out, appearing to draw strength from all around as a trainer patched the flesh wound on the American's head.

"BA-TI-ROV! BA-TI-ROV!"

The stands are filled with hearty men wearing Russian blue shirts, many of whom are former wrestlers who once competed on a world-class level, and they applaud Batirov as if the fate of their country depends on it.

"BA-TI-ROV! BA-TI-ROV!"

Each score is followed by a roar from his countrymen and Soviet Blocs alike, as well as anybody else who desires to cheer against the U.S. Batirov becomes more powerful, his holds and moves more fierce, never relenting until the bout becomes his, punctuating his dominance with pounding forearms across Abas' face and fish-hooking his fingers into the American's eye and nose.

One point from a tech fall, Batirov gets up with a look of tasting blood. From every corner of the arena, whistles and chants rain down and his coaches, double in size and age, hoist him closer to the crowd, closer to the gods, to the highest level any wrestler could reach, as the Russian lives a moment few competitors will ever know. At the age of 20, Adam Batirov, on this day and for the rest of his years, is an Olympic champion.

One of the men who knew the Abas best, watches as he walks down the steps alone, disappearing into the nearest tunnel. "I've never seen that happen to Stephen," his training partner Yero Washington says calmly from the stands. "He got beat."

"As I walk through the valley of the shadow of death
I will fear no evil."

-PSALM 23:4

Twisted Fate
XLV

Imagine walking into an arena where nearly everyone wants you to lose. Imagine walking into an Olympic atmosphere after once being a youth athlete who used to ride the back of the school bus and study your opponents to the point where your high school coaches wonder if you have envy, wonder if you're paying them too much respect, but you keep analyzing the competition anyway because you want to know, you want to be prepared, even though these are not titanic monsters of the mats, but rather adolescent teenagers from Ceres, Modesto and Escalon, small towns peppered across California's San Joaquin Valley, kids from high schools in your local area, kids that have been competing long before you and because of their experience you feel they have an edge, in fact, you give them that edge and it costs you, it cost you a higher state placing, its cost you the recognition that teenagers crave, it cost you the big-time athletic scholarship because you weren't a CIF state champion, didn't even win your sectional tournament that you knew you had the talent for, because there's a part of you that didn't fully trust in yourself nor your ability to brush aside whoever the competition was.

So you end up in some shithole town in the upper reaches of the

California state, in a place whose borders could not contain your talent, but you were as tied to two years in Lassen as the local prisoners were to their sentence, because the coaching and competition at Lassen College is legit as a juco gets and you need academic units in the classroom and you need to prove yourself on the mat. So you handle business, keep your nose clean, and mop up the NJCAA ranks, get your name out there as a national runner up to go along with earning sufficient grades and then Oklahoma State comes calling, John Smith is offering an opportunity for success that few could, and finally you've made it, you're a Cowboy, and within the next year you head into NCAA's top-ranked, top-flight shape with the all the required physical skills to slay a beast of a tournament, but perhaps lacking the head for it, you but don't even place at the NCAA championship, you never earn the All-American status that seems to come naturally to anyone who is a starter for OSU, you're labeled a head case and the doubts about your place in the sport after college are strong. Few believe in you, your coach does though, John Smith believes you got what it takes to be a successful freestyler even though your weight class is jammed with eight former NCAA champs, proven winners, guys who did what you didn't and some twice over, but Smith's word counts, so you stick with his program and ignore the rest.

You stay in Stillwater and keep training, and after a year or two of uneven results, you arrive at the U.S. World Team Trials and all your talent and speed and mental toughness comes together in a situation where it usually fell apart, and you knock off all those bastards that did what you failed to accomplish before, three former NCAA champions, Bono-McIlravy-Zadick, beat them down in two days, and people look at you different, have more respect when they say your name now that your're the world team member, but you fail at Worlds, get smoked, not winning a match and the doubts about you resurface and remain up and through U.S. Nationals and the Olympic Trials, but you show em' again in Indy, you show the United States who's boss at 145-pounds, you earn the Olympic slot but the media disregards your medal ambitions, one calling you the step-child of an Olympic Team filled with multiple NCAA champions, but you're here anyway, at the Games in Athens, and the American weight class of 145-pounds is called in the arena, across the airwaves, loud enough for the world to hear.

"FROM THE UNITED STATES OF AMERICA..."

But the devil of doubt creeps back and you have to smash it again as the eyes of Ano Lorissa Olympic Hall descend upon you as you cross an arena floor where glory was to be had, yes these were the gates to Olympic eternity and you have to put doubts in their place otherwise they'd prevent your ability from taking over. You hear your name, it lingers after the announcer calls it off, and with a raise of the hand you step forward identifying yourself, your country, that you are the challenger for the Olympic gold, that you are one of the last two men standing, not one of those guys like Dane Bettencourt that beat you back in high school for the section title, not some wrestler from Oklahoma that knocked you off in college, but now in a moment that will define you, your place in the sport that is your life, it's not about a wrestling match anymore, the next six minutes are about immortality.

And you got here because you beat that damn Russian in the semi's that was supposed to beat you, beat him cold, no matter how much his powerful sporting delegation protested and tried to alter the ruling, and you sprinted off the mat, floated off really, as the arena booed with venom in their voices, spewing profanities in a foreign language while you were giddy with a victory that must have seemed so unfathomable to your high school coach Paul Bristow who is sitting in the Olympic stands, the one with the scratchy voice and reading glasses that recalls you fondly as a skinny 95-pound Atwater high school freshman, but a decade later you've grown into a perfectly symmetrical Olympian who doesn't look anything but.

You're fast and strong and coached by the best, but that matters little in an arena that is full of athletes who look like the world's greatest, because it's what's inside the head that will actually crown you one. But there's still a part of you that knows too much about your opponent, in this case the heavy favorite Elbrus Tedeyev of Ukraine, a three-time champion of the world who is waiting to meet you on the mat, waiting to beat you for the gold, the guy whose leg-lace technique you're familiar with, because you're still prepared, you're still curious, so you scouted everything that Tedeyev did. You watched videotape. You hatched a plan. But a part of you still has doubts in the moment and if you can understand that then you can understand what Jamill Kelly was feeling as he steps back in line after being introduced for the Olympic gold-medal match.

John Smith turns to Kelly and smiles easily, patting him on the back as if to diffuse the pressure and somehow make things normal. For Smith it was. He had come and conquered the Olympics twice and looked so casually at ease in this situation, wearing a polo shirt and khakis that one might have thought he was out golfing.

But there was no downplaying it in Kelly's head. This is what he had dreamed about and there were no guarantees he would ever be here again. Years of training and a four-year buildup can prepare one for it, but winning the Games is about winning the moment.

As the match begins, Kelly knows what Tedeyev is going to do, but that didn't stop him from doing it anyway. Over a minute in, he turns Kelly twice, gaining an early 3-0 lead. On the edge, the Ukrainian cradles Kelly's head and leg together and nearly tosses him out of the circle. Chants come and go but Smith's voice cut through the clamor. Kelly knows what his coach is telling him to do, but while his mind says yes, his body says no and the Olympic atmosphere finally catches up to Kelly; instead of competing to win, Kelly wrestles not to lose.

He doesn't attack. He doesn't set-up. He waits and by the time he scores on a double-leg, it is too little-too late as he trails 5-1. The Ukrainian is too good, too experienced for a letdown in his third Olympics and is quickly dancing over the mats. Kelly, like Abas, leaves immediately past a row of photographers who no longer find interest in capturing him. They shoot the joyous Tedeyev instead, who grabs the gold Ukrainian flag and sidesteps around the mat, fanning it up and down like he was trying to ignite a flame.

Shortly thereafter, Abas emerges from the locker room in his warm-ups. Abas takes his place on the medal stand and waves to the crowd, long enough to acknowledge the American fans but brief enough to not acknowledge satisfaction. Minutes later, Kelly takes his turn. Once second in his high school section, Kelly is now second-best in the world, but the American tightens his jaw and stands dispassionately during the proceedings because he is too angry to realize where he is. Kelly can't escape the frozen-up nervous feeling he had on the mat and knows he could have done more; he feels he let everybody down. It wasn't until he saw John Smith smiling and clapping like a dad reassuring a son that Kelly realizes what he accomplished. After listening to the gold medalist's national song, the athletes make their way around the arena. Fans throw flowers and the athletes halt at each corner to receive applause. At the last turn, they walk under an exit and head for drug testing that takes place behind closed doors.

***

In ancient Greece, athletes were immortalized by statues, paintings and poet's descriptions. Now, they are digitally photographed and their images are printed in papers throughout the world; their feats instantly recorded, downloaded, and replayed on web sites that were modern day time capsules. But for Sanderson, the subject of many great athletic feats in the past, he has to be engaged in the beauty of the sport, in its holds and maneuvers, attacks and counters, in its complex strategies that he has mastered at every level, this is simply the highest peak.

Sanderson is an athlete who has the genius of being in the present. When his streak began to grow and take a life of its own at Iowa St., Sanderson's opponents were aware that stepping on the mat with him was tangling with potential greatness, if they could derail Sanderson, their name would hang in the air long after they disappeared from the scene much like Larry Owings did after defeating Gable in 1970. Many embraced the challenge, but no one could do anything about it because over 159 NCAA matches Sanderson was that focused, that skilled, that good.

One lucky hold, one well executed move and a wrestling match can be over. Winning requires a channeled aggression, precision technique, excellent positioning; a tight-wire balance of the physical maneuvering. Russian gold medal favorite Sajid Sajidov's loss earlier in the day had to do with getting caught in a wrong position, choked out in a front headlock, and the man who took advantage of it was the lone thing standing between Cael Sanderson and the gold medal.

At McQ's sports bar in Indiana, a place Sanderson has never heard of, never gone to and probably never will, the volume is turned up and the American chants begin. In Heber City, Utah the local faithful that had known and witnessed Sanderson over the years watched with pride and hope. In Athens, with Dan Gable watching, with John Smith watching, with everyone in the arena watching, Cael Sanderson walks out for the gold-medal match.

NICHOLAS HOPPING

Thousands of eyes follow Sanderson as he climbs the platform, but they did not witness the work that has gone into his success. He had run to the top of Pikes Peak Mountain, taking 14,000-feet not all at once, but one step at a time. He had spent time in the room before and after the scheduled practice repeating monotonous technique. By virtue of his preparation beforehand, Sanderson has insured himself that he was going to win.

Shifting back and forth during the introductions, Sanderson lightly kicks out each foot and glances at the scoreboard. He slaps Douglas' hand, then Jackson's, and steps on to face Evi Jae Moon of Korea. The Korean fans stand and begin to beat drums as their wrestler scores first, but in the ensuing struggle Sanderson swiftly flips him on his back, and takes a lead he will not relinquish. And if the story is reading anti-climatic it's only because the moment was. In Athens who could deny the inevitable result, an athlete of Sanderson's caliber couldn't be bet against; a Jordan, Montana, Zidane or Messier of sport.

The last minute El-Moon hardly attempts a shot and all the excitement that remains is to see how the American will react. *Will Sanderson be like an Olympic sprinter bursting across the finish line? Or a gymnast upon hearing the final tallying of their scores? A pure, unadulterated moment of joy that overcomes athletes at the pinnacle of accomplishment?* But somehow Sanderson holds it in because he has wrestled this match before, back in Wasatch where news of his triumph will spread like wildfire, and in Ames where he went to college and never lost and now finally in Athens where Jackson and Douglas burst onto the mat to embrace Sanderson who moves slowly, awestruck, before raising his arms in triumph. Jackson and Douglas lift Sanderson by the waist and into the air, three Cyclones merging on the mat, equal parts of relief, awe, and fulfillment coming together.

During the medal ceremony, he bashfully waves to the crowd while fidgeting with the olive wreath that was placed on his head. As the 184-pound medalists begin to make the traditional walk around the mats, bronze medalist Sajid Sajidov quietly breaks off from the group on the first turn. After patting the Sanderson lightly on the back, he parts to his right, takes the medal off his neck and proceeds down the steps. Jackson, who is talking with Douglas, walks over and congratulates him but Sajidov hardly feels worthy of praise. Many considered him to be the best wrestler in the world but his defeat earlier in the day ended such talk. When his bronze medal bout ended with him as the winner, the reaction was hardly such. The Russian coaches did not rush the mat to embrace him nor did the Russian star bask in the cheers of the crowd. Not once did Sajidov offer any clue that he captured an Olympic medal.

Or maybe he did.

Sajidov's kids could go to school and brag to their classmates that their father was the third best wrestler in the world but based off his reaction after beating Romero in the consolation bout, Sajidov clearly wanted to do with the bronze medal. He exited the arena with his head buried in his hands, tears escaping his eyes, moving as if all feeling had been replaced by numbness, and if one were clueless to the proceedings beforehand and had only raw emotion to go off, it wouldn't be a stretch to say that the announcer in the arena was a municipal judge reading off Sajidov's name in connection with a lengthy jail sentence. The Russian will have a long time to think about redeeming himself, it would be another four years before Sajidov could clear his name.

Sanderson continued his lap around the arena and by the time he was finished with the sport, his body bore its effects. His face resembles one that has been shaven with a dull razor and no soap, all nicks and cuts, bruises and red marks, all of which seems to be of little personal consequence as he stares stoically into the crowd of journalists. If this is the last to be seen of Sanderson competing, he will be remembered as a champion on the mat who was unsure of how to react to the glory afterwards. "All I could think about was not embarrassing myself," Sanderson would say later.

True to the end, Sanderson clenches his jaw. He wouldn't allow the media more than the exterior, there were pieces of him that he would never show, but when his eyes meet those of his wife Kelly, who is standing behind a the row of photographers that shoot him repeatedly, he cracks a grin while she does the same as lights pop and flash off his pale face; the effect of the gold medal hanging from his neck not yet realized.

By virtue of his feats, he has stamped himself into the memories of countless fans, leaving a lasting impression the way a great painting or a memorable song can spur others to great things. His exploits will be a reference for coaches to pass on to future generations of wrestlers, they will recall his skill in rooms across America, just like Gable, Smith and other American greats before him.

At 9:20 p.m., the music stops and flags are lowered and removed from the empty arena. Results remain posted on the scoreboard, but the day that defined these men, one they had spent their entire sporting lives working for, is over.

Point Break
XLVI

There are athletes in this arena, great athletes who have dominated on every level but the very highest, failing to eclipse the final peak of athletic supremacy. And then there is Buvaysa Saytiev who once reaching the top, never leave.

Saytiev has been a sure thing in world championships and the Olympics and finding the Russian superstar in the weight has been a death sentence for opponents championship aspirations.

And one could see it. One could see something in Saytiev's cold, gray, detached eyes that he was not from sunny San Diego, that he did not train along sandy Florida beaches, that he came from Chechnya, a land plagued with conflict.

In the Olympic arena there were various groups of society: sportsmen, business men, mafia men and killers, men who swayed power in political arenas and who instilled fear in dangerous neighborhoods. It was no wonder that the best wrestlers came from the hardest places, like Iran and Turkey, Ukraine and Georgia, places of extreme measures and climate, that were scorched by sun and had brutal winters that saw little of it, places that honored champions with

Olympic gates and cheered the sport with religious fervor, where wrestlers were protectors of villages and settlers of disputes.

Their family bloodlines had traces of poverty and oppression, had genetic codes of survival and instinct, and these men, these hardened athletic figures were partly a by-product of Chechnya's rebel wars with the motherland of Russia, these conflicts were a prelude to their fighting spirit, and that just because they were now competing in a glistening new arena under the soft white lights that lit up Olympic mats did not mean that they had always wrestled in such pristine settings, dined with silver spoons, wore sponsored athletic gear, were under professional trainers' watchful eye, so they did not yell into TV cameras nor walk to a pompous beat because it would have belied the very nature of why these men had made it here.

Saytiev, the Chechen fighter, does not move like the other athletes on the mat, he doesn't think like most of them either. Before stepping on, Saytiev recites a Boris Pasternack poem to himself.

> *"The object of masterpiece is to give yourself away*
> *It's not about the noise, it's not about the success.*
> *It's embarrassing that just because you've created*
> *something that you're on the lips of other people.*
> *Just because you've achieved something that doesn't*
> *mean that everyone should be talking about you just*
> *because you've won. It is only a piece of you defined."*

Saytiev is a complex man with complex thoughts. He walked with authority of a fighter but appeared more driven by finding personal truth in a sport than winning shiny medals. There was a time in his life when he was constantly drunk with alcohol and driven to states of depression. He speaks of fame as a curse and has the goal of praying five times a day, but is often surprised by where his anger comes from.

Perhaps the crowd can tell that Saytiev is different and that's why they watch, or maybe that had nothing to do with it at all, maybe philosophy and psychology and the search for being was inconsequential for the spectators, and maybe the crowd focused on the Russian star for the same elementary reason people watched in bars, school playgrounds and locker rooms when a conflict arose, they watched because somebody was about to get their ass kicked.

Saytiev steps onto the Olympic platform of Greece, onto the surface of the world's most ancient sport, on to the execution of another opponent. He stands straight-legged and to the side, slightly hunched, daring the opponent to attack his legs like a cocky boxer dropping his hands and baiting the opposition to take a swing. His posture is a slap in the face of any conventional wrestling stance where the wrestler would hunch low and guard his legs as a last line of defense. Saytiev defies protocol in search of a challenge, but this was not going to happen in the first round so he is creating ways to be engaged.

The Russian does a quick Ali foot-shuffle, before sliding in and tossing his opponent off the mat. No points. The referee calls no points. And Saytiev just nods. That unfazed, detached, all-knowing nod that comes with winning every major championship he has entered, other than the 2000 Olympics, since 1995. He walks back to the center, composing himself in the gladiator arena as if he would be deeply insulted to be scored upon. When the action continues, he moves like a contract killer around a wounded target; completely focused, emotionless, only looking to finish the job. Against the Greek, Saytiev gives the local fans no choice but to stay out of this one, no chants of their countryman's name, not even the Gods could save him; its 5-0 before it should be.

While there are differing methods for producing a champion, there is only one way to think: absolute. Doubts are toxic, poisoning the mind, stealing the edge. Sometimes that mental edge was all a wrestler needed. Without it, reactions are less quick, moves less certain. Whether it is a belief or an attitude, Gable had it, Smith held it and Saytiev owned it; on international wrestling mats, it is a competitive language spoken by the universal elite.

So it might be that Sanderson was down two points with a minute to go, or Saytiev was locked in a close battle where any false move was fatal, but each would find a way. Both wrestlers had an innate sense of what the opponent would do, relying on a heightened sense of feel for where he was going, dominating the battle of mental chess.

Who would make the first move? Who would set off a chain of actions and reactions? Counters, twists and turns? Touches and shifts in movements as simple as pounding the back of an opponent's neck could potentially throw off one's rhythm, mess with his timing. Instead of creating moves, instead of searching for attacks, opponents were reduced to counter wrestlers. This psychological exchange is being witnessed on Saytiev's mat. The predator and the prey are each distinguished by their posture in stance, their expression of face, their sureness in movement or lack of it. The Russian advances. If there was ever any doubt.

*"The United States is like the guy at the party who gives
cocaine to everybody and still nobody likes him."*

-JIM SAMUELS

August 29
XLVII

The disapproval came down in powerful rushes, the voices of hate strong as the breadth of an afternoon drunk. They were directed at an athlete, not because he had defeated, tormented or humiliated their countries favorite wrestler, no, the arena in Athens was directing its wrath at the athlete because where he was from, what he represented and his country's sagging world popularity at the moment. In the arena, they were cheering against the Americans.

The Olympics was one of a monumental build-up and blowout for the athletes. Everything leading up to this event was in the past and in the arena nothing was certain. For the Americans who had controlled the elements in their matches, for those who had dictated their opponents, their work was already complete; Abas, Kelly and Sanderson had medals around their necks, but for the last three Americans left in competition, the Olympics could get as risky as a game of roulette and which way the ball would bounce, shift, tilt and fall, was yet to be determined if they let it reach that point.

Kelly's overturned call against the Russian to the benefit of the American had angered many powerful members of the international wrestling community, many of whom stood and jeered at the edge of their VIP seats, clinging to the metal railings, shouting down at the refs, flexing whatever influence they could. A similar ruling justified or not, was unlikely to favor the Americans for the remainder of the tournament.

If one had walked the Southside Chicago streets where Joe Williams had come from, had experienced the areas he was exposed to, had dodged the street gangs that he had to, had taken the measures he did to be successful; typing up his homework, living with his high school coach when his father wasn't around; and now saw the mats he was competing on, one match away from the Olympic podium, one might say that it was a miracle, a tremendous accomplishment, a feat worthy of gold itself but that wasn't the case here, not in this arena where the crowd was pledging against him and the country he represented.

There were other elements in play as well. Williams was a young father and wrestling was his livelihood, how he fed a table, and throughout the Olympic training camps he approached it as such. As his peers went to play basketball on a day off Williams could be found on the mat. It was a sport that Williams had always loved while growing up, but the child's play was over because the Olympics were big business and there was no denying that the next several matches were the biggest job opportunity of Williams' life because a gold medal would be overwhelming credibility for any coaching position he pursued in the future.

Right now, it was the next three battles in the circle that would dictate how people treated him for the rest of his life, the difference between being introduced as Joe Williams the Olympian or *JOE WILLIAMS OLYMPIC GOLD MEDALIST*, the difference being a big one, making this moment, this match even bigger.

As he stepped onto mat three for his quarterfinal bout against Gennadiy Laliyez of Kazakhstan, there was the sentiment that the Americans would not be receiving the benefit of the doubt. But the U.S. coaching staff never stressed for their athletes to rely on calls. They stressed the importance of controlling one's destiny, total responsibility, total control, this was the beauty of the sport. Somebody in the stands could insult William's mother, someone in the arena could bash the country he represented, but as a wrestler, no committee, no jackal in the stands, no teammate could change a thing on the mat; Williams owned his destiny as the arena announcer called out his name.

Having conquered the NCAA three times, having dominated the U.S. for several years, Williams has only one level remaining in which to prove himself. Before heading out, Williams turns and systematically leans down, grabs the water bottle from Tom Brands, takes a swig and spits it out like mouthwash. Judging by his movements, one can tell Williams, like most wrestlers at this level, had wrestled this match beforehand. There wouldn't be much improvisation, this was going to be a systematic defeat of his opponent, and every detail, down to his pre-match routine, was scripted beforehand.

"Move him Joe!" Brands yells from the corner. *"Move him!"* But Williams is not moving. He's taken down and turned for two points. As they go back to their feet, Jackson hollers out, *"Pick up the pace Joe!"* And, as if a switch was flipped, Williams comes back with a double-leg takedown and turn to tie the score 2-2 tie. At the break, Jackson wipes Williams back down with a white towel while coaching in rapid-fire tones as Brands shifts nervously on the side.

Williams snatches the right leg, then the left, and drives forward, but as they crash to the mat the Kazakhstan wrestler deftly hits a switch move and swiftly turns from prey to predator. Williams is run out of the circle, but both manage to stay on their feet. No takedown is called and the ruling is turned over to video review. It is not just the Russians but the Japanese fans that are cheering against the American. But Williams catches a break. The call stands. No points. The score stays locked at two.

The wrestlers wait it out, circling each other until the second period evaporates. In overtime, in the clinch, Williams is worked off the mat and the ensuing scoring is debatable. For the second time in the bout, Williams is gambling with his fate, letting the ball roll onto the officials table and tilt and sway in whatever direction out his control. As officials huddle around a TV monitor the feeling grows more helpless as Williams stands in the middle of the mat, not wrestling, not fighting, not claiming what is his, but just standing there, listless, facing the officials for the ruling to come and as the procedure draws out the more one knows this chance shouldn't have been taken, and that the American's number might not get called. Men in the VIP section lean over the railing and shout at the table of referee's beneath them, pleading to favor the Eastern European wrestler as officials peer into the small screen. After the review, they turn to the mat to give their verdict.

A half-hour later Williams is sitting stone-faced in the stands next to his wife and various members of his family; on the mats, Buvaysa Saytiev and a Kazakhstan wrestler battle in the semi-finals. He still wears his black sweats and wrestling shoes, but he will not be in a rematch with the Russian star or even have a chance to medal. Williams still has the physical look of a world champion contender, but there is no hiding the absence on his face, one could tell a terrible loss had overcome him, the type of empty sadness usually reserved for funeral parlors, the kind of expression one saw and immediately felt guilty for smiling.

Outside the Olympic Hall, the sun is beating down on Joe Williams' older brother as he walks gingerly along the exit as fans hurry by to catch taxis and buses. The air is hot, the pavement more so. Williams, tall and beefy, bears little physical resemblance to his Olympian brother. He walks slowly by himself, away from the rest of the Williams clan that made the trip from Chicago. Tears trickle down beneath his sunglasses and disappear as soon as he can wipe them away. One session of wrestling remains, but his brother Joe, the pride of the family, will not be leaving Athens with what he came for.

Later, Jackson is blunt in his assessment. "In training, Joe did everything we told him to do, but that's not how we trained, that's not how we coached him to wrestle, he did it to himself. I would have rather seen him come out of the first period down by one, two points that way he would be aggressive. Even with 20 seconds left, he didn't attack. You leave a match to chance and chance might happen."

When the referee's call came, Williams turned to Jackson but there was nothing he could do; the decision was final. The crowd cheered as the American moved to the center, silently shocked, shaking his head meekly, walking off slowly as most wrestlers do after losing a defining match: deflated, stunned, not wanting to leave, as if all that training, all that dreaming, had been one big lie.

"Anger cannot be dishonest."

-MARCUS AURELIUS, ROMAN EMPEROR

Soviet Divide
XLVIII

The tension between Russia and former Soviet-bloc countries runs deep. While some of these wrestlers train together and compete in the same tournaments, friction remains and was evident during a bout pitting Belarus against Russia that the influence of mother country still loomed large.

Shortly after ten in the morning, politics and sport reach a breaking point when Buvaysa Saytiev is the controversial winner in a tightly contested bout against Murad Gaidarov; awarded the victory after just six seconds of overtime. The Belarusian has to be pushed back on the mat by his coaches to shake hands. The referee, trying to diffuse the tension, instructs Gaidarov to calm down by putting a palm to his mouth, but he refuses and storms down the steps, flipping off the jeering crowd. When he reaches the warm-up area after the ruling, he has to be restrained from entering the judge's area.

When he and Saytiev meet at the exit they continue the heated exchange until one wrestler says a word too many, and they both lurch at each other with such a vicious intensity the one anticipated they were going to tear out each others flesh like wolves. Their coaches quickly intercede, there is a brief struggle but no punches are thrown.

Wrestling was not a sport that drew in the curious fans who wanted to take in as many Olympic venues as possible; the crowd was the world's roughest at the moment. The arena was full of sun-deprived Eastern Europeans, thick-necked Iranians, the battered ear and strong-jawed alike, filling the stands. Faces that couldn't be looked at for too long and others that could be model's if not for the scars and cuts and ears that needed Photoshop. Some of the men were goons, people you would call the cops on and if you were stuck in an elevator with, you would fidget and shift and possibly even hit the button for the nearest floor to take the stairs, but the wrestler could feel this, because while you had a four-year degree and $600 loafers from Sak's Fifth Avenue, these men could sniff out weaknesses and on the mat you'd be exposed because this is what the sport does-it exposes people, this is what the sport gives-it empowers individuals, and there were a fair amount of wrestlers who had all the arrogance of small-town sheriff and while these type were certainly not easy to deal with, there is a certain line of thinking that says it was easier to manage big-egos than it was to put up with those who were afraid to test themselves, make mistakes, those who didn't want to be embarrassed because they felt no woman was going to love them if they ever saw that, but if you took a beating and you didn't quit, then you deserved respect and women can sense that out like the goon in the elevator could sense fear.

The Olympic arena was full of these men, full of silent gladiators only they were no longer silent, they were roaring, cheering at the worlds greatest and only sporting event, the only pursuit worth chasing was how they saw it, and the action is now heated, the ruling is questionable and Russia and Belarus aren't forging diplomacy on this one, they aren't drafting international treaties, because Russia sees the ruling one way and Belarus interprets it another and now the divide is thick, the sounds are raged and Saytiev is shuttled away like a President after an assination attempt, which does little to stop the commotion.

Spectators spill to the bottom of the stands as if their seats were replaced with a slide. One man hops the railing, lands on the arena floor and quickly jumps into the rumble between Eastern European coaches and representatives. Cameramen scramble for position. An American official tries to isolate the incident, using his outstretched arms to block a horde of photographers who have formed a wall, but there would be no hiding this.

The man from the stands is flushed out of the tunnel like a rat from a sewer and is quickly served the treatment of a snitch in county; punched, kicked and beaten by three men who chase after him as he flees to temporary safety in the stands. Meanwhile, a separate fight reaches the warm-up room.

The athletes halt their routines and distance themselves from the commotion. One man's shirt is torn. Another cries out in frustration of the politics of the match that set off the fight, doing little to quiet the talk the Eastern European sporting federation bought off athletes and referees; rumors that have been swirling through the back hallways of Ano Lorissa throughout the tournament. There are accusations that Cuba's Yoel Romero was paid off to throw the bronze medal bout against the Russia's Sajidov and those who believe it point out the fact that Romero, who had been turned once on the mat in two years, was turned twice by Sajidov in six minutes.

For Olympic purists, the idea of athletes being bought out seemed so foul that one wanted to refuse the idea, spit it out, but it was still there, still slimy on the surface and not in the gutter where they felt it belonged. Matches are stopped for a half-hour while Olympic officials sort out the incident.

***

One hour before the most significant match of his life, Daniel Cormier enters the Olympic warm-up room. Amid the atmosphere of anxious competitors, Cormier shakes out his own butterflies. He checks the TV screens that broadcast the matches. Mo Lawal comes in and helps rub out the kinks in his back and when Cormier is seven matches away from competing, his training partner shakes his hand, wishes him luck and walks away. Cormier is on his own but this solitude is not unfamiliar, he is a wrestler, this is the path he has chosen.

The American moves across the surface that is much like any of the warm-up rooms he has been in. Although several dialects are overheard between various coaches, little is discernible from the voices. It's a physical room, primal as a prison yard, and movement is the language that tells the story. Follow with the eyes and everything is in clear interpretation. Specimens from around the world, alpha males of their countries sporting ranks, prepare to fight it out for Olympic medals. The cool, confident Russians, dangerously regal in white jumpsuits and red stars, self-assured in their dominance, eying the the remaining competitors with passivity; the powerful and relentless Americans, covered in patriotic stars and stripes, ready to add to the lead of their Olympic medal count.

Two men. Trained to destroy. Prepared to let loose. Two men who were the stock of their countries' athletic trade, stand side-by-side catching glances, stealing looks, sizing each other up, convincing themselves invincible, silently squashing any notion of defeat, the greatest wrestlers ready to smash each other on the mat but momentarily restrained, forced to be dignified, but winding closer to the moment of release, each step in the tunnel the less their coaches are saying, each step the crowd grows louder, the vibrations of the bleachers, the thunder of the clapping, the passionate chants above, beyond, surrounding the gladiators and ready to feast on them whole. If the American wins the next two bouts, he takes the gold and his face will be known, the television will give him his 15 minutes, the newspapers will make him a celebrity, he will be on NBC, CBS, Oklahoma State will put his name on the wall that no one will dare remove, all the friends, all the doubters, all of Metairie, Louisiana will know that Daniel Cormier is the Olympic gold medalist.

If you're as dedicated as Cormier has been over four years, if you're a true competitor, then this moment is better than sex, will climax any athletic experience you've ever had, and if you're nervous because it's your first time remember to treat it like it might be your last, all you have to do is take out the burly Russian that stands right next to you.

Khadjimourat Gatsalov, thick as a linebacker and rough as a bear, is not saying a word, just listening to directions from the Russian coaches who have his ear. But shifting, loosening, moving just enough to keep his body warm and ready, alert and prepared because once he walks out of the tunnel, its go time.

In previous bouts, Cormier exhibited skill and stamina, performed with fury and finesse in equal doses, dismantling his first two opponents. For the U.S. coaches and Cormier, this was expected. But as Cormier waits next to the young, powerful Russian, he now faces an opponent every bit as strong and relentless as himself.

One of the humbling truth's of elite fighters is the notion that there's always someone out there who's better, but in this arena, under the Olympic lights, the top contenders didn't believe it, couldn't believe it, they had to believe they were the other side of that equation, that they were the great conquerors that were here to do the humbling and their Olympic coaches patting them on the back and whispering confidence in their ears don't tell them any different. The American's tell Cormier he is the best in the world and right next to him, in their own language, the Russian's tell Gatsalov the very same.

Flanked by Jackson and Smith, Cormier occasionally looks to read their faces. Jackson exhibits as much assurance as the knowing Smith at his side. If it were them in this position, Cormier knew what they would do; he heard his coaches' voices without them ever speaking. *'Were gonna take this dude out! Were gonna get him!'* Jackson was known to say. He knows what Smith would say because the Cowboy coach has been on his side since he got to Stillwater. But Cormier is not wrestling with Smith and Jackson, so he begins to talk to himself, *'OK, this is it Daniel, you're wrestling for the gold medal, you're life's dream.'* As the line inches closer to the entrance of the arena, he repeats the words to himself, *"I'm gonna get it done, I'm gonna get it done."*

But Jackson sees a different look on Cormier's face. "You could see in his eyes that he was nervous," Jackson would say later. "Opposed to the killer look, it made me scared right away." Jackson had always seen Cormier compete hard and expects as much when they walk out. He wants Cormier to make the opponent pay for all his hard work. He wants him to let go, scrap for every point, let his talent take over and turn the match into a brawl. Jackson knows if he does that, if Cormier is physical and makes it a high-scoring match, he will win; in Jackson's mind there are no two ways about it, he expects the U.S. 211-pounder to dominate.

But as they walk out under the glaring lights, as Cormier moves into the Olympic atmosphere, something is lost in the plan. The Russian dictates. The Russian controls. The Russian seizes the opportunity and the American has met his match. While Cormier gets close to scoring while holding Gatsalov in a front head-lock, he can't spin around and score, getting blocked at the last second. On their feet, he constantly reacts to Gatsalov's fakes, leaving him off balance. In the clinch with his grip slipping, he desperately tries to throw, but lands on his back instead. One can hear the apprehension on Jackson's voice, *"Make him work Big D!"* But the urges do not change things. Cormier, normally the aggressor, never settles in. The Russian constantly fakes and moves, setting the tempo, controlling the high-paced action. *"Smack him!"* Jackson yells to Cormier during a blood stoppage. *"You gotta get him here!"* One can hear the anxiety in Jackson's voice. He believes in Cormier. He wants to go out there and show him. But coaching, tactics, and focus is lost in the battle and there's nothing the American coaches can do. Cormier is in trouble.

He's down and fading fast, time's leaving him, and the work he put into preparing seems inconsequential because ambition is staring him cold in the face and everything Cormier said he wanted in the interviews with reporters about taking the world as his athletic ambition was present, but the moment was not magical, it was not glorious, it was not divine, this moment of ambition hurt, this moment had scorched lungs, but this is what Cormier said he wanted, this is what he put in time for, because several months past, when his daughter's death wrecked his heart, wrestling was the only thing that could get Cormier from laying in bed in continual dread.

In overtime, Cormier could save it all with one mighty throw from the clinch. As the two Olympians brace and maneuver to lock in the clinch, squirming to hold a grip, Gatsalov says something to the official that Cormier cannot understand. The American briefly lets up and the Russian swiftly takes advantage, adjusting to the side for a tighter hold. The whistle has yet to blow and Cormier has no chance and the action that follows is all too predictable:

Cormier is bear-hugged to his back.

The Russian clenches his thick fist.

John Smith walks off muttering words of dismay.

Cormier's wife, Robin buries her head in her lap as a friend and two family members wait by her side. She had seen Daniel at his lowest low after Kaedyn's death. She had gone to work when he stayed behind in his room all day, worried about how her young husband would recover. And Robin Cormier had certainly seen Daniel pick himself up after a couple weeks of mourning, get back into the Stillwater room, whip himself into shape and make an Olympian out of himself. So there was no reason for her to believe that Daniel wasn't going to go the distance, take the tragedy and turn it to gold, that's how these things end in the movies right? But in Athens, in the arena, in a sport that crowns the individual king, the failed reality of this pursuit was finally bleeding through.

Ten minutes later, with ushers clearing the last spectators out, Robin Cormier's head rises from her knees as a friend hands her a white napkin.

***

During the final session, Cormier is the last American in contention for a medal; Guerrero and Williams were eliminated earlier in the day. He can earn the bronze if he defeats Alireza Heidari, a thickly built, gel-haired, Sylvester Stallone look-alike from Iran. At the 2003 World Championships, Cormier lost his temper, shoving Heidari in the waning seconds of an ugly loss, but in Athens, the rematch begins differently. Cormier holds his cool in the early stages of the bout and leads 2-0 in overtime, needing only one more point to secure the bronze medal.

But slowly, cruelly, things begin to crack as Heidari is never put down. Suddenly, the attitude of each wrestler, heads in differing directions. Cormier tries to hold on while Heidari refuses to give up, attacking the American until he backs off the mat. Swayed by the Iranian masses, the referee's thumb begins a slow ascent, the crowd's approval fueling its rise, until it peaks above his shoulder. Passivity on Cormier. One point for Heidari. The crowd roars.

"Hei-da-ri! Hei-da-ri! He-da-ri!"

Heidari rushes forward, attacking the legs. Cormier, already retreating, knows what's coming and has his hands down to block, but is defenseless against the surge of Heidari who rides a tidal wave of momentum to topple over his American counterpart.

"Hei-da-ri! Hei-da-ri! He-da-ri!"

At this point, it's too late for the American to salvage. Seconds after taking him down to tie the match, Heidari ends it with a turn.

"Hei-da-ri! Hei-da-ri! He-da-ri!"

The crowd is beating on drums, stomping with their feet, crying out their countrymen's name, relishing the American's loss as much as the Iranian's victory. The noise is deafening as Heidari rejoices, blowing kisses to the crowd. The American walks slowly to the media area, bends over and rests his thick forearms on the gate facing a TV camera. He looks up as if ready to begin an interview, but, physically and emotionally drained, puts his head down again. Fourth in the world never hurt so much.

"When Alexander looked at the breadth of his domain, he wept for there were no more worlds to conquer."

-HANS GRUBER, DIE HARD I

Dominatsiya
XLIX

Inside the warm-up room, the Russian Olympic wrestling team congregates. The mats are deserted and all but a few seats in front of the TV are as well. Gym bags are scattered along the walls. FILA officials wait for Gatsalov, the 211-pound Olympic champion, to emerge from the doping control room.

Russian sporting president Mikhail Mamiashvili playfully slaps gold medalist Adam Batirov on the back. A Russian coach does a victory jig as others watch in laughter. Anatoly Beloglazov, Sergei's twin brother, moves between several groups, exchanging handshakes and accepting congratulations from trainers, athletes and well-wishers alike. Two-time Olympic gold medalist Buvaysa Saytiev can't walk too far without being stopped to have his pictures taken; volunteer workers, coaches, fellow wrestlers, everyone wants to be next to the Olympic Champ.

Batirov, Saytiev and Gatsalov will return home as heroes with financial royalties and a lifetime of respect coming their way. In all, Russia and the Soviet Bloc countries have captured 35 out of a possible 56 Olympic wrestling medals, unofficially winning the tournament with 52 points; the U.S. was second with 45, Cuba finished third.

On the competition mats in the arena, volunteer workers have taken over the surface, posing on top of medal stands as friends and colleagues snap photos with disposable cameras. The arena is emptying, the Olympic closing ceremonies are nearing, the celebration is beginning.

Back at the American College of Greece, the gym is silent. There are few clues that U.S. Olympians ever trained in this facility. No discarded water bottles or damp white towels lying around the locker room. No wrestling mats plastered across the surface or athletic trainer waiting dutifully on the sidelines to treat the next cut or injury. There had once been four gold medalists coaching a group of seven hopefuls. There had been rowdy basketball games between Olympic coaches. There had been the presence of a former U.S. President, Olympic dignitaries and school janitors alike. Now, it was just another empty gym in an Olympic city full of them.

Later in the evening, the lobby of the Park Hotel is clustered with large duffel bags near the double-door glass entrance. A USA Wrestling employee hustles in and out of the lobby preparing the logistics for departure. In the nearby lounge, the families of Williams, Cormier, McCoy and Guerrero share food, drink and laughter together while coaches and training partners mill about, playing poker and nursing bottled beer.

As fireworks explode over the stadium signaling the end of the closing ceremonies, the Americans' gear is loaded and shuttled to the nearby airport. Every so often, one of the wrestlers glances at the TV monitor but they appear emotionally detached from the event and more preoccupied with the latest hand of cards they've been dealt.

A blimp floats over the Olympic stadium as the sun sets on the XXVIII Olympic Games. Clouds of smoke arise from the stadium; spotlights shoot back and forth, invading the night. After much propaganda and world-wide concern, the Olympics go off without the feared terrorist incident. The impending deficit worries, the question of what to do with the several empty stadiums throughout Athens, are put off for another day. Now, more than ever, it's time to party.

Lounging on balconies over drink and cigarettes, packed into clubs and disco techs, all over Athens the city is alive. And the Greeks celebrate as only the Greeks can, into the wee hours, not a care in the world.

In the midst of the night, a shuttle van slowly pulls out of the Park Hotel parking lot and rumbles down the narrow street as fumes of smoke billow from its exhaust, carrying America's wrestlers to the airport as the world's largest party rages on.

At 1:45 a.m., they are gone.

Epilogue
XLX

Upon returning from Athens, Olympic assistant coach Zeke Jones accepted a head coaching job at West Virginia. John Smith continued his success at Oklahoma St., winning NCAA titles in 2005 and 2006. Minnesota, fueled by J. Robinson, won the NCAA title in 2007 before Tom Brands, after being hired over from Virginia Tech, led the Iowa Hawkeyes back to prominence with a NCAA team title in 2008.

Sergei Beloglazov accepted a position with Sunkist wrestling in Arizona, before moving back to Eastern Europe to coach the Russian Women's Olympic wrestling team. Kevin Jackson remained in Colorado Springs as the U.S. national freestyle coach, implementing a new plan to beat the Russians, a plan that would develop a new crop of hopefuls, a plan to bring the U.S. more Olympic gold.

FILA and USA Wrestling implemented rule changes intended to make the sport more fan friendly, but wrestling's popularity in America is still waning. Sucessful NCAA programs Oregon, Fresno St. and Arizona St. have been cut in the past three years and Title IX continues to butcher the sport. Other than the NCAA Championship broadcast on ESPN, national television viewership is virtually non-existent. Real Pro Wrestling, a venture into a professional wrestling league, failed after a brief existence.

The Olympic team later reunited at the White House for one of its last official gatherings and many debated whether they should continue training for another Olympic cycle or move on to coaching or business ventures. Four years is a long time for a wrestler. If they choose to continue, the Olympics will be their driving force on early morning runs and will push them through days when their body doesn't want contact. But in a sport that wears on bodies, minds and families, nothing is certain. New, younger opponents will emerge. No one can tell what life's uncertainties can bring. From one Olympic cycle to the next, nothing is guaranteed.

Daniel Cormier, with unfinished business on the mat, was taking another shot at Olympic gold. While Jamill Kelly and Eric Guerrero retired from competition, Stephen Abas, on the podium in Athens, was already thinking about taking the next step; after vacationing in the Greek islands, he resumed his training at the OTC. Joe Williams and his wife Kim Vinton, had a second son, Wyatt Steven, and he continued training. Kerry McCoy retired from wrestling, moving on to coaching and athletic department duties at Lehigh before being hired as the head coach at Stanford in 2005 and eventually taking over the same position at the University of Maryland.

As his legend grew by the moment, already the subject of a thousand conversations, Cael Sanderson retreated to Canada to fish and relax for two weeks. He would return to a hero's welcome in Ames, then his hometown of Heber City where he pulled the Athens gold medal out of the tube sock he kept it in, showing it to crowds that honored him with an official Cael Sanderson day.

After being recruited by Ohio State for their head coaching position, Bobby Douglas retired and Sanderson took over as head coach at Iowa State in 2006. He took over the Penn St. program in April 2009. Sanderson has not competed since Athens, but as John Smith said in Athens, "He'll be back, I guarantee you he will be back and there's only one guy in the U.S. that can beat him."

On January 12, 2004, back in Stillwater, Mohammed Lawal began another practice in the Oklahoma State wrestling room. He warmed up fast, drilled hard and went live with a practice partner. One thousand, three hundred and twenty days remain until the Beijing Olympics. *The clock is ticking...*

Mikhail Mamiashvili, Russian Wrestling President and 1996 Gold Medalist

211-pound Olympic Champion
Khadjimourad Gatsalov of Russia

163-pound Olympic Champion
Buyvasa Saytiev of Russia

126-pound Olympic Champion Adam Batirov of Russia

Olympic Silver Medalist Jamill Kelly, USA; Gold Medalist Elbrus Tedeyev, Ukraine; Bronze Medalist Mahach Murtalzaliev, Russia

Olympic Heavyweight Gold Medalist Artur Taymazov of Uzbekistan

NICHOLAS HOPPING

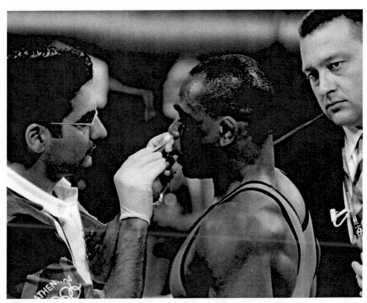

Joe Williams being treated during his Olympic quarterfinal bout

Joe Williams USA v. Gennadiy Laliyev Kazakhstan

Stephen Abas, Zeke Jones and Adam Batirov being introduced for the 126-pound gold medal match